Social Change in the Twentieth Century

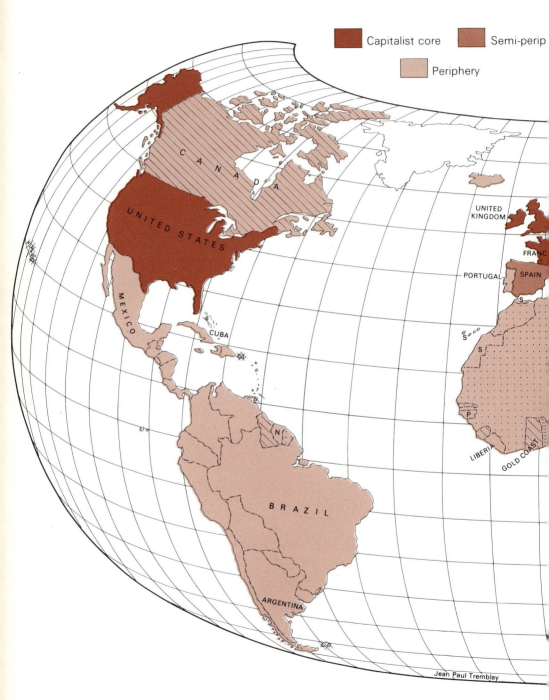

THE WOR

Capitalist core   Semi-perip

Periphery

Jean Paul Tremblay

1913

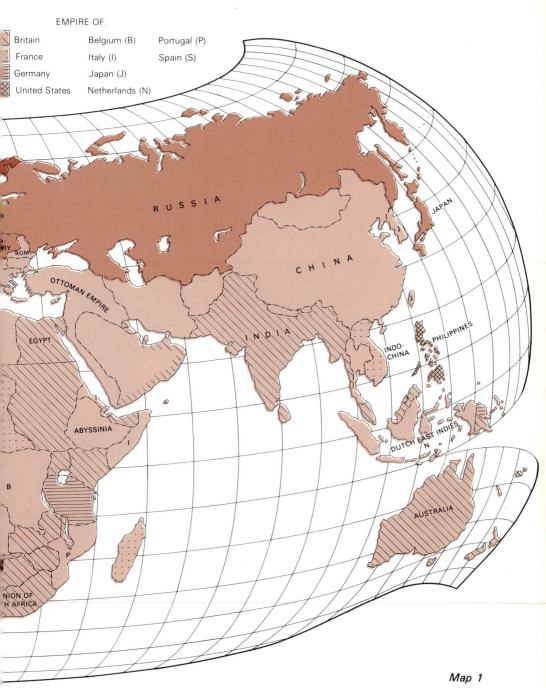

RY
ROM

RUSSIA

JAPAN

OTTOMAN EMPIRE

CHINA

EGYPT

INDIA

INDO-
CHINA

PHILIPPINES

J

ABYSSINIA

I

DUTCH EAST INDIES
N
P

B

AUSTRALIA

P

NION OF
H AFRICA

Map 1

Social Change
in the Twentieth Century

DANIEL CHIROT

University of Washington, Seattle

Under the General Editorship of ROBERT K. MERTON
Columbia University

HARCOURT BRACE JOVANOVICH, INC.

New York   Chicago   San Francisco   Atlanta

ISBN: 0-15-581420-6

Library of Congress Catalog Card Number: 76-56889

Printed in the United States of America

TO MY TEACHERS

Laurence Wylie

Sigmund Diamond

Immanuel Wallerstein

Preface

Social change means different things to different audiences. Those interested in, say, the women's movement wish to read about social changes related to this topic. Others, interested perhaps in ecological questions and the issue of conservation, might seek books about rather different kinds of social change. No single work can cover all worthwhile issues.

This particular book is about two closely related types of social change. First, it seeks to explain why certain kinds of change within societies affect the international balance of power. Second, it examines how changes in that balance, in turn, cause changes in the individual societies that make up the world. These two types of change make up an unbroken causal circle; neither one is comprehensible without the other.

Most people would agree that the world is now made up of interdependent units, and that no country is a self-sufficient island. But the extent of mutual interdependence and its consequences for the daily lives of all the world's people in the twentieth century are not as widely appreciated. Also not generally perceived is the fact that the bonds of interdependence and the international balance of power have changed, and continue to change rapidly. These changes need to be discussed and understood by everyone, if only in preparation for the dramatic effects they will have on our domestic lives.

This book focuses on issues of social stratification, the distribution of power, and international relations. It is my contention that these form the basic framework within which all other types of change occur. Other aspects of change are not necessarily less interesting or less important to individuals. But the distribution of power, both within societies and among them, determines the direction and speed of all social change. I hope to demonstrate that no contemporary society is independent of the rest of the world, and that studying social change without studying its international context is both theoretically unsound and dangerous.

In addition, I believe that there is a strong possibility of catastrophic change in the capitalist democracies, now the richest and most advanced societies in the world; this catastrophe will come about because of changing international forces. It is conceivable, however, that a better understanding of the world context in which change occurs can help to avert catastrophe. I hope, therefore, that my book contributes, even if only a little, to such an understanding.

Acknowledgments

A number of people were of help to me in the writing of this book.

Immanuel Wallerstein, of the State University of New York at Binghamton, originated many of the ideas that make up the book. Some of my interpretations are not ones with which he agrees, and my political opinions are not always ones he shares. I hope that the original clarity and strength of his ideas have survived my interpretation.

I thank one of the world's most considerate editors, William A. Pullin, for seeing me through this project.

Guenther Roth, Pierre van den Berghe, Sam Preston, Rod Stark —all colleagues of mine at the University of Washington—and Ev Wilson—a former colleague at the University of North Carolina—gave me a great deal of valuable advice.

Lewis A. Coser, of the State University of New York at Stony Brook, Ralph H. Turner, of the University of California at Los Angeles, Peter T. Schneider, of Fordham University, and Jane Schneider, of York College, were helpful critics.

Carolyn Johnson, of Harcourt Brace Jovanovich, and Cindy Chirot helped me to revise my manuscript and make it comprehensible.

Mary Whiting, Karen Wayenberg, and Beulah Reddaway typed the manuscript.

Most of all, I thank Robert K. Merton, of Columbia University, for his advice and continuing encouragement.

Daniel Chirot

Contents

I

Comparative Sociology:
Past Failures and New Ideas

Social Change and the Study of Development

In the United States in the late 1950s and early 1960s there was a great deal of interest in the problems of underdevelopment. After 1960 this interest was particularly strong among the nation's college students. There were two major reasons for this trend.

First, the United States was deeply involved in the affairs of most countries of the underdeveloped world. The main reason given for this involvement was that it could stop the spread of Communism. This policy, which originated soon after World War II, has generated much debate. Was it really a defensive strategy against Soviet aggression, or was it an aggressive plan to encircle the Soviet Union? Was it primarily a military strategy, or was it designed mainly to protect raw-material sources and export markets for the American economy? Was the policy idealistic and designed to help the world, or was it selfishly motivated and designed to help the United States at the expense of poorer societies? These questions cannot be answered easily, if at all. Moreover the fact remains that by the late 1950s, the United States had been engaged in this policy of involvement for well over a decade, and the prevailing view at the time, both among scholars and within the general population, was that the motivation was primarily idealistic rather than imperialistic.

Second, during the 1950s, a liberal interpretation of underdevelopment was articulated in the country's major universities. By the late fifties it had matured enough to form the basis of an activist ideology for Americans seeking a more satisfactory policy toward the underdeveloped countries. The liberal interpretation explained why certain countries were underdeveloped, and what should be done to help them escape from this condition. According to this explanation, the underdevelopment of a country was the result of its deficient value system and economic structure. The people of advanced European societies and of the United States had progressed because they had developed a modern, rational business system and ethic. This had enabled them to accumulate capital, invest it, and achieve rapid economic growth. The West had gone through a series of stages: capital accumulation, ever-increasing industrialization, a drive toward industrial maturity, and a constant move toward a modern and wealthy economy with high consumption.[1] In order to go through these stages a society needed a strong puritan ethic (to save and invest, not simply to consume), and it needed to develop sophisticated skills, an educated work force, and a highly motivated population. A democratic political system seemed best suited for this. It produced a more highly motivated population and better satisfied the demands of a literate, skilled population, which would not tolerate the kinds of inequality typical of older, traditional monarchies and empires. Democracy was therefore likely to be more stable than other political forms, and it was also the one most likely to honor skill and ingenuity (rather than royal grants and inherited position), both tending to motivate and promote rapid economic growth. The danger came in the early stages of the process of development, when, though not yet democratized or very wealthy, a society was already experiencing changes. The frustrations caused by the retention of old social inequalities that blocked progress could easily turn many people in underdeveloped countries into Communists. Communism, therefore, was a disease of the early stages of development, and it had to be the task of the United States to help societies pass through this stage as quickly and as safely as possible.[2]

The preceding paragraphs simplify the arguments of such scholars as Walt Rostow, Gabriel Almond, Karl Deutsch, Talcott Parsons, and many others who promoted these ideas. The activist, ideological side of this interpretation was that Americans should concentrate on helping underdeveloped countries in order to block Communist expansion. While military strength was important (both to discourage outright Soviet attack and to prevent subversion in underdeveloped countries during the critical stage of early development), it was not sufficient unless a great deal of aid accompanied defense efforts. Thus, mere blocking of Communism was not enough; it had to be accompanied by a program of financial aid.

Foreign aid was to accomplish four goals:[3]

1. The outdated, traditional values that predominated in the underdeveloped world and that blocked saving, investment, and rational organization of the economy had to be changed in order to promote progress.

2. Antiquated, insufficiently democratic political structures had to be modernized in order to facilitate progress and to head off radical leftist revolutions.

3. People had to be trained in order to provide an adequate supply of skilled labor and managerial personnel.

4. Capital funds had to be provided, through loans or gifts, in order to speed up the process of development.

All this was no small task. Only someone who recalls those years from the perspective of that time, rather than from the perspective of today's more cynical atmosphere, can believe that learned professors in the liberal academies actually stood in front of their students and said that *it could be done,* and that it was the duty of young Americans to do it. In today's intellectual circles the question has been raised whether these bold statements were cynical covers for American imperialism or whether they were honest ideals. Again, who can answer? But the fact remains that a significant number of America's educated youth believed the message and were enthusiastic about it. With the election of John Kennedy in 1960, that enthusiasm was translated into a set of concrete programs, of which the most symbolically important was the Peace Corps.

The enthusiasm and interest of those years produced a wave of interest in comparative social sciences and great sympathy with the struggles of African, Latin American, and Asian peoples against poverty and backwardness.

But the "Peace Corps" ideology did not work. The other side of the coin was that during this fragile transitional stage underdeveloped countries had to be protected from Communism, a task that was to involve much unpleasantness. Along with the Peace Corps and the Alliance for Progress to help Latin America, there also had to be a build-up of conventional and nuclear armed might. If atomic and hydrogen bombs could deter the U.S.S.R., still more strategies were needed to fight subversion. So, along with the Peace Corps, Kennedy built up the Special Forces and other instruments of military intervention. The later full-scale, though undeclared, war in Vietnam was the logical result of this dual and originally quite logical and consistent liberal doctrine of development. This darker side of the theory and practice of aid led to massive draft calls, a general loss of faith in the mission of the United States, and, ultimately, a loss of interest and enthusiasm among the very group that should have been in the activist forefront of the "Peace Corps" ideal.

At the same time, other problems developed. It became evident that the United States had its own internal problems. The urban race riots that began in 1964 and became severe in 1965 dramatized this point. The later race riots coincided with an upsurge of college-student protest, which became particularly acute in the late sixties. This protest was the product of the military draft, the overcrowding of universities, and the general sympathy of students with protesting ethnic minorities. It was also deeply associated with a loss of the well-intentioned faith that had predominated during the early sixties.

These simultaneous, or near-simultaneous, events had many important consequences. The one that is most pertinent here is that the liberal theories about remedying regional underdevelopment of the late fifties and early sixties were largely discredited and that, far worse, there was a general loss of interest in the whole area of comparative social science. After all, the reasoning went, when the United States was involved in so many domestic problems and when the end result of the "Peace Corps" ideology was the Vietnam war, how was it possible to sustain an interest in such theories? They seemed impracticably idealistic at best, and cynically evil at worst.

In the place of the liberal theories of underdevelopment, older, Marxist (and particularly Leninist) theories were revived. Underdevelopment, according to these theories, was caused by colonialism and imperialist exploitation. Therefore, the solution was not aid, or even a "super Peace Corps," but revolution against the dominant imperial power, the United States. Similarly, poverty in the United States was not the product of ignorance and disorganization among the poor, but rather the product of willful exploitation by the capitalist system. It was no accident, said the neo-Marxists, that the Vietnam war and race riots were occurring simultaneously—they were both aspects of the same capitalist world system. In many ways, this theoretical framework certainly seemed to explain the world of the late sixties much better than the benign theories of the liberals that had dominated academies ten years earlier. But while neo-Marxism made great advances in universities (thereby turning the old liberals of 1960 into the new reactionaries of 1970), it did not revive the interest in comparative social studies that had been so evident in the early sixties. Why not?

First, it is evident that Americans care to hear only a certain amount of derogatory information about their country; beyond this, they experience a feeling of apathetic futility. Certainly, it is much more difficult to sustain interest in negativism than in positive, hopeful theories. Second, since much of the neo-Marxist attack on liberal theories of development is primarily an attack against the United States, it stands to reason that liberal concerns would turn to internal problems rather than to comparative studies. So the neo-Marxist theories have diverted the attention of many to domestic problems, and away from an examination of societies in general.

Third, the cynicism that developed during the middle and late sixties, originally directed at the liberal theories of the world which led to the Vietnam war, carried over into the 1970s and was applied to all social science theory. While old theories lost their appeal and believability, the specialized scholars of comparative social science have since been unable to popularize an acceptable and interesting new synthesis.

Yet such a synthesis is much needed, particularly for the purpose of teaching comparative sociology and reawakening interest in the study of foreign societies. As American students have lost interest in such studies, they have turned to studies of their own psyches as well as the study of sex-roles, and of exotic life-styles. This might be more acceptable if the United States lived alone in the world, or if change in other areas of the world could be confined. But in fact, changes in other parts of the world influence American society, just as changes in the United States influence the rest of the world. At the very time that this is becoming most evident, American students appear to have little interest in broad, comparative study, and are therefore likely to end up inexcusably ignorant of the world at large. Worse, ignorance of the world means ignorance of the United States, since the good and bad in any society mean little if compared to abstract standards, and take on meaning only when compared to other realities.

In other words, it is essential to offer a new synthesis for comparative sociology. Because of the production of specialized studies in the 1960s and early seventies, and because of the actual experiences of these years, it is possible to offer such a synthesis. Actually the synthesis virtually exists, and in recent years several scholars have developed it to the point where it can be simplified and used to teach comparative sociology to nonspecialists.

The purpose of this book, then, is to provide in elementary form a theory of social change that connects changes in the highly developed world with those in less developed societies. The key fault of the dominant theory of the early sixties was that it saw the problems of underdevelopment purely in terms of the internal forces working in each society, failing to take into account the existence of international networks that greatly influence all societies. Underdevelopment involves more than a set of outdated institutions and values; it also involves being in a weak position in these international networks. Between the excessively demonic vision of the United States presented by the neo-Marxists and the excessively benign theory of the liberals, in which the United States is a rich old uncle trying to teach his nephews the secret of success, lies a workable synthesis that may promote interest in comparative sociology by showing how important it is to an understanding of the world, and thus to an understanding of American society.

The Basis of Analysis: The World System

To begin the presentation of that synthesis, it is perhaps best to return to the dominant theoretical model of the early 1960s and the reasons given for the poverty or wealth of certain societies:

1. Poor societies held outdated, traditional values that were insufficiently oriented to hard work, savings, and investment. Rich societies held rational, scientific values, and they had high rates of savings and investment.

②　Poor societies had antiquated political and landholding structures that were not sufficiently democratic to satisfy the aspirations of their people, particularly their more talented, ambitious people. The resulting frustrations produced political turmoil, which was bad for development since it discouraged investment and diverted energy away from economic activity. Rich societies, on the other hand, had more equitable and democratic governments. Talented people could rise relatively freely, popular demands could be met, and governments tended to be stable. This provided a good climate for economic growth.

③　Poor societies had an inadequate supply of skilled labor and managerial personnel. Rich societies were abundantly supplied, and they had more highly developed educational systems that could produce an ever-growing number of skilled persons.

As a result of these three factors, poor societies lacked the human and financial capital necessary for economic development. Fundamental changes in their traditional cultures, political systems, educational systems, and economic arrangements were necessary for progress. Rich societies were quite the opposite. They could look forward to increasing prosperity and success because they had the capital, skills, stability, and values that promoted economic growth and social well-being.

There is nothing objectionable about these statements. Descriptively, they are largely correct. But they are based on a major assumption, namely, that each society is basically independent of all others, and that poverty or wealth in any one society is caused by its internal characteristics. According to these principles, any effort to help poor societies would have to start with internal reform. Similarly, reform in poor societies is both possible (given sufficient effort) and unlikely to create greater world conflict, since it is in everyone's interest to eliminate troublesome places in the world that destabilize international politics. According to this liberal theory, only the Soviet Union and its allies could profit from the continued poverty in Latin America, Africa, and Asia.

Yet, the facts in the twentieth century have not fit this theoretical perspective. For one thing, even in 1900 (and all the more in 1950) there were very few "traditional" societies left in the world. Virtually all people, aside from the few isolated groups in the most remote parts of the Amazon, in a few parts of Africa, and in certain inaccessible parts of Asia, had already experienced prolonged and extremely unsettling contact with the highly modernized, industrialized, and politically dominant Western world. This was actually an old pattern, for since about 1500, an ever larger part of the world had come into contact with the dynamic, growing, and modernizing Western European societies. By 1600, large parts of the Americas, most of Eastern Europe, and the coastlines of much of Africa and Asia had come into contact with the West, and this contact had already produced substantial change, particularly in America and Eastern Europe. By 1800, the scope of contact had increased. Much of inland Africa had been influenced by the coastal slave trade carried on by the Westerners, and in Asia, Western influence had spread inland from the coasts, particularly within India. By 1900, the process was virtually complete, and most of the world was actually directly or indirectly controlled by Europeans (or by Europeans transplanted in the Americas). By 1900, this prolonged conquest and penetration had produced a veritable world division of labor. Certain societies acted as the international upper class, the rich, economically diversified and industrialized powers who dominated the world scene (even though they fought quite bitterly among themselves); and other societies acted as an international lower class who provided cheap labor, certain raw materials, and certain agricultural products while they remained poor, weak, and economically overspecialized in the production of one, or at best a very few export products. Between these extremes, there were a few societies that acted as an international middle class, a group trying to catch up to the rich and at the same time trying to subjugate some of the poor societies in order to use them in their catch-up effort.[4]

The world seen in that light becomes a very different place from the world seen in the light of the originally stated theory of poverty and wealth. There is no doubt that in 1500, a few Western European societies had developed internal traits that set off the enormous growth and political expansion that followed; nor is there doubt that during this period of expansion other societies in the world had traits that made them unable to resist Western expansion. But by 1900, there were relatively few truly "underdeveloped" societies. Certainly, by 1950 there were even fewer. Rather, by the twentieth century there were some societies (the rich) that had developed as a powerful upper class, and there were others that had been developed as a poor and weak lower class. The characteristics of the poorer societies were no longer due to traditionalism, but to the direction in which they had been developed. These societies were poor not merely because of internal conditions but because of their relationship with the rich societies. Long contact and adaptation to the West had not produced the same kind of progress that had occurred in Europe and North America. That is not to say that had they been left alone, non-Western societies would have entered the twentieth century as advanced industrial societies. But they would not have entered the century as an international lower class. Furthermore, had the industrialized societies not succeeded in imposing an international division of labor, they would not have been able to reap such large benefits from their progress.

By this reasoning, the twentieth century's advanced societies had, and continue to have a direct interest in turning less advanced societies in certain directions and not in others. That is, rich societies have not been, and are not presently, interested in turning poorer societies into independent and prosperous ones. Rather, they are interested in keeping the poorer areas dependent, and overspecialized in the production of certain cheap goods. Balanced development in any poor society, therefore, is likely to meet the active resistance of the rich societies. This is not necessarily the product of any direct "plot" by the rich against the poor (even though it sometimes seems to be exactly that), but rather, the result of interconnected forces within rich societies and within the entire world system. If this is so (and it will be the task of this book to prove this point, since it cannot be accepted simply at face value), the liberal development theories of the 1950s and 1960s *had to be wrong.*

Sociologist Immanuel Wallerstein uses the term "core societies" for the rich societies that started the great outward push of the West, and it was their success that changed the rest of the world. These societies were at the center of world power in 1900. Only in the twentieth century has that power been challenged. The poor societies can be called "peripheral." They were coerced into the dominant world system run by the core societies, but they remained on the edges of the system, at least in terms of raw power, and also in terms of the benefits distributed by the world economy. A map of the world in 1900 shows that spatially, the terms "core" and "periphery" were quite suitable. The economic center of the world was then the North Atlantic, Western Europe, and the United States. A very few societies located in this center ran the rest of the world. The United States, the United Kingdom, Germany, and France, along with the small but highly industrialized societies of the Netherlands and Belgium owned almost all of Africa and huge parts of Asia; and they dominated the economies of those parts of the world which they did not directly own (most of Latin America, China, and large parts of the Middle East and Eastern Europe).

Switzerland, Sweden, and Denmark, though not colonial powers (only Denmark had a few small colonies), were certainly highly developed, well-off, and politically independent. They were, along with Belgium and the Netherlands, the "minor" core powers.

Around the core, but not really in the periphery, were several other European societies. Spain, Italy, Austria-Hungary, and Russia all had their own colonial domains. They were richer than most of the remainder of the world, but much poorer, and much less industrialized than the core powers. All of them, in one way or another, aspired to the status of core power. They were the "semi-peripheral" societies. Japan was the first non-European country to make a serious claim to core status, but in 1900 it had not yet reached this position. Canada, Australia, and New Zealand were in the peculiar position of being wealthy societies that were somewhat under the political and economic control of the United Kingdom, but they were far more independent and powerful within the British Empire than most of the other colonies.

Aside from the rather small number of countries in the core and the aspiring or semi-peripheral countries, the rest of the world was peripheral. Whether peripheral societies had their own government and played the international political game (like the Ottoman Empire, China, or most of the Latin America countries) or were outright colonies (like India or most of Africa), they were very weak and were the subjects of constant manipulation and interference by the core and semi-peripheral countries.

The core, semi-periphery, and periphery formed the different elements of the capitalist world system of 1900. The term *capitalist* is appropriate for several reasons, but mostly because it describes the prevailing economic organization of the core societies and, by extension, the economic means by which the core dominated the rest of the world economy.

Within core societies, capitalism meant the operation of a relatively free market, in which economic value and activity were determined by the impersonal mechanism of trade. The rights to private property were defended by the governments of core societies, and labor, land, capital, and the product of these could be bought and sold with few hindrances. This system, with many recent modifications, and the considerable increase of government power in restricting free internal trade and the use of private property, survives in the late twentieth century in core societies.

Outside the core, and between core societies (as distinct from within core societies) capitalism operated far less as an open, free-market system. There were tariffs that restricted the flow of goods between countries; and core societies held colonies in which they attempted to monopolize trade and exchange, and in which coerced (nonwage) labor was common in mines and plantations.

The main controllers of the means of production in core societies, the large capitalists, formed the economic, and in most cases the political elite of these societies. Since core societies in the early twentieth century played such a powerful role throughout the world, and since they were largely, if not entirely, dominated by a capitalist elite, the term "capitalist world system" is appropriate on political as well as economic grounds, even though capitalism operated quite differently in the periphery than in the core.

It is evident that the shape of the world system has changed since 1900. There continue to be core, semi-peripheral, and peripheral societies, but many societies are actively trying to escape the periphery. They are therefore more like the semi-peripheral societies than like the weak and dependent peripheral ones. A few semi-peripheral areas, most notably Japan, have joined the core. These developments have entailed enormous social change within particular societies and for the world system as a whole. The old capitalist core remains rich, *NB* and very powerful militarily, but it no longer has the absolute control it once had. A rival potential world system, the Communist system, has come into existence, led by one formerly semi-peripheral society and one formerly peripheral society, that is, by Russia and China. In today's world, the most common type of society is the semi-peripheral society, both within the remaining capitalist world system and within the Communist system.

All internal social change is not causally linked with changes in the world system, but much of it is. Also, many internal changes have influenced the world system, or systems, and this has fed back into particular societies to produce further change. A careful study of changes in the world system from 1900 to the 1970s will help explain a great deal about the general process of social change.

Definitions and Labels

Before the discussion proceeds, its principal terms should be defined.

State] a large social system with a set of rules that is enforced by a permanent administrative body. That body claims and tries to enforce sovereignty. That is, the state claims to be the highest source of decision-making of the social system within its jurisdiction, and it rejects outside interference in making or enforcing its set of rules. The many smaller systems within the state are not sovereign, nor are large international organizations like the United Nations, since states routinely reject their dictates. The "state" is a political concept that refers to the exercise of power or the ability to make and enforce rules.

Nation] a group of individuals who feel that they have so much in common (interests, habits, ways of thinking, and the like) that they should all become a particular state. Unlike the term *state*, the term *nation* refers to the subjective feelings of its people. By this definition, almost all the present nations would like to become nation-states, but many nations are actually parts of other states, and many states are not nation-states. On the whole, nation-states can count on much greater loyalty from their citizens than states that contain many nations, and this gives them greater strength in their international deal-

ings. (The term *international* should really be *interstate*, but there is
no point in using an unconventional word when a conventional one is
adequate.) Core societies tend to be nation-states, while most semi-
peripheral and peripheral states are not. But there are important exceptions.

Society: the population controlled by a state, or the population that
forms a nation, or both. For example, one may speak of "Austro-
Hungarian society in 1900" even though Austria-Hungary was then a
state composed of several nations and parts of nations. At the same
time, one may speak of "Czech society in 1900" even though the
Czechs were then a nation in the Austro-Hungarian state. Some societies are territorially limited to a single geographical area and a single
state, while others are not. The term *society*, unlike the terms *state*
and *nation*, is not limited to a single, precise definition because societies overlap with different states and nations.

Country: a well-defined geographical area. The term simply refers to
a spatial concept.

If all the world consisted of well-established core countries,
these definitions would be superfluous. France, for example, is at once
a state, a nation, a society, and a country. Its boundaries are quite
precise (even though in the past this was not always true), and the
overwhelming majority of the French people know that they are
French rather than German or Italian. But there are many unclear
cases in the world, and this causes terminological problems that sometimes have severe political implications. For example, Eritreans and
Somalis within the Ethiopian state of 1977 do not consider themselves
part of the Ethiopian nation. Ethiopia's Somalis would like to rejoin
the Somali state, and the Eritreans would like to form their own new
state. The Ethiopian state rejects these claims and tries to impose
loyalty on the entire state. Other examples include almost any European colony in Africa in 1900. Senegal, for example, was part of the
French state, but neither the French nor the Senegalese thought of
Senegal as part of the French nation. Furthermore, Senegal was a
recognizable country in 1900 even though most of its people thought
of themselves as Wolof, Tukulor, Serer, or some other tribal grouping.
These tribal groupings were something quite close to what has been
defined here as nations, even though they probably had little intention of setting up distinct states. A *tribe*, in a sense, is a *pre-nation*.
These terms do not explain anything, and the definitions given
here are more axiomatic than analytical. But without a few clear
definitions, analysis is difficult. Some other terms have already been
defined.

Core societies: economically diversified (in the twentieth century that means industrialized), rich, powerful societies that are *relatively* independent of outside control.

Peripheral societies: economically overspecialized, *relatively* poor and weak societies that are subject to manipulation or direct control by the core powers.

Semi-peripheral societies: societies midway between the core and periphery that are trying to industrialize and diversify their economies. While they are weaker than core societies, they are trying to overcome this weakness and are not as subject to outside manipulation as peripheral societies.

The notion of independence of any society is totally relative in this century. Not even the core societies are truly independent (as was demonstrated by the oil boycott of 1973–74) because their strength depends, in part, on control of resources that come from peripheral and semi-peripheral areas. Loss of such control has always been, and continues to be, a potential danger. It is even conceivable, though highly unlikely, that in the next century the core societies of the twentieth century will become the periphery of a new world system. Some core societies of the past (for example, Spain in 1550) have subsequently become peripheral societies, and over the last century, some societies (like Japan) have moved from peripheral to core status.

World system: A world system consists of a set of interconnected societies. The state of being of each of these societies depends to some extent on its relative position in the world system, which has strong, middling, and weak members. The world system of 1900 was a *capitalist* system. In the late twentieth century there is a capitalist world system and some competitors who challenge its hegemony.

Class: a group of individuals, or a group of social systems united by a common economic interest. There may be a great deal of conflict within a class. The rich do not always cooperate with each other against the poor, for example. Nor is the reverse always, or even generally, true. But the members of a class have a common position within any economic system (whether at the intrasocietal or at the intersocietal level). Any economic system has at least two, and generally more than two, classes whose interests diverge. When the members of such a group unite to act according to their economic interests, they are acting on a class basis. For example, blue-collar workers may unite in a union against the controllers of capital, or the oil-exporting states of the world may unite against the oil-importing states. Class conflict, either within a society, or internationally, is a major basis of conflict in the twentieth century, though not the only one.

Culturally based conflict groups: individuals, or groups united by a common ideological, but not economic, interest. The basis of this mutual interest may be language, religion, ethnicity, or simply political ideology. If all Greeks in Cyprus join together (say, against the Turks in Cyprus) because they are Greek, rather than because they are capitalists or laborers, rich or poor, they form a culturally based conflict group. Similarly, if the Arab states, whether oil-exporting or oil-importing, join together because they are Arabic and Muslim, they form an international culturally based conflict group. Nationalism is the most important such basis for union in the twentieth century, but it is not the only one. Many culturally based conflicts are deeply rooted in antagonistic economic relations, and thus class and culture often act simultaneously to produce particularly bitter conflict. On the other hand, class and culture may also act against each other to produce peculiar alliances. For example, in the southern United States, throughout most of the twentieth century, poor white tenant farmers were set against poor black ones, even though they had common economic interests. The alliance of poor whites with white land-owners against blacks may have served the class interests of the landowners, but it hardly served the class interests of the poor whites.

Generally, in the twentieth-century world, the divisions within the world system have been based primarily on the economic division of labor (class), as well as on cultural and ideological considerations, chiefly nationalism. The existence of these two types of cleavage, which may be contradictory, has made events rather unpredictable. This also applies to internal conflict within particular societies, and therefore, to the process of social change in general.

The Organization and Central Question of This Book

The main theme of this book is the changing world system, and how the shifting balance of international economic, political, and cultural forces shape and are shaped by changing class structures within core, semi-peripheral, and peripheral societies. The temporal format adopted, treating the early part of the century, the period between 1914 and 1950, and concluding with the shape of the world system in the latter part of the century, is both convenient and necessary. The contemporary world system is not comprehensible without background information on the changes wrought by capitalist penetration and influence in the early part of the century. Not only social scientists but people everywhere still conceive of the world and its societies in terms derived from earlier experiences.

Throughout this book there run critical questions to be answered: To what extent is the prosperity of the core dependent on domination of a periphery? Has capitalism become so tied to the exploitation of peripheral areas that it will not survive the nationalist, anti-core revolutions in the old colonial periphery? To what extent is the struggle between capitalism and communism an outcome of the earlier domination of core capitalism throughout the world? Finally, given the evident inability of core capitalist societies to control the world as easily in the late twentieth century as in the early part of the century, how will this influence domestic changes within the core? While these questions may be treated distinctly, they are all parts of another, broader question: Will the core adapt to its reduced international circumstances and survive, or will it finally collapse? What will this mean for the United States, and for different types of societies outside the core?

Social change will be studied here as the interaction between international and domestic change in various societies. This means that not all types of social change will be treated, but only those that are central to the issues raised by this critical question.

II

The Capitalist World System
in the Early Twentieth Century

By 1900 the capitalist world system reigned supreme. With a very few exceptions, its economic and political might had spread throughout the world; and its influence had changed social, economic, and cultural life as well as the balance of political forces within and between societies. How capitalism achieved such supremacy is of great interest, but it is not the central topic of this book, which takes for granted the strength of the West at the start of the twentieth century. Still this chapter will begin by reviewing, very briefly, the antecedents of that success, and then proceed to look at the international balance of economic and political forces. Such matters will set the stage for the later examination of why the capitalist system has become weaker in the present century.

Antecedents: 1450–1900

The capitalist world system originated in the second half of the fifteenth century when Portugal and Spain began an astounding series of conquests throughout the world. First, the Atlantic islands were colonized, then the coast of West Africa, the coasts of the Indian Ocean, the Americas, parts of the Indonesian Archipelago, the Philippines, and ultimately, even parts of coastal China and Japan were brought into a gigantic trading network. The Italian historian Carlo Cipolla has called this the start of the age of Vasco da Gama[1] (the first Portuguese to reach India by the sea route around southern Africa). An age that was to last into the middle of the twentieth century, it was based on the superior sailing and military technology of the Westerners, and ultimately, on their superior economic organization. When that superiority faded, the "age of Vasco da Gama" began to fade. But only now is that long period of Western domination reaching its end.

As early as 1494 the Pope formally divided the entire world outside of Europe into two parts, the Portuguese and the Spanish halves. The fact that the Iberians controlled only a few coastal trading points and forts should not blind us to the immensity of the networks established soon after. Nor should the early decay of Spain and Portugal obscure the novelty of this development.

China, in the early fifteenth century, had come close to establishing a Southeast Asian and Indian Ocean sea-based trading empire, but it failed to follow up its early lead.[2] In the thirteenth and fourteenth centuries the Mongols had conquered an immense land empire linked by caravan routes, but it, too, declined quickly, and its collapse left the former provinces of the empire relatively isolated, as they had been before the empire. In West Africa, the same period saw the rise of large, trade-based empires, Mali, Kanem-Bornu, Songhay. But again, their collapse left the same scattered villages that had existed before. Nor is the history of large empires limited to the period immediately preceding 1450 or to the Eastern Hemisphere. Ancient China, Rome, Persia, Macedonia, and India all had large empires, as did the Andean Incas and the Mexican Aztecs. But all these empires stopped far short of absorbing the entire world.

The Iberian Empires also collapsed, but when Spain and Portugal faltered, the Dutch, the English, and the French took their position. The great European trading network begun in the 1400s was never unified into a single state, but its parts were joined to the controlling core states of Western Europe by economic bonds that ultimately proved far more durable than the bonds of classical empire. The effects of this network spread inland from the coasts, and outward from the mines and plantations established in the Americas. They spread into all parts of the world, destroying or fundamentally altering all societies except for a handful of isolated and remote peoples. By 1900 the entire world had been brought into this giant Western economic system, and only one non-Western society remained in a position to escape Western domination, Japan.

How and why this happened remains a prime question of modern history, if only because the development was, in a way, so improbable. A neutral observer in the 1400s could hardly have predicted such an astonishing future. China was as technologically advanced as Europe, and in some ways more advanced. The Turks seemed militarily more dynamic and successful. No European country was very big. Portugal had fewer than one million people, Spain about 7 million, England under 3 million, and even France, the most populous state in Europe, included no more than about 12 million. China had at least ten times as many people as France, and more than all of Europe put together. India, soon to be almost united in the 1500s by the Moguls, had at least 100 million people.[3] In short, Europe did not, in the fifteenth century, seem ready to conquer the world. But the Western societies had several peculiar traits that allowed them to revolutionize the world.

First, they had in capitalism a form of economic organization that was highly oriented toward constant economic growth. Not all of Western Europe was capitalist in 1450, or even in 1500; far from it. But several key areas were. The North Italian city-states, primarily Venice, Genoa, Florence, and Milan, were probably the most advanced capitalist societies of the middle fifteenth century. A number of cities in the "Dorsal Spine" of Europe, along the trade routes between Italy and the Low Countries and through Germany to the Baltic, were also capitalist, as were the manufacturing and merchant cities on the Baltic Sea and the coast of the North Sea and English Channel.[4] Capitalism was, at that time, a form of economic organization that emphasized economic profit for the sake of *profit*, not for the sake of political power. It combined a highly rational method of bookkeeping and banking with a peculiar lack of interest in political conquest. Traditional empires were based on tribute, on the extraction of a surplus from subject populations to support the elite, or on the taxation of trade routes to support the elite. Capitalist enterprise, on the other hand, aimed at the extension of, and maintenance of, access to markets in order to increase profits. The method of increasing taxes in traditional empires was to raise them. The method of increasing profits in capitalist enterprises was to expand the velocity and quantity of exchange. While the distinction may seem both oversimplified (which it is) and trivial (which it is not), its consequences were enormous.

In 1204, Venice, the protocapitalist city-state and the precursor of European capitalism, effectively conquered the Byzantine Empire. But of this conquest it kept only the Byzantine trading rights, a few key islands, and some coastal forts. Maintaining control over a whole populous and largely hostile empire would have been too expensive. Venice was wiser than many of its successors. Time and time again capitalist societies that have fallen to the lure of classical, territorial empire have found themselves overwhelmed by the costs of maintaining large armies on foreign territory, and have frittered away the profits of their domination. Spain, in particular, ultimately failed to follow the Venetian example. Starting off with Genoese capital, it amassed a huge empire in the Americas, only to ruin itself in the sixteenth and seventeenth centuries trying to maintain this empire. Its colossal wealth notwithstanding, Spain lost its economic strength to smaller capitalist societies that developed their business rather than try to extract obedience and tribute from hostile foreigners.[5]

In classical empires, a political elite, as opposed to a business elite, dominated policy. This elite was composed of soldiers, glory-seeking emperors, and learned but antibusiness religious officials. In the small capitalist centers of the fifteenth century, politics was subordinated to business, and an economic elite of merchants, financiers, and manufacturers dominated policy making, always with an eye to profits. The key to capitalist success was not simply the ability to organize individuals. After all, the Romans, the Incas, the Mongols, and the Confucian bureaucrats of China were all superb organizers. Rather the success of these capitalist centers was due first to their ability to focus on profits to the detriment of most other considerations.[6]

Second, by the fifteenth century, Western Europe also had an advanced technology. Perhaps it was not more advanced than the technology of China, but it certainly exceeded the technology in most of the world at that time. The agricultural revolution of the Middle Ages, the more effective harnessing of horses and use of water power, and the fifteenth- and sixteenth-century advances in shipbuilding, artillery, and navigational techniques were the prerequisites of Western success.[7] Furthermore, the unique dominance of capitalism in a few crucial urban centers of Europe meant that in these centers religious elites were not particularly powerful in determining intellectual currents. Rather, intellectual inquiry was free and divorced from traditional religious ideologies. Thus, in these centers, science and technology could progress much more quickly than in the centers of traditional civilization outside of Europe. The combination of weak religious elites and dominant, practically minded business classes produced a rapid expansion of knowledge that allowed Europeans to advance far beyond other people in their mastery over nature. If, in 1400, Western Europe was possibly still behind China in technological development, from 1600 to about 1950 Western Europe (and its cultural extension, North America) moved far ahead of the rest of the world in both science and technology.

Third, Western Europe had the great good fortune of never uniting. The failure of 1000 years of effort at putting the Roman Empire together again meant that no single imperial structure was able to dominate Europe. This lack of domination aided economic advance; for imperial structures drain away business profits, stifle free thought and subjugate it to political order, overtax their subjects, attempt to impose religious and cultural uniformity, and seek glory and pomp. The closest modern Europe came to being united was in the 1500s when Hapsburg Spain used its enormous treasure of American silver in an attempt to conquer the continent. Where it conquered —in Northern Italy, parts of Southern Germany, and Iberia—science and industry were ruined, the business classes were bankrupted, and rigid Catholicism was imposed. The Spanish success of the 1500s caused the demise of Mediterranean Europe (killing, in the process, the promising early capitalist North Italian city-states) and left the way open to the smaller, less grand, and less Catholic political units of Northwestern Europe.[8]

After 1600 first the Netherlands then England took over the

capitalist trade routes opened by the Iberians and their Italian financial allies. France, though never dominant, also participated. To a lesser extent, a few minor Northwestern European societies did also.

The pattern was fairly simple in principle, though exceedingly complex in detail. Starting with a small technological advantage and with a primarily capitalist orientation, the core states of Northwestern Europe engaged in commerce throughout the world. They took raw materials and cheaply produced agricultural goods in return for their efficiently produced manufactured goods. They used their superior fleets and business organizations, and ultimately, superior military power in order to keep trade routes open and to expand markets. In peripheral areas, most particularly in Eastern Europe, they linked their commercial interests with the interests of local nobles. The nobles, in turn, forced an agricultural surplus out of their populations in order to have goods for commerce with the West. This resulted in serfdom for the peasants.[9] To some relatively unpopulated areas, particularly the Caribbean and Brazil, the Westerners brought African slaves (purchased on the coast of Africa from Africans who collected slaves as trade goods in order to purchase European products) and set up slave plantations to produce tropical agricultural commodities —chiefly tobacco, sugar, and cotton. In other parts of the Americas, Indians were enslaved to work in the mines. The spread of capitalism, while it brought progress and wealth to Western Europe, brought large-scale serfdom to Eastern Europe, slavery and serious depopulation to large parts of the Americas, and continual slave wars in substantial portions of Africa.[10] In Asia the great size and relative technological sophistication of India and China made the process slower, but eventually, the results were similar. India fell under the control of a British merchant company, Indonesia fell under the control of a Dutch merchant company, and finally, in the nineteenth century even parts of the immense Chinese Empire were subverted by the combined force of the capitalist market, cheaply and efficiently produced Western manufactured goods, and the selective but efficient use of European military force.

Everywhere, non-Westerners resisted. But the introduction of Western goods and market forces, combined with European firepower, almost always won. European losses were temporary, since the drive to expand profits meant that sooner or later the Westerners would return where they had previously been excluded. And when they returned, they would have even more advanced weapons, even more seductive and more cheaply made goods to sell, and an even greater chance of winning.

In the eighteenth century Europe began to industrialize. Using its capitalist organization of business, its control of large amounts of capital gained in foreign trade, and a superior technology, England led the way and rapidly revolutionized the technology of manufacturing. Other Western European societies, France, Germany, Belgium, Switzerland, the United States, and eventually the Netherlands and the Scandinavian countries, rather easily imitated England. By the early twentieth century they were all substantially industrialized.

But this further advance of the West in the nineteenth century, while it seemed to set the seal on Western superiority, actually initiated an opposite reaction that was not to become evident until the late twentieth century. The reasons for this are complex and more appropriate to later sections of this book. Here it will serve to note that just as the neutral observer in 1450 was unlikely to predict the future success of Western Europe, so, very few observers in 1900 ever imagined that by the late twentieth century the West might be losing its dominance. It seemed that in 450 years Western Europeans and their North American kin had made *all* the significant progress in the world, and that everyone else had stagnated. Looking ahead, there were few indicators that the capitalist world system might ever be threatened.

✳ Position in the World System and Level of Development

In the early 1900s four core societies dominated the capitalist world system. One, the United Kingdom,* had been the leading core society for most of the nineteenth century. Another, the United States, a peripheral society in the late eighteenth century, was on the verge of becoming the major core power of the twentieth, though it would not fully assume that role until the 1940s. Its main long-term rival was Germany; but while Germany ultimately came to pass Great Britain, it never overtook the United States. The fourth core society was France. It was not economically, militarily, or politically as powerful as the other three, but it was of considerable importance, possessing great cultural prestige as well as extensive foreign investments that placed it well within the core of the capitalist world system.

Five other European societies also shared membership in the core even though none rivaled the four main societies in power and influence. These were the Low Countries of Belgium and the Netherlands, Switzerland, Sweden, and to a lesser extent, Denmark.

There were five semi-peripheral societies in 1900, though one of them, Spain, had already been pushed into virtual peripherality by its defeat in the Spanish-American War of 1898. Austria-Hungary,

---

* *Great Britain* refers to England, Wales, and Scotland, while the term *United Kingdom* includes these plus Ireland (from 1801 to 1921) or these plus Northern Ireland (after 1921).

like Spain, was a declining power, having been reduced to secondary importance by its loss in the Austro-Prussian War of 1866. In 1918 it disintegrated entirely and vanished. Italy, like Germany, was a relatively new political entity striving to attain core status. But it had a weak economic base, and never quite succeeded. Russia and Japan, the two other semi-peripheral societies, were very different from the first three. Both had enormous political and economic potential and considerable strength in 1900, but both suffered from economic backwardness.

The rest of the world comprised the periphery. This included Portugal, China, and the Ottoman Empire, all of which controlled large territories but were clearly peripheral in the interactional capitalist system in that they were subject to its core economies and political pressures. The small Eastern European countries of that time were similarly peripheral. Latin American societies were formally independent, but their economies were also tied to the European core, and they were very weak in international political dealings. Canada, Australia, and New Zealand, and in some respects, parts of South Africa as well as Argentina and Uruguay were more prosperous than other peripheral societies. But they remained partially dependent on core power, and their economies were colonial adjuncts to those of the core. Almost all parts of Africa and Asia were poor, weak, and directly ruled as colonies of the core. (See Map 1.)

On the whole, position within the capitalist world system correlated highly but not perfectly with level of social, economical, and political development. The core societies were more highly industrialized, more urban, had better-educated populations, were richer, and formed more solid nation-states than non-core societies. Each of these aspects of development is discussed separately below.

Industrialization

In 1900 the four main core societies produced some three quarters of all the world's manufactured goods even though they had only about one eighth of the world's population (about 208 million people out of a world total of 1.6 billion). With the five minor core societies producing something on the order of 5 percent of the world's manufactured goods and containing 2 percent of the world's population, rounded totals show that in 1900 about 15 percent of the world's population produced 80 percent of its manufactured goods. The 85 percent of humanity outside the core produced only the remaining 20 percent of all manufactured goods.

Along with having more-developed industries the core societies had all those advances that go along with industrialization. They had far better communications than non-core societies (more railroads,

TABLE 1

Manufactured Product and Population in Core Societies, 1900

Percentage of World Manufacturing Product	Great Britain 20%	U.S. 30%	Germany 17%	France 7%	Total 74%
Percentage of World Population	2.3%	4.8%	3.5%	2.4%	13%
Total Population	37 million	76 million	56 million	39 million	208 million

SOURCE   Richard B. Morris and Graham W. Irwin, eds., *Harper Encyclopedia of the Modern World* (New York: Harper & Row, 1970), pp. 707, 849, 874.

roads, canals, better postal and telegraphic systems, and so on), far more productive agricultures, and incomparably larger capacities to produce military hardware.

Semi-peripheral societies were less industrialized, though all of them had considerable industrial capacities. Their industrial output, both on the average (in terms of product per person) and in absolute terms, was small compared to the four main core societies. Their agriculture was not as advanced (except, possibly, for Japan's), their communication systems were weaker, and their capacity to produce arms was smaller.

Among the peripheral parts of the world, Canada, Australia, and Argentina each had the beginnings of an industrial economy, and their agricultures were relatively advanced. But the rest of the peripheral world had a minuscule industrial production, and virtually all aspects of technology were far behind technology in the core parts of the world.

Division of labor and urbanization

Core societies were also more developed in that they had more advanced divisions of labor. There was greater internal economic specialization than in less developed societies, and also, as a consequence, greater concentration of population in cities. A smaller proportion of the population remained in agriculture, in large part because of superior agricultural technology. Each farmer in the core

TABLE 2

Labor Force in Agriculture Around 1900

Major Core Societies
Great Britain (1901)	9%
Germany (1907)	34%
United States (1900)	37%
France (1906)	43%

Semi-Peripheral Societies
Italy (1901)	59%
Hungary (1900)	59%
Spain (1900)	67%
Japan (1902)	69%
Russia (about 1900)	around 80%

Seven Peripheral Societies
Australia (1901)*	25%
Canada (1901)*	43%
India (about 1900)	above 70%
Mexico (about 1900)	70%
Poland (1897)	70%
Brazil (about 1900)	73%
China (about 1900)	around 80%

SOURCE   Simon Kuznets, "Quantitative Aspects of the Economic Growth of Nations," Part II in *Economic Development and Cultural Change*, Vol. V, 4 (supplement), (July 1957): 82–95. For India: Kingsley Davis, "Social and Demographic Aspects of Economic Development in India," in Simon Kuznets, Wilbert E. Moore, and Joseph J. Spengler, eds., *Economic Growth: Brazil, India, Japan* (Durham: Duke University Press, 1955), p. 273. For Poland and China: Paul Bairoch, "Agriculture and the Industrial Revolution 1700–1914," in Carlo M. Cipolla, ed., *The Fontana Economic History of Europe*, Vol. III (London: Collins/Fontana Books, 1973), pp. 468–69. For Russia: Carlo M. Cipolla, *The Economic History of World Population* (Baltimore: Penguin Books, 1967), p. 29.

* Australia and Canada have been included as reminders that peripherality is not identical to low development, though the two are highly correlated. All core societies were and are highly developed, but according to many indicators, a few peripheral societies were rather more developed than one might expect. In 1900 this was the case for several "English overseas" societies—Canada, Australia, New Zealand, and in part, South Africa. It was also true for Argentina, Uruguay, and in part, Chile. These peripheral societies were all more developed in certain respects than the semi-peripheral societies, in other respects, they were less developed. Much of the same might be said about some of the wealthy petroleum exporting societies of the 1970s. While rich, and in some ways highly developed, in other respects they remain strongly peripheral—for example, Kuwait. Later elaboration of the terms "core" and "peripheral" will make this clear.

societies could produce enough food to feed many people, while in less developed societies, each farmer produced much less, and a far larger proportion of the population continued to live in rural villages. This, of course, was very closely associated to the relative degree of industrialization.

Urbanization statistics for this period are troublesome because different states defined "urban" differently. But a better comparative measure of the degree of division of labor is provided by the percentage of the labor force in agriculture. While obviously some village dwellers did not engage in agriculture, and while some city dwellers did, this statistic is highly correlated with urbanization as well as with degree of industrialization.

Education and literacy

Core societies, on the whole, had much more highly educated populations in 1900 than did the rest of the world. Their literacy rates were close to or above 90 percent; while in most other societies, school systems were poorly developed or, as in most of Africa, virtually nonexistent. The world's major universities and research centers were to be found in core societies, and most of these countries also had highly productive and diversified book-publishing industries as well as many newspapers with large circulations. These facilities were both the result of, and a further cause of, the high educational levels.

Many English overseas societies were highly developed in this respect as well; so was Japan, which probably had a higher literacy rate in 1900 than France.[11] The semi-peripheral societies all maintained major universities, as did some of the peripheral European societies and some of the Latin American ones. China, India, much of the rest of Asia, and parts of Africa had long records of achievement in their traditional intellectual centers, and India in particular contained a substantial number of Western-educated intellectuals. But in general, in most of the peripheral world, as well as in the semi-peripheral societies (Japan excepted), illiteracy was still very high (that is, well over 50 percent, and in most of Africa well over 90 percent), there were few newspapers and little publishing of books, and the average educational level was low.

Wealth

Core societies of the early 1900s were also, on the whole, much richer than other societies. This was a consequence of their higher technological levels and their more productive industries and agricultures. Per capita income statistics for the period are more a matter of educated guesswork than certainty; but even if one allows for a

TABLE 3

**Estimated Per Capita Gross National Products,*
1900–1910**

Major Core Societies	
United States	$1330†
Great Britain	840
France	740
Germany	640
Average	890
Three Minor Core Societies	
Denmark	$730
Netherlands	690
Sweden	510
Average	640
Three Semi-Peripheral Societies	
Italy	$290
Russia	about 200
Japan	140
Average	210
Five Normal Peripheral Societies	
Mexico	$160
Philippines	140
Egypt	130
Ghana (Gold Coast)	130
India	60
Average	120
Three Rich Peripheral Societies	
Australia	$960
Canada	940
Argentina	440
Average	780

SOURCE   Simon Kuznets, *Economic Growth of Nations* (Cambridge: The Belknap Press of Harvard University, 1971), pp. 11–40. For Russia: Olga Crisp, "Russia 1860–1914," in Rondo E. Cameron, ed., *Banking in the Early Stages of Industrialization* (New York: Oxford University Press, 1967), p. 184.

* Gross National Product (GNP) represents the monetary value of a country's total goods and services.
† All numbers rounded to nearest $10 in 1965 U.S. dollars. Multiply by about 150% for mid-1970s dollars. Averages not weighted by population.

high degree of error, they tend to reflect enormous differences between core and non-core areas.

The same qualifications exist here as with other indicators of development. Aside from the English overseas societies (it is obvious, by now, that they were extremely deviant peripheral societies by most standards), some non-core societies were relatively wealthy—Argentina, for example. Even the Gold Coast (today's Ghana), then a British colony and a very peripheral society in the world system, was probably almost as wealthy on a per capita basis as Japan, even though, in every other way, Japan was both more developed and much closer to joining the core.

Political development: the nation-state

The main core societies were nation-states. Though Germany included a substantial Slavic minority in its eastern parts, and though Great Britain ruled a culturally distinct and hostile Ireland, the four major core states each contained a substantial majority of people who shared a language, a general way of looking at the world, and most importantly, a common allegiance to and belief in the legitimacy of the state. This was also true of some non-core states (in particular, Japan), but in most of the rest of the world the boundaries of states correlated poorly with the boundaries of cultural groups that identified themselves as distinct nations or tribes. In European colonies in Asia and Africa, the state was controlled by Westerners, not by local people. In much of Latin America (most notably in Mexico and the Andean countries) there was an enormous cultural and linguistic gap between the Amerindian populations and the Spanish elite. The Ottoman Empire, Austria-Hungary, and Russia ruled culturally disparate people who were frequently hostile to each other and to the state that ruled them. Even such old and presumably well-established states as Spain and China were to experience separatist civil wars in the twentieth century, and these often came close to establishing new states. In each of Eastern Europe's new Balkan states, large portions of the dominant ethnic group still lived outside the state that claimed them.[12]

Although the four major core societies were relatively well-established nation-states, some of the minor core societies were not. Sweden, in 1905, split into two countries, Norway and Sweden. In Belgium parts of the Flemish (Dutch-speaking) half of the population felt oppressed by the dominant Walloon (French-speaking) half, and this would produce ethnic conflict throughout the century. The Swiss state was weak and consisted more of a coalition of loosely joined cultural groups than of a single nation-state. Even in France, the United States, Great Britain (leaving aside Ireland), and Germany there were major cleavages between various ethnic groups and regions. Some Welsh and Scots felt that they ought not be part of a British state; some Bavarians did not wish to be part of Germany; and in the United States, many new immigrants as well as many members of racial minorities were poorly integrated into the dominant culture and gave little loyalty to the state. Also, Japan was probably as much or more a nation-state than any of the major core societies. Thus it is apparent that nationhood is a less reliable indicator of development than most economically based factors. Nevertheless it can be said that the major core societies of the early 1900s were far more strongly organized into nation-states than the overwhelming majority of peripheral and semi-peripheral societies.[13]

Just as the highly industrialized societies had an economic and military advantage, so the stronger nation-states had a political advantage in that they could count on the loyalty of a relatively large proportion of their inhabitants in times of conflict with other states. States that were not yet fully nation-states could be undone by the simple tactic of "divide and conquer." Hostile cultural groups were unreliable supporters of the state that ruled them, and they often turned directly against it. This was shown during World War I when military pressure caused a disintegration of Austria-Hungary and Turkey (the Ottoman Empire), and even, to some extent, Russia. Local nationalists revolted against these states and hastened their collapse. On the other hand, the German nation-state held together despite a severe defeat. In much of Africa, Europeans could run their colonies with little military power because the local populations were so culturally distinct and disunited. Even in China and India, cultural diversity and lack of allegiance to a single state made foreign control much easier.

Development: conclusions

In brief, at the beginning of this century the core societies of the capitalist system, particularly the four main ones, were more developed than the world's other societies. Certain indicators of development reveal a few major deviations from this rule, but these discrepancies also emphasize that development is not the *sole* determinant of core status. Furthermore, the existence of these discrepancies should not conceal that in general in the early 1900s the distinction between the developed core and the less developed periphery and semi-periphery was very clear. If, in one way or another, the English overseas societies and a few Latin American societies were better off than other states on the periphery, most of the world's population was more consistent with expectations. These favored societies contained very few people, and when considered with all of Latin

America, Asia, and Africa, must be judged atypical and of little statistical importance.

As for semi-peripheral societies, the pattern, while not unbroken, is clear. Some such states, notably Spain, Italy, and Austria-Hungary, were less developed than the core societies but far wealthier (as well as more industrialized, urbanized, and literate) than the vast majority of peripheral societies. Others were not. Russia, on a per capita basis, was at a low stage of development, even though it had large industries and cities and a well-educated urban elite. Japan was also a very poor semi-peripheral society in some respects.

These qualified conclusions on developmental differences between societies in the capitalist world system make evident the need to discuss the other dimensions as well. They are, in some cases, equally important.

World Investment, Trading, and Economic Patterns

Core societies were not simply more developed than non-core societies in the early twentieth century, they also owned a good bit of the world; for their citizens held large investments in peripheral and semi-peripheral societies. In 1913, citizens of the United Kingdom, France, Germany, and the United States owned about 85 percent of all capital invested abroad (that is, of all capital not provided by native investors). And in some peripheral societies, foreign capital accounted for a very high percentage of the total monetary investment in domestic concerns. Thus, with respect to foreign investment, the United Kingdom was still the preeminent core society in the early twentieth century. Some 35 percent of its investment was in Canada and the United States, 9 percent in India, 8.5 percent in Australia, 8 percent in South Africa, and 8 percent in Latin America. France and Germany were primarily investors in Europe, most of their investments being in the non-core states of the continent's southern and eastern regions. Twenty-five percent of all French foreign investment was in Russia, and 10 percent in Spain and Portugal. But both France and Germany also had major investments in Latin America (primarily Brazil and Argentina) and in the Ottoman Empire. In 1900 the United States was still a very minor foreign investor, but by 1913 its share of world investment had increased and was growing rapidly, allowing it to become, by far, the world's major foreign investor soon after mid-century. In 1913, 26 percent of United States investment was in Canada, 25 percent in Mexico, and 13 percent in Cuba. Belgium, the Netherlands, and Switzerland were minor foreign investors. Spain, Italy, Austria-Hungary, Russia, and Japan each also had small invest-

TABLE 4

Foreign Investment in World Regions in 1913
(In Percentages)

Place of Investment	Investors' Home Country					
	U.K.	*France*	*Germany*	*U.S.*	*Other*	*Total*
Europe	9	39	21	6	25	100
Canada	70	2	4	26	0	100
United States	60	6	13	—	21	100
Latin America and Caribbean	42	18	10	19	11	100
Oceania	96	4	0	0	0	100
Asia	50	18	10	4	18	100
Africa	61	22	12	0	5	100
Total World	44	20	13	8	15	100

SOURCE   William Woodruff, *Impact of Western Man: A Study of Europe's Role in the World Economy 1750–1960* (New York: St. Martin's Press, 1966), pp. 154–55.

ments in a few areas abroad. But the four major core societies were extremely dominant in foreign investment, just as they were in the production of manufactured goods.[14]

To gain an idea of how powerful core investments were in certain peripheral economies, consider that in 1913 the Argentine economy had an annual Gross National Product on the order of two to three billion dollars (calculated in 1965 U.S. dollars, which have been estimated as worth about two-thirds less than 1913 dollars), but in that year, some nine billion dollars invested in Argentina were owned by foreigners.[15] In other words, outside investors owned Argentine land and facilities worth about three times the country's annual production.

That proportion may not take on its full meaning until compared to a hypothetical situation. If the United States in the 1970s were in an economic position similar to Argentina's in 1913, foreign investors would own something on the order of three trillion dollars worth of the country's assets—and all the shares of the New York Stock Exchange put together are currently worth only about one trillion dollars. In other words, if the United States of the 1970s were in the economic plight of Argentina in 1913, all its major corporations and much of its other investment opportunities would be owned by foreigners.

Argentina was the extreme case, but even in Canada and Mexico in 1913, foreign investment was worth about twice the annual GNP. In India, foreign investment (almost entirely British) equaled 25 to 30 percent of the annual GNP. But in the United States in 1913, where the GNP was about 120 billion dollars (again, in 1965 dollars), foreign investment amounted to only about 20 billion, even though, in absolute terms, foreign investment in the United States was worth far more than a similar one in any of the peripheral economies.[16] Thus the *relative* foreign investment (relative, that is, to GNP) in Argentina was about 18 times greater than such investment in the United States; that in Canada or Mexico was about 12 times greater, and even that in a very poor economy (such as India's) was twice as much. This reflects one of the key differences between core and peripheral economies: the latter are heavily dominated by foreign investments, while the former are not. France, Great Britain, and Germany had even smaller foreign-investment ratios within their economies than the United States.

While the economic impact of huge foreign investments within a society can be measured quite easily, their psychological impact cannot. Consider this current case. In the United States in the 1970s many are worried about the possibility of a "takeover" of the national economy by Arab and Iranian petroleum interests. Yet these petroleum exporters have, at most, several billion dollars to invest, and into the 1980s it is unlikely that they will have more than a few hundred billion even if they manage to save an unusually large portion of their earnings (which is itself a questionable proposition). How much can they "take over" in an economy that has a Gross National Product of a trillion and a half dollars a year? Possibly enough to worry many Americans. But certainly not enough to turn the nation's economy into a foreign owned operation. One can imagine how dependent and vulnerable some United States citizens would feel if foreign investment reached two or three times the annual GNP.

Investment in non-core economies took many forms. A few peripheral and semi-peripheral areas—Argentina, Brazil, Mexico, Canada, Australia, Russia, the Ottoman Empire, India, China, and South Africa—contained most of the world's foreign investment. Chile, Cuba, Egypt (mostly the Suez Canal), and the Netherlands East Indies (Indonesia) as well as Japan also had considerable foreign investment. Throughout most of the peripheral portions of the world, foreign investment was, in absolute terms, small. But even there, most of what little investment there was in the modern (that is, import-export) sector was very heavily controlled by the core societies.[17]

In some non-core societies the land itself was owned by citizens of core societies, but except in a few plantation societies, this was a relatively rare phenomenon. More commonly, core investors controlled the means of transportation (chiefly railroads), key mineral resources (gold, tin, petroleum, and so on), and large commercial houses that dealt in the import-export business. In China, for example, foreign investment was concentrated almost entirely in the coastal cities that handled foreign trade rather than in the interior. In the Balkans the French, Germans, and Austrians controlled railroads and banks, but little land as such. In Argentina, the entire railway system was owned by the British and comprised that country's single largest foreign asset. French investment in Russia was mostly in the form of railway and government bonds, and in India, 49 percent of foreign investment (for the most part British) was in government bonds, 37 percent in railways, 7 percent in coffee, tea, and rubber plantations, and 7 percent in other types of investments.[18]

The presence of foreign investment in non-core economies in the early twentieth century has often been used to explain the poverty that prevailed there.[19] But this argument is clearly a misguided reading of the facts, for those non-core areas that held the largest foreign investments per capita were also the most prosperous non-core societies. The bulk of foreign investment was attracted by the presence of valuable export commodities, and the more of these that existed, the wealthier the society.

While financial dependence did not create poverty, it did create peculiarly lopsided economies and a slow pace in economic diversification. It kept some economies dependent on the export of a few valuable resources, making these economies extremely vulnerable to the effects of changes in the needs of the core economies. Foreign investment went into the development of a few, specialized sectors: products that could be exported to core economies, transportation networks that carried these products to ports, and government structures that maintained the social order and administrative machinery needed by the export sector. Thus the more prosperous they became, the more peripheral economies tended to become highly specialized. This was the exact opposite of the trend in core economies, where increasing prosperity brought increasing diversification. While core economies were governed basically by domestic needs and markets, peripheral economies were governed by events occurring outside their societies.

A look at their export patterns in the early 1900s shows the skewed nature of peripheral economies during this period. Argentina and Uruguay exported meat and cereals, Brazil exported coffee and rubber, Cuba exported sugar, French Indochina and British Burma exported rice, the Gold Coast exported cocoa and gold, India exported jute, cotton, and tea, Nigeria exported palm oil, Egypt exported cotton, Mexico exported various minerals and petroleum, South Africa was a major mineral (chiefly diamonds and gold) exporter, and

TABLE 5

Percentage Distribution of Exports by Value for Selected Peripheral Economies, 1913

Romania
Cereals	76%
Petroleum	10%
Lumber	4%
Other	10%

Egypt
Cotton	80%
Cottonseed	7%
Cereals	6%
Other	7%

Brazil
Coffee	61%
Rubber	18%
Other	21%

Gold Coast (Ghana)
Cocoa	46%
Gold	31%
Timber	6%
Other	17%

Southern Nigeria
Palm products	74%
Tin	8%
Other	18%

Dutch Indies (Indonesia)
Sugar	23%
Petroleum	17%
Tobacco, Tea, Coffee	20%
Copra (Coconut)	8%
Other	32%

SOURCE   W. Arthur Lewis, ed., *Tropical Development 1880–1913* (Evanston: Northwestern University Press, 1970), pp. 103, 148, 209, 258. For Romania: Daniel Chirot, *Social Change in a Peripheral Society: The Creation of a Balkan Colony* (New York: Academic Press, 1976), p. 122.

so on. In each peripheral economy, one or, more often, a few primary products dominated exports. (Primary products are agricultural and mineral products; while secondary products are manufactured items, and tertiary products are services, like banking.)

Core societies were not limited to primary exports. The United

States, for example, exported a wide range of raw materials in 1913 (31 percent of its total exports) and of raw agricultural products (7 percent), but it also exported manufactured (that is processed) food-stuffs (13 percent of exports) and a wide array of other manufactured products (49 percent of exports). In the same year the United Kingdom exported large quantities of manufactured textile goods (27 percent of exports) as well as iron and steel products, manufactured chemicals, and machinery (together 18 percent of exports). Its only significant primary export was coal (11 percent of exports). France and Germany also had supplied a wide array of exports. Of the core societies only Sweden was still highly dependent on the export of a few primary products, and even this circumstance was changing very rapidly and would cease by the 1930s.[20]

But as the export figures for 1913 indicate, even huge and geographically highly diversified peripheral areas like the Dutch East Indies specialized in a relatively small number of primary export products. This was true even in India. It was equally true of the wealthy export economies of Canada and Australia which specialized in mineral exports and cereals and meat or animal products.

Of course in the less developed societies, not all the economy was engaged in the production of key export commodities. (Those sectors of the work force not so engaged tended to be involved in very poor, technologically stagnant, and unproductive subsistence activities.) Still the dependence on a few exports and the dominance of foreign investments tended to produce serious malintegration. That is, the various parts of the economy and society of a particular state tended to interact directly with the core economies, without interacting with each other. Thus they became a series of isolated enclaves more tightly connected to distant European or American markets than to other economic sectors or provinces of the same country.

For example, in Brazil, there were three distinct economic regions, and these hardly interacted. Donald Coes has written:

> Between 1870 and 1900 [railway] lines were opened in nearly every [Brazilian] state. . . . British capital was invested in many of the larger private lines. . . . One of the fundamental weaknesses of Brazilian railway development was the lack of any real national integration of the system. . . . A number of different gauges were used, making it impossible to interchange rolling stock, and even today this problem persists. Since most railways were built to bring produce down from the hinterlands to the ports, no railways ever linked the various regions of Brazil with one another.[21]

That is, Brazil's southern coffee area, Amazon rubber area, and very poor, virtually subsistence and sugar-producing northeastern area each operated independently. The lack of interregional transportation has been used to explain a phenomenon that would otherwise defy explanation: namely, that even though the coffee area was short of labor, and the northeast was over-populated and poor, the coffee area imported labor from Europe (mostly from Italy) while underemployed northeasterners remained in their own region.

If the case of Brazil was extreme, this general situation was typical. In Colombia:

> Railway construction divided the country further and made each of its component parts look outward. Since it was cheaper to bring merchandise to Medellin from London than from Bogota, each commercial region . . . was more or less independent and what it did not produce it brought in from abroad.[22]

It is evident from this that even in the early twentieth century, the term *underdeveloped* did not properly describe the nature of peripheral economies. To be sure, peripheral economies were less industrialized, and peripheral societies were less literate, less urban, and poorer than core societies. But peripheral societies also had enclaves that were participants in the world system, and these enclaves were not so much underdeveloped as developed in a particular direction—as subsidiary producers of primary goods for the world market. The non-enclave parts of peripheral economies and societies were largely undeveloped since, with the lack of intrastate exchange, they did not benefit significantly from the relative prosperity of the enclaves. Foreign investors, who dominated the enclaves, were hardly interested in a particular state's balanced development. Rather, they sought to develop whatever areas of a state seemed most likely to generate profitable exports. Ultimately, the undeveloped subsistence sectors of peripheral societies were to turn into huge labor reserves for the enclaves, but in the early twentieth century, this had happened only in a few of the more highly developed peripheral economies in Latin America, Asia, and Africa. (In this respect, the peripheral English overseas economies again stood out as exceptions: they had no undeveloped subsistence sectors and no labor reserves. Thus, like Argentina, Uruguay, and Chile, they had to import labor from Europe. The absence of a significant, retarded subsistence sector later became a great benefit to these societies.)

The full implications of this kind of development can be seen in other examples. Some of the early twentieth century's agricultural peripheral economies were so dependent on the world market that they had lost the ability to feed themselves, even though they were overwhelmingly rural. Senegal, for example, had become sufficiently specialized in peanut production (for exportation to France, where peanut oil was an important commodity) that it had to import food (mostly rice from another part of the French colonial empire, Indochina). Java in Dutch Indonesia, which was a major exporter of several tropical products, was also an increasingly important rice importer. There is nothing wrong with economic specialization as such; however, a society that is highly dependent on the export of one or a few products risks widespread economic damage from a substantial drop in the price of even one of its products, the economy having few (and sometimes no) alternative exports toward which it can turn.

In the core societies, there was a great deal of regional specialization. The agricultural middle west in the United States, for example, specialized in cereal and meat production and exchanged these items for industrial products from the northeast and Great Lakes regions. Iowa in 1910 was no more economically independent than Senegal. But specialization within a well-integrated society is quite different from specialization within a peripheral, enclave economy. First, Iowa farmers could put much more political pressure on the United States political system in times of trouble than Senegalese peanut farmers could put on the French political system. This meant they could extract greater economic concessions. Second, as the demand for agricultural labor declined in the agricultural parts of the United States, it was fairly easy for people to migrate from rural areas to industrial areas. In peripheral economies, where there were no industrial areas, if the price of peanuts, or coffee, or rubber went through a depressed period (a frequent occurrence for primary commodities), the agricultural worker was stuck with a bad bargain.

The Brazilian economist Celso Furtado has shown that when coffee prices fell, there was a long-run tendency for Brazilian coffee producers to produce even more coffee, rather than to switch to another product. They had no viable alternative. However in a balanced economy, if demand for one product falls, investors have other opportunities and labor finds other jobs. Highly specialized regions in core economies have many of the same problems as peripheral economies, but their problems are much less acute.[23]

In the long run, the only solution to such overspecialization is economic diversification. But in peripheral economies, this step was extremely difficult. Diversification requires time, well-integrated markets, and large amounts of capital. These were all in short supply in the peripheral economies of the early 1900s, particularly because so much of the investment capital that was available was foreign and more interested in the extraction of a few export commodities than in general economic integration and balanced growth. Given the low levels of skilled labor in peripheral economies, this is not surprising.

Why should core investors invest in, say, Brazilian or Senegalese industry when these were unlikely to be as efficient and competitive as the more advanced industries in core economies? As long as peripheral economies remained part of the world capitalist system, their economic diversification was not a profitable proposition even if it was necessary for their eventual well-being and for the well-being of their societies.

In 1900 the semi-peripheral economies—those of Italy, Spain, Austria-Hungary, Russia, and Japan—were not as over-specialized agriculturally as the peripheral economies, and they all had considerable industries. Japan especially was on its way to having a strong, well-integrated, and highly diversified economy. But throughout the early part of the twentieth century, semi-peripheral economies were in constant danger of being turned into peripheral ones. Russia, for example, was turning into a major wheat exporter and was forced to import much of its manufactured needs and a great deal of its investment capital. In this respect, the semi-peripheral economies were economies whose fate had not yet been decided. They could develop in the manner of core economies, but they also risked being reduced to peripherality. This dilemma was a source of much of the political tension that existed within these societies.

Cultural Elements of Position in the World System

It is perhaps in the cultural and intellectual sphere that the essence of the differences between core, semi-peripheral, and peripheral societies is most evident. Unfortunately, ideas are hard to measure, and because of that, the defenders of non-Western cultures have repeatedly stressed that "Third World" cultures have retained their superiority in the face of Western military, economic, and technological success. Virtually every peripheral culture has produced apologists who have claimed that their culture is more "humane," more profoundly philosophical, or more poetic than the crassly materialistic capitalist cultures of the West. Of course, apologists for Western thought have claimed for a long time that in some way the West is more "civilized" than the rest of the world. This was particularly true in the early twentieth century when most Westerners accepted the racist and ethnocentric notion that the West had a "civilizing" mission to perform in the world, and that non-Western cultures were, in some sense, backward, and for many, "savage."

All attempts to prove that *any* culture is more humane, civilized, or philosophically attuned to universal truth than any other are fruitless except as a means of boosting cultural pride. Rather, the key question is: What cultural patterns have shaped change in the twentieth century? The answer is clear. Because of the overwhelming economic and military strength of the West, each contemporary culture has had to adapt to Western ways or perish. World science and technology, as well as methods and theories of social, political, and economic organization have been dominated by the core societies. This is in keeping with their expected role, for, by definition, a core society causes other societies to change (whether by force, or by example). Core cultures are dynamic, and they originate ideas that others adopt or try to adapt to their own local conditions. In the late twentieth century, Western societies have lost the dominance they once had in this sphere. Japan, China, and Russia have provided non-Western (and, in the case of Russia and China, noncapitalist) models of change, and India has served as a model of effective anticolonialism (that is, anti-Western political behavior) for many societies. In addition, Islamic cultures have recently regained some of the dynamism they exhibited before the rise of the West. But all this has happened as non-Western areas have moved from peripheral to semi-peripheral or even core status. These changes have been possible because Japan, China, Russia, India, and other non-Western societies have adopted certain core ideas and techniques in order to compete more successfully.

In the first decade of the twentieth century, virtually all new ideas came from the tiny number of Western societies at the core of the capitalist world system. Latin American societies could try to imitate French intellectual fashions and political forms, German military organization, or British business organization, but innovation in Latin American cultures was just that—imitation—not domestic dynamism. Latin America was not alone. A number of peripheral and semi-peripheral societies tried to overcome their relative weakness through conscious imitation of the West. Japan, while retaining much of its traditional culture, was highly successful economically because it adopted many Western techniques and forms of organization. Even in Russia, the ideological struggle between the proponents of native village culture and Western culture was soon to be resolved by the triumph of Marxism, that is, Western socialist ideology. (Marx, it should be remembered, was a German who lived and worked in France and England, and who was, for some time, employed by a New York newspaper.) In China, the revolution that was brewing in the first decade of the century, and which finally broke out in 1911, was led by people imbued with Western ideals. Even Gandhi, the archetypical nativist, was trained in British Law, and India's first ruler after Gandhi, Nehru, was in some ways culturally more British than Indian. Similarly, Ho Chi Minh's ideology was formed largely during his residence in France and the United States.[24]

The fact that many new anti-Western cultural forms have become very influential since 1950 should not obscure the fact that in the early twentieth century, core cultures were overwhelmingly dominant. This was not the result of any innate or absolute superiority, but rather the result of Western military, political, economic, and technological success.

Core societies, then, were intellectually dynamic just as they were economically dynamic. Semi-peripheral societies, on the other hand, had cultures sufficiently dynamic to influence a few neighboring areas (Japan at this time was beginning to influence China, and Russia strongly influenced cultural developments in other Slavic, Eastern European societies), but their influence was far smaller than that of core cultures. Successful semi-peripheral cultures were also highly *syncretic*. That is, they combined traditional cultural patterns with imported Western ones in a fairly successful way. This sort of synthesis had not yet been achieved in peripheral cultures.

Peripheral cultures in the early 1900s, like peripheral economies, were peculiarly malintegrated. Each had a small elite that had accepted many Western ideas (and that existed in what one might call cultural enclaves since its members tended to live in the few main commercial cities dealing with core societies); however the large majority of each population retained more traditional ways of viewing the world, and between the elites and the masses there was relatively little contact or understanding. The members of the "cultural enclaves" based their notions of reality on what they had learned from Western intellectual sources. By and large, their understanding of core societies was greater than their understanding of their own societies.

Furtado explains a typical example. In Brazil, he notes, late nineteenth- and early twentieth-century Brazilian politicians and economists repeatedly failed to understand the nature of the Brazilian economy because they had learned their economics and politics from European books and universities. Consequently the country's frequent economic crises were met with responses that would have been proper in Europe, but which were totally unrealistic in Brazil. This pattern was most evident throughout Latin America in the sphere of political ideology. European (particularly French) constitutional models and political ideologies were espoused, but these had so little bearing on Latin American realities that the end products were always highly distorted, and generally inefficient.[25]

Throughout the peripheral world, this pattern was repeated over and over. It was only when intellectual elites in peripheral areas learned more about the realities of their own societies that they could hope to suit Western ideas to local conditions. But the process of producing successful syncretic cultures was difficult. Just as foreign investors dominated the peripheral economies, so foreign languages (French, German, English) held sway in non-core cultures, at least in terms of prestige. Everywhere, elitists tried to imitate the ways of the French, Germans, or English. Russian and Romanian nobles spoke French, wealthy Argentines or Brazilians sent their children to local French, German, or English schools, aspiring Chinese modernizers went to school in the United States or Japan, or at least to Western-run schools in China, and of course, in the European colonies of Asia and Africa, the tiny, new school systems were patterned entirely after schools in the ruling country. Before cultural peripherality could be overcome, there had to be greater cultural integration within peripheral societies, and this required cultural, as well as political, nationalism and pride. As the twentieth century advanced, cultural nationalism gradually replaced many of the enclave cultures which had predominated earlier. But at the start of the century, this was only beginning to happen.

Cultural peripherality can have economic consequences. With respect to Canada, the economist W. T. Easterbrook has observed:

> . . . Heavy reliance on borrowing techniques and capital from external sources, and concentration on processes related to the exploitation of a limited number of basic resources, seriously restrict the possibility of creative action on the part of the entrepreneurship of "persistence" areas, whose induced investment is reflected in the more or less routine technological change characteristic in such areas. . . . Technological progress, an accompaniment of growth, manifests little or nothing of the transforming power which, in some areas, takes us to the heart of economic change.[26]

Cultural peripherality and economic peripherality were closely related in the early 1900s, and the lack of new ideas and "transforming" technologies in peripheral areas, which was a consequence of peripherality, further perpetuated that condition.

Core cultures, as indicated, were far more dynamic than peripheral or semi-peripheral cultures; how else did they differ? Aside from the crucial fact that they were well integrated (that is, widespread within each core society rather than being restricted to a few elite individuals) and well suited to conditions that prevailed in their own societies, what was their specific content? Simply put, core cultures of the early twentieth century placed great emphasis on business rationality (the propriety of, and need to maximize, economic profits through continual technological advance), scientific growth (the worthiness of constant expansion of knowledge), and the legitimacy of capitalist organization (the propriety of a business-oriented social and political system in which private property and the right to maximize profits was insured). Not all Westerners shared these values: on the conservative and reactionary side of the spectrum, there were many who claimed that capitalist culture was humdrum and crassly materialistic, while on the left there were many who questioned the justice of capitalist organization. But the dominant elites in core societies and probably the large majority of the core populations accepted these notions without much question. Rational capitalism and science had brought unmatched progress and growing prosperity. Science had not yet solved all problems, but it promised greater and greater success. The endless search for profits and knowledge might lack poetic beauty, but who could argue with success?

Why, given this success, did peripheral cultures fail to copy Western ideas successfully? The problem was that they often did copy, but only in the cultural enclaves dominated by core economies. *non- enclaves* Meanwhile, large portions of the peripheral world's population remained outside these enclaves. These masses neither accepted nor understood Western ideas, and this produced the great cultural splits suggested above. The key is that the ideas and techniques worked out in the capitalist core were not *directly suitable* in peripheral or even semi-peripheral societies. Just as close ties between peripheral and core economies did not (and could not) change peripheral economies into strong, independent, diversified economies, but rather into overspecialized, dependent economies, so close cultural ties between core and periphery produced small elites blinded to local realities and unable to adapt Western thought to local needs. French or British educational systems could not work effectively outside the enclaves, where the native language and customs prevailed.

The basic ideology of capitalist economic and political organization, moreover, was not suited to peripheral societies, for it perpetuated and strengthened peripheral economic and cultural malintegration. In other words, accepting core ideas made the periphery even more dependent and divided instead of more independent and integrated. What was needed was an acceptance of economic and scientific rationality *combined* with a rejection of core capitalist ideology and with the creation of ideas and techniques suitable to the majority in each non-Western population. This was a difficult task indeed.

By 1900 only one non-core society, Japan, had succeeded in carrying out this kind of "cultural revolution." For all its incorporation of Western ideas, particularly Western science, technology, and military organization, Japan was never a slavish imitator. Old Japanese values were upheld, the new synthetic culture was successfully taught to and absorbed by the Japanese masses, and Japanese intellectual leaders never alienated themselves from Japanese reality by empty imitation of the West. While the elites in most non-core societies pretended that they were like the French, Germans, or English, the Japanese elite never went through such a stage. Just as Japanese contact with the West never produced a dependent enclave cultural pattern, so the Japanese economy never experienced a purely colonial, dependent stage. Economic and cultural success were closely related, and both were the result of Japan's success in keeping itself more independent of Western political and commercial control than any other non-Western society.[27]

As a last point on culture and position in the capitalist world system it is worth noting that the English overseas colonies (and earlier, the United States) evolved their cultures in a peculiar way. While these areas were peripheral, they had no large, non-Westernized masses. Even though they were the receivers of ideas from Great Britain, they did not suffer from the malintegration characteristic of societies in which only a small minority was Westernized. Thus, the effort needed to blend Western culture with the culture of Australia, New Zealand, or Canada (or, for that matter, the United States) was not very great, since from the very start most people in these places were former Europeans. A synthesis did have to occur before each of these societies could escape peripherality, but in all instances the product was not that dramatically different from the original, imported model. The cultural peripherality of these societies, like their economic peripherality, was enormously different from comparable patterns in other peripheral areas. Just as Canada, Australia, and New Zealand escaped many of the economic traumas of other peripherals, so they escaped the trauma of cultural revolution as the only means to a workable synthesis of Western and domestic ideas. In this sense, the English overseas societies (and the United States) cannot be considered typical, nor do they serve as useful models of how to overcome peripherality.

The Distribution of International Power and Changes in the World System

Throughout the first decade of the twentieth century the main core powers dominated the world to an extraordinary degree. Only in a few areas did the minor core powers and the semi-peripheral powers also exercise some influence. Almost all of Africa and Asia was under the direct or indirect control of the main powers. Most of Latin America was politically independent, but the large foreign investments in Latin American economies, the ties of economic and cultural dependency, and the occasional direct military interventions by core powers reduced this independence considerably.

World population and power in the first decade of the twentieth century showed the following patterns:

TABLE 6

Control of Population, 1900–1910: Europe
(Including the Entire Russian Empire),
26 Percent of the World's Population, or 425 Million People

Percentage of the Population
Controlled by:

United Kingdom	10%		
Germany	13%	major core = 32%	total core = 38%
France	9%		
The minor core societies	6%		
Austria-Hungary	11%		
Italy	8%		
Spain	4%	semi-periphery = 54%	
Russian Empire (Asian parts included)	31%		
Peripheral Europe (Portugal° and Balkan States)	8%	periphery = 8%	

SOURCE   The estimated population figures for Tables 6–10 are from Woodruff, *Impact of Western Man*, pp. 103–04, 110; Gunnar Myrdal, *Asian Drama: An Inquiry into the Poverty of Nations* (New York: Pantheon, 1968), p. 1396; Henri Bunle, *Le mouvement naturel de la population dans le monde de 1906 à 1936* (Paris: Institut national d'études démographiques, 1954), pp. 170–90; Irene B. Taueber and Edwin G. Beal, "The Demographic Heritage of the Japanese Empire," *The Annals of the American Academy of Political and Social Science* (January 1945), pp. 64–71; Ernest Jurkart and Louise K. Kiser, "The Peoples of the Mohammedan World," *The Annals* (January 1945), pp. 94–106. Figures for Africa are based on contemporary (1960s) population figures (*Statistical Abstract of the U.S.: 1974*, pp. 815–17) with the assumption that population has grown equally throughout the continent since 1900. Because that assumption is doubtful, African figures are only very approximate. China's population is assumed to have been about 400 million in 1900. The population of the Ottoman Empire is based on extrapolation from 1920s and 1930s data in Jurkart and Kiser and the assumption that two-thirds of the population lived within the boundaries of modern Turkey. Other figures are based on the more precise estimates in the cited sources.

TABLE 7

Control of Population, 1900–1910: America
(North, Central, South, and Caribbean),
9 Percent of the World's Population, or 145 Million People

Percentage of the Population
Controlled by:

United States	52%	core
All the rest (including independent and colonial areas)	48%	periphery

TABLE 8

Control of Population, 1900–1910: Africa
(Taking into Account European Conquests through 1911):
7 Percent of the World's Population, or 120 Million People

Percentage of the Population
Controlled by:

United Kingdom	50% ⎫	
France	23% ⎪	
Germany	7% ⎬ colonies of core societies = 86%
Belgium	6% ⎭	
Italy, Spain, Portugal°	7%	
Independent (Ethiopia and Liberia)	7%	

° Because of its foreign, particularly its African Empire, one might label the Portugal of 1900–10 a semi-peripheral society. That has not been done here because the country was very small, weak, and poor by European standards. The fact that it retained an empire in the twentieth century is an interesting historical accident, but hardly of central importance in determining its world status.

China, the largest state in the world in terms of population, was still theoretically independent in the early twentieth century, however its main coastal cities were directly controlled by the core powers and by Japan. These foreign countries, including the United States, had considerable direct influence in Chinese politics, to the point of directly administering some of China's most important governmental departments. Most of the rest of Asia, excepting Japan, was even more directly colonized.

TABLE 9

Control of Population, 1900–1910: Asia
(Not Including Russian Empire in Asia),
57 Percent of the World's Population, or 915 Million People

Percentage of the Population
Controlled by:

United Kingdom	34% ⎫	
France	2% ⎪	
United States	1% ⎬ colonies of the core = 42%
Netherlands	5% ⎭	
Japan (including Japan proper and its colonies by 1905, Korea and Taiwan)	7%	semi-periphery and its colonies = 7%
China (semi-independent)	44% ⎫	
Ottoman Empire (semi-independent)	2% ⎬ other peripheral = 51%
Rest of Asia	5% ⎭	

Oceania (mostly Australia, New Zealand, and many small Pacific islands) included only about one-half of 1 percent of the world's population, and it was controlled largely by the British.

Taking the world as a whole, then, one finds the following approximate population distributions:

TABLE 10

**Division of the World's Population
into Political Categories, 1900–1910**

Core Societies	15% (13% in the four main core societies)
Semi-Peripheral Societies and Their Colonies	18% (15% in the Russian, Japanese, and Austro-Hungarian empires)
Colonies of the Core (not counting colonization within Europe)	28% (25% controlled by the four main core societies, and almost 20% by the United Kingdom alone)
Other Peripheral (independent and semi-independent) Societies	39% (about 25% in China)

The peripheral powers were of minor importance in world politics, and it is clear that only seven states comprised the list of significant powers. Four of these were core states and much more powerful than the others—the large but still relatively poor and unindustrialized "big three" of the semi-peripheral world. These seven states directly controlled 53 percent of the world's population, and indirectly controlled much of the remainder, particularly China.

Whether in terms of direct colonies or the total power exercised through a combination of military, cultural, and economic strength, all the main core powers, and perhaps some of the lesser ones, were imperialistic. That is, they all had foreign dependencies and protectorates, and their governments and many of their citizens thought that they needed such dependencies for national survival. The British were the primary imperialist power, and in many ways the United States was the least imperialistic of the four large core powers. But even in the United States there was a strong feeling that now that the continental frontier had been absorbed, it was time to push on to new areas and expand the American economic and political role in the world. Imperialist forces in Germany, a country with only a small foreign empire, claimed that foreign expansion was obligatory for national survival.

The governments of semi-peripheral states shared the desire to expand and be imperial. Austria-Hungary's last formal annexation (of Bosnia-Herzegovina) occurred in 1908; Russia and Japan went to war in 1904–1905 over clashing imperial claims in China and Korea; the Spaniards, after the loss of most of their empire to the United States in 1898, made an attempt to recreate a small empire in Africa; and Italy was trying to take over Ethiopia and parts of the moribund Ottoman Empire.[28] Expansionist imperialism was not an innovation in the twentieth century, but the feeling that imperialism was a prerequisite of national survival was somewhat new, and needs closer examination.

The concept and fact of imperialism

In 1850 the main core economy, the United Kingdom's, dominated the entire world, and the powerful British fleet intervened frequently in various peripheral areas in order to keep British markets and trade routes open. Even with this scope, however, the United Kingdom had only two large colonies populated by a majority of non-English, culturally distinct people, nearby Ireland and distant India. For the most part, the British controlled a series of islands, trading stations, and coastal-port enclaves. Yet other British colonies were areas increasingly populated by English settlers rather than by culturally alien peoples.

France at that time had almost no colonies and was limited to a few trading outposts and islands and to a part of Algeria. Germany was not yet united and was not to engage in colonial adventures until the 1880s. The United States was pushing westward, displacing Amerindians. This expansion, like the British expansion across Canada and into Australia, was both cheap and easy since the native population was far too small and technologically primitive to put up much resistance. Even the United States war with Mexico that ended in 1848 was fought over largely empty territory into which United States settlers wanted to expand. As for the former giant Spanish and Portuguese empires, they had shrunk to insignificant levels.

In short, the world of the middle nineteenth century was not politically imperialistic. The British dominated the world economy, but did not try to control large hostile foreign populations, thus, in proper capitalist fashion, limiting the costs of empire. In that sense, the British-dominated capitalist world system was still primarily an economic empire rather than a direct political one. India and Ireland were, of course, major exceptions, but both were leftovers of previous periods of colonial expansion.

The logic of capitalism suggests that imperialism is profitable only if it does not entail costs that exceed economic profits. Certainly, the maintenance of a few trading enclaves and islands was a much sounder commercial policy than trying to impose direct rule. Not surprisingly, British political opinion in the middle of the nineteenth century tended to oppose direct imperial expansion, and it was not until 1857 that the British Government was forced to admit that it, not a private merchant company, actually ran India.[29]

In the 1870s something changed, and the French, the Germans, and the British set out on a hysterical race to divide up what was left of the world (and there was still quite a lot left at that time). Africa was the most obvious target, but the uncolonized parts of Asia were also desirable, and the only reason many of them escaped conquest was that the big powers could often not agree on who should take what. (This, for example, is what saved Iran, Afghanistan, and Thailand from colonial rule—all were border states between various European empires.) Presumably, had it not been for the rapidly growing influence of the United States in Latin America in the 1890s, there would have been an equally heated race over control of and division of this particular part of the peripheral world.

As the main core powers, followed by some of the minor core powers and by the more active semi-peripheral powers, expanded, the new interests of different countries quickly conflicted. This intensified rivalries between the main powers, and from the 1890s to 1913 it led to a series of near-wars between core powers and actual wars between various semi-peripherals. In addition, as the colonial empires grew, they lost much of their economic rationale; they were, in fact, no longer particularly profitable. In that sense, the empires created in the late nineteenth century began to resemble earlier, precapitalist imperialistic structures much more than the businesslike economic domain of Britain in the middle of the century. Large armies and navies were built by the main powers, and the weaker semi-peripheral powers strove to keep up in order to avoid being reduced to peripheral status. The French and British almost went to war over the Sudan, the French and Germans almost battled several times over Morocco, a French-Italian war was threatened over Tunisia, Russia and Austria-Hungary were permanently at each other's throats over division of the Balkans, Russia and Japan did go to war over China and Korea, and the United States attacked Spain in 1898 for the sole purpose of gaining a colonial empire and securing American investment in Cuba; in general, international tensions reached an extremely high level in the first decade of the twentieth century.[30]

Why did this happen? A theoretical explanation was offered by the British Liberal J. A. Hobson in 1902, and in a somewhat modified version, was adopted by Lenin in 1916 and greatly popularized by him. Often called the Lenin theory of imperialism, it continues to be the major theoretical explanation of imperialism, including United

States imperialism in the 1960s and 1970s. In essence, the argument goes something like this:[31]

1. By the late nineteenth century the growth of capitalism in the core economies had led to the inevitable concentration of ownership of the economy into a few giant monopolies. While this process had its start in the middle of the nineteenth century, according to the theory, it did not mature fully until about 1900.

2. These giant monopolies came to be controlled by and to merge with large financial institutions (banks) which sought to maximize the return on their capital. These institutions were so big and rich that they effectively controlled the politics of the core states.

3. Maximization of profits, however, required constant economic growth, which in turn required ever larger amounts of raw materials. Raw materials, plentiful throughout most of the nineteenth century, were presumably becoming scarce in the later part of the century because of the tremendous growth of industrial capitalism.

4. The new investments in the core economies did not lead to maximization of profits because national wealth was too unequally distributed, and the working-class masses and the rural population did not have enough money to soak up increased production. In other words, demand was weak, and capital was over-abundant, and in order to maximize return on investments, capitalists had to invest abroad, or alternatively, convince their governments to increase demand by wasting huge sums on armaments.

5. This caused the financial monopolies in the core societies to engage in a series of desperate attempts to control new sources of raw materials and new markets in order to ensure the continuation of high profits. Quite quickly, this led to a division of the world among the four major capitalist powers and a few minor powers.

6. But all this had to lead to war. For by 1900, or certainly by 1910, the world had been "filled up," and there were no easy new colonies to take. The continued demand for cheap raw materials, for new markets, and the build-up in arms of the past several decades had to lead to a giant explosion.

As Lenin explained, that is exactly what happened. World War I broke out in 1914, with Germany on one side and France and Britain on the other. The semi-peripheral powers, and finally many peripheral societies, were brought into the war as well, but essentially, according to Lenin, it was an intracore conflict over the division of the world capitalist system.

By the Lenin-Hobson reasoning, that system was different in 1900 from what it had been at any previous time, because, for the first time, it was in some sense "overcrowded." This meant that the capitalist world system was bound to enter a period of desperate struggle. The consequences of failure for any core power were likely to be fatal. Loss of cheap overseas resources and abundant markets would produce financial collapse. This in turn would lead to domestic depression, and this would provoke the working class to revolution and to an overthrow of capitalism itself.

Was the explanation correct? Certainly the history of the capitalist world system from 1450 to 1945 supports this interpretation of history in some major ways. Repeatedly, England, the Netherlands, Spain, and France engaged in war to control access to markets and raw materials. In a sense, the period from about the late seventeenth century until 1815 was taken up by the real "First" World War, between France and England, to determine who would become the primary core society. This war was fought in Europe, in the Americas, in India, off the coasts of Africa, and in the Middle East. Finally, France lost, and there was a period of *relative* world peace until Germany began to rival the British in a time when the world had no room for new capitalist empires. Germany's, and later Japan's, attempts to become the leading core powers clashed directly with the British, and ultimately with the inheritor of British world power, the United States. So the period 1900 to 1945 saw the outbreak and resolution of a "Second" World War (fought in two parts—the conventionally labeled World War I, from 1914 to 1918, and the conventionally labeled World War II, from 1939 to 1945). This world war was particularly bitter because there was no room left for expansion after 1900. It ended with the United States as the main core power in the capitalist world system.

Further support of the theory is provided by the fact that indeed, as explained by Lenin, the outbreak of the twentieth century's great world conflict was preceded by a gigantic increase in foreign investment by the core economies. From 1900 to 1913 alone, foreign investments by the core powers increased about 50 percent; and there is every reason to accept Lenin's estimate that this rate of increase had been maintained since at least the 1870s and that from 1870 to 1913 core investments abroad had increased at least threefold; if not more.[32]

On the other hand, there are some puzzling facts that do not support the theory. For one, the overwhelming bulk of core capitalist investment and trade *did not* go to the newly opened colonies in Africa and Asia. As mentioned above, the United Kingdom's investments were located primarily in its old colonies (the English-speaking overseas colonies, South Africa, and India), in Latin America, which was not owned directly by any foreign country and which was actually open to investment from all the core societies, and in the United States which was not a colony at all. French investment was heavily concentrated in Europe, particularly in Russia, which was certainly not a French colony, and in Latin America and the Middle East, not in the new French colonies in Africa and Asia. British, French, and German investment in the new African colonies (excluding South Africa and the Suez Canal) was actually very small. So why establish empires there? Of course, it is entirely possible that Africa was merely seized with an eye to eventual profits, not with short-term interests in mind. And the jockeying for power probably revolved more around possible control of the truly lucrative colonial areas than around the newly conquered African and Asian territories, which were sideshows to main world developments.

A second, more puzzling fact is that the world was not close to running short of raw materials and agricultural products. Even within the core societies, there was little evidence of shortages. At least in the United States, huge reserves of raw materials were still untouched. And Lenin correctly noted that there was still enormous potential for growth within the core economies, both in agriculture and in the production of consumer goods for the masses; however he felt that monopoly capitalism would not invest in these areas because, in the short-run, the probable profits were lower than those to be gained from new discoveries of cheap raw materials in the periphery. But throughout the twentieth century, capitalism succeeded in doing just what Lenin had said could not be done. It invested enormous amounts in domestic production and greatly raised the standard of living of all segments of the core societies.

The Thomas Theorem

Despite these two obvious flaws, Lenin's theory is at least somewhat convincing simply because the core societies behaved *as if they thought it were true* (without, of course, having read Lenin). Indeed after 1870 there was a desperate race to amass empires, and not surprisingly, a substantial increase in armaments spending. Thus, as the following table suggests, between 1875 and 1914 the major core economies grew quite rapidly, and their military spending rose even more quickly than their rates of economic growth.

The growth of arms expenditures in France was not much larger during this period than the growth of the French economy, but in the United Kingdom, Germany, and the United States, arms expenditures grew considerably more rapidly than the respective national economies. Comparing the rates of military growth can be a bit misleading however; for in the 1870s the United States possessed a rather small military machine, and it is easy to achieve a large percentage increase starting from such a small base. But even with this fact taken into account, it is clear that the military expenditures of the United States grew very dramatically in the late nineteenth century—and despite the fact that the country had no conceivable enemy. This

TABLE 11

Expenditure on Arms: Growth, 1875–1914, with 1875 = 100

	1875	1907	1913	Average growth per decade	Average growth in GNP per decade
United States*	100	394	536	56%	40%
Germany (base year 1881)	100	272	331	45%	29%
United Kingdom	100	210	289	32%	23%
France (base year 1873)	100	177	202	19%	16%

SOURCE Walter Minchinton, "Patterns of Demand 1750–1914," in Cipolla, *The Fontana Economic History,* Vol. III, p. 106; U.S. Bureau of the Census, *Historical Statistics of the United States, Colonial Times to 1957* (Washington: U.S. Government Printing Office, 1974), p. 718. For GNPs, see sources of Table 3.

* Calculations for the United States are based on growth of total spending by the departments of Army and Navy. Those for other nations are based on actual growth of direct arms spending. Assuming that the percentage of the United States military budget devoted to direct arms spending remained roughly constant during this period permits comparison. In actual fact, these estimates probably understate the growth of direct arms expenditures by the United States. (Veterans benefits are, of course, not included.)

seeming overpreparedness reflected a growing sense of impending crisis caused by the race for empire.

Through the latter part of the nineteenth century, the ideological climate in all the core societies, and in the semi-peripheral ones as well, became increasingly, stridently imperialistic. This was particularly true in Germany and Japan, but as is shown by the declarations of such leading citizens as Theodore Roosevelt, even the "least" imperialistic of the big powers had many important people who considered expansion vital to ensuring a nation's "place in the sun."[33] The statement of a German in 1879 sums up this view, but it could just as easily have been written by a contemporary in any of the other core or semiperipheral societies:

Every virile people has established colonial power. . . . All great nations in the fulness of their strength have desired to set their mark upon barbarian lands[,] and those who fail to participate in this great rivalry will play a pitiable role in time to come. The colonizing impulse has become a vital question for every great nation.[34]

If it cannot be demonstrated that Lenin's theory of imperialism was really supported by the economic facts, then how can one account for the fact that it seems to fit what happened quite well? Many in the core and semi-peripheral societies believed that endless expansion and permanent security of raw material sources and markets were necessary for economic survival. And everywhere, this feeling combined with the great cultural arrogance that defined peripheral cultures as inherently "uncivilized" and core cultures as inherently "superior." Thus, since the prevailing opinion in core and semi-peripheral societies was that imperialism was vital, the main world powers behaved as if it were indeed vital, and proceeded inevitably toward world conflict. Or as the American sociologist W. I. Thomas observed, "If men define situations as real, they are real in their consequences."[35]

In short, during the first decade of the twentieth century, the world system consisted of a set of giant powers locked in a struggle to gain mastery over the peripheral world. And while the peripheral societies were largely pawns in the struggle, the consequences of that struggle for these societies were quite far-reaching.

Knowing something about the operation of international relations in this period does not, however, tell one very much about the social changes that were occurring within particular kinds of societies, nor how these changes interacted with developments in the world capitalist system. An understanding of these topics requires a turn to internal class and political structures within the various parts of that system.

Internal Stratification, Politics,
and the *World System*
in the Early Twentieth Century

Just as position in the capitalist world system correlated highly but not perfectly with level of development, type of economy, role of foreign investment, military power, and certain cultural patterns, so it correlated highly but not perfectly with social stratification and domestic politics. Rather than attempt to explain all the variations in the social stratification and politics of nations in the early twentieth century, this chapter will concentrate on those patterns that most closely reflected the capitalist world system.

Culturally Based Stratification

Virtually every state in the modern world once had many ethnic groups within its boundaries. Most still do. In nation-states with diversified and developed economies, however, these various ethnic groups have invariably been brought into close contact with each other for relatively long periods of time. This has caused many neighboring groups to merge and vanish as distinct entities. In the highly developed main core societies of the early twentieth century there were fewer ethnic groups than in the non-core areas. Even in the United States, an immigrant society with many ethnic groups, the dominance of one group, the Anglo-Saxons, was taken for granted, and most new immigrants used this group as their model of proper adaptive behavior. Still, ethnic homogeneity was far from total, and the presence of various ethnic groups in all the core societies provided one base for the organization of domestic political conflict. This was particularly true when an ethnic minority was composed chiefly of individuals in the lower economic classes. Eastern and Southern European immigrants in the United States, Southern Blacks in the United States, Celts in the United Kingdom, and Slavs in the Prussian part of Germany were the main examples. In each case, class (economic) and ethnic (cultural) differences combined to create particularly persistent divisions.

It is not correct to say that development ends ethnic divisions, not *as long as there exists a culturally based division of labor in which certain culturally defined groups continue to occupy only certain economic positions*.

Similarly, in every early twentieth-century society, certain regions were richer or more powerful than others or both. This produced regionally based ideologies (regional nationalisms) and regionally based political groups, and the weaker or poorer regions struggled against the stronger or richer ones. When a weaker region was populated by a particular ethnic group, regional want and ethnicity combined to create a particularly strong regional nationalism. The most extreme example of this in an early twentieth-century core society was the Celtic area of the United Kingdom: Wales, Scotland, and, most importantly, Ireland, which was in a state of endemic revolt against British domination.[1] Other examples included the Southern United States, which long after the Civil War was still set somewhat against the rest of the country, and the southern and eastern parts of Germany, subordinate areas with enough regional nationalism to bring them into conflict with the Prussian-dominated state. *Development does not end regionally based hostilities if it perpetuates regional inequalities in power and wealth.*

Finally, religious differences, if they correlate with class, ethnic, or regional differences can also become an important base for political conflict. In the early twentieth century, religious division was particularly strong in the United Kingdom, where Ireland was predominantly Catholic and Britain predominantly Protestant. The fact that Ireland was much poorer, ethnically different, geographically distinct, and religiously distinct split the United Kingdom, since the correlation of all these divisive elements produced extreme conflict. Germany and the United States also exhibited a Catholic-Protestant split, particularly Germany, where the south tended to be Catholic. In the United States, the fact that many of the new immigrant groups were not Protestant exacerbated ethnic and class tensions. *Development does not eliminate religious conflict if religious differences remain correlated with major ethnic, regional, or class differences.*

In a sense, every core society was like a mini–world capitalist system, that is, composed of a dominant industrial-financial core and dependent, generally overspecialized peripheries. France, the United States, Germany, and the United Kingdom were all this way. Where peripherality correlated most strongly with culturally unique traits, as in the United Kingdom, serious problems arose. Where it correlated least, as in France, neither regionalism nor ethnicity produced severe problems.

Whatever cultural divisions existed in core societies, however, they were minor compared to those that existed in most non-core societies. The majority of the population in each core society were integrated into its national culture and shared an allegiance to the state. In the core societies, Ireland was the only exception, and Ireland had long been exploited as a British colony. There, economic, cultural, and political divisions were so highly correlated, and so intense, that Ireland ultimately split away from the United Kingdom. In non-core areas, very large portions of each population, often the majority, were not integrated into national cultures that corresponded to state boundaries.

In most peripheral societies, the state had not yet achieved cultural legitimacy. That is, various ethnic, religious, and regionally based groups did not recognize the authority of the state even if they had to accept it. The fact that many peripheral societies were economically malintegrated, that is, that certain parts of the society interacted more with core portions of the world than with their own hinterlands, did not help promote loyalty to the state. The cultural malintegration of peripheral elites and masses (discussed in the previous chapter) was but one example of this tendency. Furthermore, in much of the peripheral world, agents of the core powers and other foreign interests deliberately pitted different ethnic, religious, or regional groups against each other. This tactic facilitated the foreign manipulation of peripheral areas. The pattern was most evident in the European colonies in Asia and Africa, and it represents the main difference between cultural divisions in peripheral societies and core areas: in the former, outside power and influence could effectively manipulate differences in order to control local politics. While the strength of core societies made such manipulation virtually impossible within their boundaries, the weakness of peripheral societies made outside manipulation both easy and effective.

For example, while the British could use Muslim-Hindu hostility in India to strengthen colonial rule, India was in no position to use Irish-British hostilities to manipulate British politics. In fact, not even Germany could engage in such manipulation within the United Kingdom, any more than the United Kingdom could split Bavarians from Prussians in order to weaken Germany. And while the European powers (chiefly the United Kingdom and France) had tried to weaken the United States by supporting the South during the Civil War of 1860–65, the attempt had failed; by 1900, such a policy would have been absurd. Even German manipulation of German immigrants in the United States during World War I, from 1914 to 1918, proved almost totally ineffective.

Even though peripheral societies were the exact opposite of the culturally well-integrated core societies, and *substantial majorities of the population did not participate in a single national culture that corresponded to the boundaries of an existing state*, this was considered the normal state of affairs. In most peripheral areas little effort was being made to create strong national cultures that would integrate populations and legitimatize existing states.

Semi-peripheral societies in the early 1900s (except Japan) were also highly polarized along ethnic, religious, or regional lines. Each of these societies, however, had a national culture, even if substantial portions of the population did not yet accept it. In addition, most semi-peripheral states were trying to strengthen their state machinery in order to raise their position in the world system, and to do this, they had to gain the loyalties of those parts of the population that were not yet integrated into the dominant national culture. Strengthening the state involved drafting men from all regions and ethnic groups into the army, forcing people from all regions and various ethnic backgrounds to learn the main national language, and particularly, changing long-accepted patterns of loyalty in the unintegrated parts of the population. Such efforts provoked resistance among the unintegrated groups rather than increased loyalty, for it was these groups that most opposed the centralizing tendencies and increasing demands of state machineries not yet considered fully legitimate.

Every core society had experienced such opposition. The United States, Germany, the United Kingdom, and France had long histories of internal conflict based on cultural differences between ethnic groups, religions, and regions. But all these issues had been substantially resolved by 1900 (except, again, in Ireland, where there was to be no resolution). In semi-peripheral societies, the issues were not yet resolved. Those in Austria-Hungary would persist until the state split apart in 1918, and Russia and Spain were to go through periods of intense civil war in order to resolve their cultural malintegrations (and the issues in Spain remain unresolved). The fact that Japan, alone of the non-core societies, was culturally highly integrated in 1900 gave it an immense advantage in its effort to gain core status.

To reiterate, on the whole, core cultures were substantially integrated in 1900, and non-core cultures were not. Semi-peripheral societies were in the process of trying to integrate their cultures, and peripheral societies were not even making the attempt. This made it particularly easy to manipulate peripheral politics by using various culturally defined groups against each other. In all societies, core and non-core, the cultural splits were closely related to class structure.

Core Class-Structures and Politics

The class structures of core societies in the early 1900s (and to some extent, those of the richest peripheral areas, the English overseas

TABLE 12

Class Structure in Core Societies

Elite	Major controllers of capital (big industrialists, bankers, financiers, owners of the largest enterprises)
Middle Class	Proprietors of enterprises, managerial and professional groups, supervisory white collar employees (both private and public)
Lower Middle Class	Lower white collar employees (mostly clerical and sales)
Working Class	Blue collar workers (manual laborers) and lower service workers (servants, janitors, etc.)
Agriculturalists	Owners and managers of farms (at the top), tenants and hired laborers (at the bottom)

societies) can be represented as shown in Table 12. This scheme is hardly perfect, however. Owners of small shops and independent artisans were more lower middle class than middle class, and some might even be put at the upper limits of the working class. Among service workers the line between lower-middle and working class was hard to discern. Among agriculturalists: a few major landowners were members of the elite; prosperous farm owners were part of a rural middle class; and some tenants were quite prosperous, while some were at the very bottom of the class system. Nevertheless the scheme is useful for present purposes because it corresponds to a certain reality—better than, say, mere income distribution statistics, since individuals have always identified themselves as members of a particular class by their position in the occupational hierarchy as well as by their income. Poorly paid Protestant parsons in the United States, for example, have hardly considered themselves members of the working class even if they made less money than some blue-collar workers. (This is not to say that, aside from the diffuse agricultural class, income did not correlate quite well with class—except at the edges of each class.) Table 13, a breakdown of the actual class composition of the United States in 1910, gives a good idea of the relative size of socio-economic classes in the early twentieth-century core society.

In terms of distribution of income and wealth, the United States in 1910 was probably the most egalitarian of the core societies, even though it was inegalitarian in absolute terms. In Wales and England, 32,000 adults (0.2 percent of the adult population) owned 41 percent of all assets, and the top 1 percent of adults owned two-thirds of assets; in the United States, the top 1 percent owned only one-third

TABLE 13

Class Structure in the United States, 1910

Elite	(Not measured in census; but top 1% of population earned 15% of all income in 1913 and owned one-third of all assets in 1922)
Middle Class	4,220,000 individuals in labor force 11% of labor force
Lower-Middle Class	3,742,000 individuals in labor force 10% of labor force
Working Class	17,797,000 individuals in labor force ⟋ 48% of labor force
Farm Owners and Managers	6,163,000 individuals in labor force 17% of labor force
Farm Laborers and Tenants	5,370,000 individuals in labor force 14% of labor force

SOURCE   U.S. Bureau of the Census, *Historical Statistics of the United States, Colonial Times to 1957* (Washington: U.S. Government Printing Office, 1960), p. 74.

of assets. Similarly, in Great Britain the top 5 percent of the population earned 43 percent of all the income, while in the United States the top 5 percent earned 25 percent of all income. (Note that income is *always* more equitably distributed than assets since even the working poor who own no capital still earn something from their work.)[2] Yet, taking the United States as the most egalitarian and the United Kingdom as the most inegalitarian, it remains clear that in the core societies before World War I a small elite held a disproportionately large share of assets and income. This elite was the capitalist upper class, the main controllers of large industries, banks, commercial enterprises, and other key sectors of the economy.

Though small, the upper class was also the most powerful political class. Members of the elite certainly did not have all the political power, far from it; but their attitudes and interests were disproportionately influential, and these individuals tended to occupy many (though again, not all) of the top administrative and political positions in government. Even where such positions were not directly occupied by members of the elite, many of the actual occupants were dependent on elite support for their positions. Members of the elite were also the ones who profited most from foreign investments, for they controlled the banks, mines, railways, import-export businesses, and agricultural enterprises that dealt in the peripheral world. So, while controlling much of their domestic economies, the core elites also controlled much of the peripheral economies.

The middle class, however, was also powerful in core societies, and its members participated significantly in the political process. Most supported core imperialist policies, and some were investors in overseas economies (though on the average, of course, middle-class investors controlled much less than investing members of the elite). The majority of the middle class also shared the strong nationalism of the elite, that is, the concern for maintaining their particular core society in the front ranks of world powers. Even when middle-class interests conflicted with elite interests in domestic politics, there was considerable agreement between the classes on matters of foreign (then expansionist) policy.

The working class was different. In the early twentieth century it was only beginning to gain a place of importance in core societies. Unionization and the growth of socialist parties (or, in the United States, the growth of a labor-oriented wing of the Democratic Party) were still unrealized threats to elite and middle-class domination of the economy and the political process. Such activities were perceived by the upper classes as principal threats to capitalism; however, in fact, the working class was still quite weak relative to its size, and not yet equipped with the political parties and movements that would gain it some real power.

Nor did the working class share the position of the upper classes on foreign investments. The ideologies of the working class tended to be anti-imperialistic. This opposition derived not only from the direct domestic conflict with the capitalist elite, which controlled a large portion of such investments, but also and more closely from the perception that foreign investments were capital taken out of the domestic economy and, therefore, hindrances to a rise in the domestic standard of living. Foreign investments were also hard to control by normal political processes, and working-class parties opposed the placement of capital in areas where domestic politics could not control it. But, in a sense, these positions were limited to the leaders and intellectuals in the working-class movements; the rank and file tended to share the "nationalism" of the controllers of capital. When the crisis came, at the start of World War I, all the European socialist parties supported the war on nationalistic grounds. Only later, when war turned out to be very costly—in terms of deaths and injuries as well as decreases in the standard of living—did the working class turn against it, and against imperialistic foreign adventures as well.

Prosperous agriculturalists were also politically important, and in many ways, they behaved like the nationalistic middle class, at least with respect to international policies. In the United States, the agrarian populist William Jennings Bryan, a theoretical opponent of American imperialism, changed his mind on the issue after the country's easy victory over Spain in 1898.[3] Similarly, in other core societies, the prosperous agriculturalists, the rural middle class, were not likely sources of opposition to prevailing policy.

Poor agriculturalists, on the other hand, whether peasants in France or sharecroppers (both white and black) in the United States, were virtually powerless and without any significant political role. Less influential than even the blue-collar workers, they comprised the very lowest class in terms of political influence and wealth. But in all core societies, it was also a class that was diminishing rapidly as marginal farmers were forced off the land and pushed into cities to join the ranks of the urban working class.

In short, despite the political conflict between the various classes in core societies, particularly between the working class and the upper and middle classes, domestic politics before 1914 did not do much to alter the generally expansionist and imperialistic policies of those societies.

Before the frenzied expansionism of the late nineteenth century there had been opposition to foreign expansion in all the core societies, primarily from those who saw no profit in getting involved abroad, but rather, only needless expense. The growing conviction that national survival depended on constant expansion of markets and sources of raw materials and primary goods changed this prospect and reduced the anti-imperialist sentiment. It proved so easy to take over vast foreign domains that the costs did not seem important. As they began to be more apparent—for example, when the United Kingdom became involved in a long war in South Africa, or when Irish opposition to British rule threatened outright civil war—protest revived. But it took the immense cost of World War I to generate enough protest to change the policies of core societies, and later wars to convince majorities in the core that the game was not worth the cost.

Peripheral Class-Structures and Politics

Peripheral societies were much more heterogeneous than core societies, and generalizations about them are consequently more difficult. Even leaving aside the English overseas societies, major differences existed between the early twentieth-century's peripheral societies. The first major distinction was that some of these societies were relatively highly involved with the world system, while others had just recently been brought into the system and had experienced only very limited core influence. Those societies in which core interests had made large investments were "more-developed" peripheral societies (for example, Argentina, Brazil, Mexico, India, or South Africa); while many of the newest African colonies (particularly the interior African colonies of France) were barely involved in the world system, and were therefore poorly "developed" peripheral societies. The second major distinction (which produced different groupings than the first) was between peripheral societies that were still theoretically independent (such as China, the Ottoman Empire, most of Latin America, and Ethiopia) and those that were legally colonies (most of Africa, India, Indonesia, and so on). In direct colonies the top elite consisted of officials from the ruling core power, while in the remaining peripheral societies there was a domestic administrative elite—but usually one that collaborated (willingly or not) with core interests.

Despite these complexities, there were two obvious differences between core class-structures and peripheral ones. First, peripheral middle classes were distinctly split between the "new" element that participated in and profited from the enclave, core-dominated sector of the economy and the "old" element that did not. In the existing independent states of Asia (particularly the Ottoman and Chinese

TABLE 14

Peripheral Class-Structure

Elite	Controllers of the land (landowners, authorities with power over the land, and—where they were present—foreign officials and investors)
New Upper-Middle Class	Westernized intellectuals, civil-service and white-collar employees, Western-oriented merchants ("compradors," both foreign and native)
Old Upper-Middle Class	Small landowners, officials of traditional pre-Western bureaucracies, the clergy
New Lower-Middle Class	Clerical and service workers in foreign enterprises or the civil service
Old Lower-Middle Class	Artisans, small, non–Western-oriented local merchants, prosperous peasants
New Working Class	Blue-collar workers in enclave cities and transportation networks, in the few industries, and in mines; non-agricultural servants in the enclaves
Agriculturalists	Small peasant owners, tenants, plantation or other hired laborers

empires) the same split existed at the elite level as well. Second, the middle and working classes in peripheral societies were relatively much smaller than those in core societies, while the proportion of agriculturalists was much larger. This was, of course, a function of differing levels of industrialization.

A look at the class composition of one peripheral society, Mexico, about 1900 suggests the relative numbers of people generally found in each class. It should be remembered, however, that Mexico was one of the most developed peripheral societies, and that its working class, and probably its middle class (at least, the "modern" or new part), was relatively much larger than that same class in the least developed peripheral areas (where peasants made up a larger proportion of the population, and where the middle class was almost entirely composed of the "old" middle class).

If the upper segment of the Mexican middle class (managers and professionals) is compared to its equivalent in the United States, it was only one seventh as large. This is not a very good comparison, however, since many of the smaller proprietors of enterprises in the United States were on the margin between the middle class and the lower-middle class, but even when all the middle classes in Mexico

TABLE 15

Class Structure in Mexico, about 1900

Elite	30 land companies and 8,000 haciendas owned one-third of all the surface of Mexico, and a larger proportion of the useful land
New Upper-Middle Class	(Managerial and professional, private and in civil service) 200,000 individuals and their dependents 1.5% of the population
Rest of the Middle Classes Combined	1,000,000 individuals and their dependents 8% of the population
Working Class	2,600,000 individuals and their dependents 20% of the population
Agriculturalists	(Mostly peasants, most of them very poor) 9,100,000 individuals and their dependents 70% of the population

SOURCE Eric R. Wolf, *Peasant Wars of the Twentieth Century* (New York: Harper & Row, 1969), p. 23; James W. Wilkie, *The Mexican Revolution: Federal Expenditure and Social Change Since 1910* (Berkeley: University of California Press, 1970), pp. 24, 193, 203. Based on an estimated 13 million people in 1895–1900. The working class is estimated by subtracting all the other categories from 100 percent.

are compared to both American middle classes, the Mexican middle class was still less than half as large relative to the entire population. Similarly, the Mexican working class was only 40 percent as large as the American working class (20 percent divided by 48 percent = .42). But the rural class was more than twice as large in Mexico. If the great poverty and dependence of most Mexican peasants is taken into account, then it would be better to compare them to the poor, virtually powerless, lower agricultural class in the United States. Poor agriculturalists were about five times more numerous in Mexico.

It was more than the mere distribution of numbers that was different, however. Comparable classes in the two types of societies held very different amounts and types of power. This can be seen by examining each peripheral class in turn, starting with the controllers of the land.

The controllers of the land

Many peripheral societies did not have large landowners (notably, most of those in tropical Africa), but many did. Southeast Asia, most of Latin America, large parts of the Caribbean, much of the Middle East, and much of Eastern Europe (including the non-Russian parts of the Russian Empire, the Baltic countries and Poland) were dominated by landlords. In India and China a relatively small number of landowners controlled vast amounts of land, while a large number of peasants were very poor sharecroppers. Where there was a community of foreign landowners, they too owned much land (for example, the French in Algeria and Vietnam, the British in Malaya, the Dutch in Indonesia, United States citizens in Cuba). And even in some parts of tropical Africa, colonial authorities and native elites so dominated the production of key export crops that, even where landownership as such was not concentrated, control of the land was. Almost everywhere, the controllers of the land were direct allies of the core-dominated, export sector of the economy and polity. They extracted a marketable surplus from peasant producers and collected a large portion of the profits, either in the form of direct sales, in rents, in taxes, or in produce taken from tenants. The controllers of the land were particularly dependent on the overspecialized export agricultural economies that prevailed in peripheral societies.

Note that the power of these controllers of the land, while it seemed to be a mere perpetuation of traditional, precapitalist patterns, was really quite new in most of the peripheral world. *The rapid growth of the export sector tied the controllers of the land to the international market, raised peasant dues, and exacerbated inegalitarian landholding patterns.* In the case of Mexico, for example, despite the fact that there had been large haciendas since the sixteenth century, in the early nineteenth century most of the land was still controlled by village communities and small peasants. It was the booming export economy and the possibility of huge profits that in the late nineteenth century led to the rapid decline of peasant and community control.[4] By 1910 the large landowners and a few landholding companies controlled a far greater portion of the land than at any time before. Mexico's situation was not unique; for in most peripheral societies, the more the export sector grew, the more power fell into the hands of the landowners, and the more they could exploit the peasants. Rather than producing greater equality, this aspect of economic development concentrated wealth.

The comprador and pariah capitalists

As the export sector of peripheral economies grew, so did the import of goods manufactured in the core. In order to handle the new exchange there had to be merchants familiar with Western and domestic markets, with the new products, and particularly with the new sources of credit and the peculiarities of the Westerners themselves. In other words, there had to be a class of middlemen to bridge the gap between the core-oriented financial and economic systems of the enclaves and the large mass of illiterate peasants or plantation workers.

In China, at the turn of the century, the members of this new class came largely from coastal cities dominated by European mercantile enterprises; they were known as the *comprador capitalists*. Hsiao-tung Fei, a distinguished Chinese sociologist, had this to say about them:

> I possess no sufficient data on the family background of those who form the first line of contact with Western traders, but I strongly suspect that those "secondhand foreigners," were, at least for the early period, recruited from the outcasts of the traditional structure, who had lost their positions and sought their fortune by illegal means. Treaty ports [core-dominated coastal cities] are open to them. If they find regular employment in the community, such as servants or interpreters in a foreign concern, they gradually become compradors, . . . if they fail, they form gangs. . . . They are half-caste in culture, bilingual in speech, individualistic, and agnostic, not only in religion, but in cultural values.[5]

And sociologist Barrington Moore, writing about the same group, observed:

By shady methods they could accumulate great fortunes to live
life in cultivated ease. On the other hand, many Chinese con-
demned them as the servants of the foreign devils who were
destroying the foundations of Chinese society. From this point
onward, much of China's social and diplomatic history becomes
a record of Chinese attempts to keep this hybrid society in
check and of contrary efforts by stronger powers to use it as an
entering wedge for their commercial and political interests.[6]

Culturally alien and hated as this class may have been in China,
in many peripheral societies there were *no* local people willing or able
to take up the role of comprador capitalist. Typically, then, foreigners
from other peripheral societies would come in to fill these positions.
These were the much-hated, but extremely necessary "pariah capitalists" (literally, outcast or despised merchants and entrepreneurs).
The list of such people is long, and the animosity they aroused as re-
tailers, money lenders, tavern keepers, landed estate managers, petty
officials in colonial governments, middlemen in control of marketing
key export crops, and, later in the century, as professionals and small
industrialists has become part of the world lore of ethnic hatred. Class
and ethnicity combined to make these foreigners a particularly visible
target; they obviously benefited from the pattern of peripheral economies, and they were more accessible to local retaliation than the
resident Westerners, who would not stoop to such low jobs. The Chinese in Vietnam, Cambodia, Laos, Malaya, Indonesia, and Thailand;
the Indians and Pakistanis in East Africa and South Africa; the Middle Eastern Christians (Lebanese, Syrians, Armenians) throughout
much of the Middle East and even West Africa; the Greeks in the
same area as well as in the Balkans; Jews in Poland, Romania, the
Baltic countries, the Ukraine, and Hungary; and Chinese and Indians
in many Caribbean islands were all pariah capitalists. While a fervent
European anti-Semite might have trouble explaining to an Indonesian
peasant what it was that he disliked about Jews, he need only say
"Chinese" to elicit the same image, the same prejudices, and the same
hatreds; for wherever they were present, pariah capitalists served the
same necessary but unpopular functions. In East Africa, Indians were
first imported by the British to be railway construction workers, but
they soon became merchants. And among the Chinese in Jamaica, first
imported as plantation workers, a similar change occurred. In Romania the development of the wheat export economy in the middle of
the nineteenth century brought thousands of Jews, and it was the
growth of the plantation economies in Southeast Asia that attracted
most of that area's Chinese.[7]

Sadly, all over the peripheral (and semi-peripheral) world, the
pattern repeated itself. The controllers of the land, core investors, and

colonial administrators used the pariah and comprador capitalists as a necessary adjunct to their power, only to despise them quite as much as they were hated by local peasants. Later, when a series of anti-core, nationalist revolts broke out around the world, the sight of mass reprisals taken against this vulnerable class became common enough for many observers to conclude that this, too, was part of the traditional political pattern in "underdeveloped" countries. But like the rise to power of export-connected controllers of the land, the rise of a comprador-pariah class was only another aspect of the growth of the capitalist world system.

It is quite clear that this type of a middle class, important as it may have been in peripheral societies, could not achieve the position attained by the middle class in core societies. Fundamentally alien and deeply entangled in core interests, the comprador-pariah class could not become nearly as politically independent or powerful.

The westernized intellectuals and civil service

The rest of the modern middle class in peripheral societies was very different. It was composed of partially Westernized native civil servants and white-collar employees. In colonial Africa and Asia a native civil service was trained by the Europeans who did not have enough administrators to run their colonies, particularly at the lower levels. Even importation of "other" (that is, foreign) peripherals was not sufficient, and some locals had to be absorbed into the administration. This meant that they had to be taught Western bureaucratic techniques, and Western forms of organization. In Latin America, where this class was relatively much larger than in Africa, it comprised the bulk of the higher civil service. Anthropologist Eric Wolf has estimated that in Mexico in 1910, three-quarters of the middle class were employed in one way or another by the government.[8] India had a substantial native civil service because the country had been a colony for many decades. In China between 1900 and 1910 those Chinese with Western educations were active in attempts to modernize China and replace its traditional Imperial administration with a regime based on Western models. After the Chinese Revolution of 1911, the Western-educated intellectuals (that is, those with formal Western higher educations) gradually came to dominate the civil service.

In the early twentieth century, such intellectuals and civil servants were still somewhat like the comprador capitalists in that they combined elements of their own and Western cultures, and in general, stood in awe of Western accomplishments. By their thinking, the poverty and dependence of their societies had to be remedied by

Westernization. As long as this awe and admiration prevailed, the dominance of core powers was assured. But the administrative middle class was not like the comprador middle class in one important respect: the livelihoods of its members did not depend on the maintenance of core domination. In fact, in colonial societies, the native civil service gradually came to realize that if the core administrators could be expelled, it would become the new elite. Ultimately, as this class learned to synthesize Western and native cultures, and to apply its organizational and intellectual skills to nationalistic purposes, it became the leader of anti-core revolts in peripheral societies around the world. In the early twentieth century, most of this nationalism was still in the future.

The modern upper-middle class shaded off imperceptibly into the modern lower-middle class. Those at the bottom of the civil service hierarchy (petty clerks, office boys, soldiers, service workers, interpreters, and even servants of the Europeans) were partially Westernized, but they were not yet much of a self-conscious class. Some could rise to become comprador capitalists, others could get more education and become civil servants or white-collar employees of core-dominated firms. Eventually the modern lower-middle class came to include substantial numbers of individuals, particularly in the enclave cities. As this class grew it became a vital part of the structure that supported core domination. When it became more self-conscious, and also more nationalistic and anti-core, the whole colonial and semi-colonial system that prevailed in the peripheral world was gravely threatened. Again, however, these were developments yet to come.

The old middle classes

The small landowners, officials of decaying but extant traditional empires (for example, the Confucian bureaucracy of China), and the traditional priestly elite (for example, the Indian Brahmins, the malams in Muslim societies, or Catholic priests in Latin America) comprised one part of the old middle class. At the top, this class shaded off into the controllers of the land, and at the bottom, it was only marginally middle class.

On the whole, people in this group were opposed to the domestic influence of core societies from the very start. As foreign influence in their state's affairs grew, as comprador and pariah capitalists gained in wealth, and as economic patterns changed, members of the old upper-middle class lost their power and wealth to representatives of the new interests and to the few big controllers of the land who could adapt to new ways. In many a peripheral society, they became the leaders of the first anti-core revolts. For example, it was members of this group, supported by members of the old lower-middle class, that led the great Indian Mutiny of 1857 against the British, the Mahdi anti-British War in the Sudan at the end of the nineteenth century, and the Boxer uprising against Europeans in China in 1900.[9] By and large, however, such revolts were doomed to failure because the old middle class had only traditional, outdated methods and arms to use against the West. The superior organization of the core, or of core-supported elements, their superior armaments, and most of all, their superior economic power made such revolts futile in all but a handful of cases. In peripheral societies, only the new middle class had the skills necessary to organize successful anti-core movements.

The old upper-middle class and the old lower-middle class— artisans, small village merchants, and the more prosperous village peasants—had similar interests. Scholarly literature has perhaps over-stressed that intrusions of Western goods destroyed artisans in peripheral societies, but the point is still quite obviously true to some extent. The importation of cheap Western goods into a peripheral society disrupted the artisanate and forced a good many traditional merchants to be squeezed out by comprador or pariah capitalists. Furthermore, many a prosperous peasant was destroyed by the growing power of the landlords, by higher taxes, and by the spread of moneylenders, all problems that became more severe as the influence of core economies grew. This destruction was very obvious in Mexico,. and it occurred in India, China, much of Eastern Europe, and ultimately, Africa as well.[10]

The experience of India is particularly instructive in this regard because that country was the largest European colony and the oldest large colony in Asia or Africa. India was also the first colony to give birth to a strong, modern anticolonial movement. Gandhi, the leader of this movement through most of the first half of the century, repeatedly stressed artisan interests (thus, the movement's symbol, the spinning wheel). Gandhi's party, the Congress party, was an alliance of Westernized intellectuals, village artisans, and prosperous peasants (joined eventually by members of a growing industrializing business class opposed to British economic domination); it sought to lead the poor peasants in a fight against the British, against native large land-owners, and against the princes who ruled many parts of India in collaboration with the British. The ultimate success of this effort— India gained independence in 1947—stands in marked contrast to the failure of the Mutiny of 1857, and was due in large part to the fact that the crucial organizers and ideologues of the independence movement were Western educated, notably Gandhi and his chief follower, Nehru. Such members of the educated elite, no longer simply aping the British, successfully combined Indian elements with their borrowed Western ideology and organization. The movement's leaders could deal effectively both with the British (organizing strikes, protests, appealing to the appropriate anticolonial segments of the population in Britain, and applying pressure to vital points of the colonial administration), and with the large number of Indian peasants who had to be organized in order to bring down British rule.[11]

They had found the key. To fight domination by a core power, a peripheral society needed more than simple resentment by the old middle class, or even by the mass of peasants. It needed a new group of leaders, individuals dedicated to their country's sovereignty and capable of applying Western ideas and methodology to this end. For the most part, these individuals were to come from the new middle class.

The working class

Railroaders, miners, dockers, and laborers in the few industrial enterprises that existed made up the working class of the peripheral society in 1900. In the most highly developed peripheral economies, such as Mexico's, this class was relatively large (though still considerably smaller than its counterparts in core societies); in most African colonies, and in the poorer parts of Latin America and Asia, it was very small. Where this class was large enough, it would eventually become a meaningful political force against foreign domination. The tactics used by working classes in core societies would be applied. Strikes would be organized, railways and port facilities would be disrupted, miners would unite against management, and core investments would therefore be threatened. As in the case of core working-class movements, the first aim would be to raise wages; and later, the working class would combine with other nationalistic, anti-core groups to help overthrow foreign domination. But in the first decade of the twentieth century these tactics had not been adopted, and these combinations had not been made. Even in Mexico the working class remained very weak, and throughout the peripheral world, it played a small role in shaping events.

The peasants

Peasants made up a large majority of the population in almost all the peripheral societies of the early twentieth century; the exceptions were the few unusually rich peripheral societies mentioned in the previous chapter. Though very large, the peasant class of the typical peripheral society was predominantly illiterate, virtually unorganized, and very poor. It was also very heterogeneous with respect to culture. Peasants spoke local languages, and often these were not the main languages of the enclave cities. Their locally oriented religious practices, their ignorance of the outside world, their focus on local and regional rather than national politics, and their poverty made large-scale organization of the peasants virtually impossible.

Even in a country like Mexico, which was relatively well developed, in 1910:

> More than 70 per cent of the population lived in scattered rural communities . . . [and] . . . at least 87 per cent of the population could neither read nor write. The Indians, defined in terms of language, could not participate in the national way of life; some 1,617,994 persons, or about 13 per cent of the population, spoke only an Indian tongue and were thus excluded from markets, jobs, and civil rights.[12]

Though more numerous, Mexico's Spanish-speaking and mixed-language peasants were hardly better off; and in Bolivia, Peru, Ecuador, and Guatemala, Indians excluded from national life comprised considerably larger proportions of the population than in Mexico.[13]

But Latin American peasants were much less divided culturally than the peasants of most of Asia and Africa. There, each state or colony contained many different linguistic groups, and even many nations and tribes that were drastically different from each other and could not communicate with each other. In Nigeria, for example, the seven leading languages (and generally, language defined ethnicity) were Hausa, Yoruba, Ibo, Kanuri, Tiv, Efik, and Edo; but there were dozens of other major languages, and perhaps hundreds of minor ones.[14] India was even more subdivided. Even in China, the oldest state, there were major linguistic differences between different parts of the country; and while the elite spoke a standardized version of Chinese, most peasants did not. These regional disparities made organization of the peasants very difficult, and they were the main reason that elite direction was necessary before anything approaching mass rural movements could develop.

Peasants were more likely to organize and act as a distinct class where they were in direct and close contact with the export sector. Thus the plantation workers were the first segment of the rural population to organize along class lines. Even so, in the early twentieth century, their organization was weak.

On the whole, peasants in peripheral societies had very definite grievances against the prevailing economic system. As in Mexico, their precapitalist form of organization was based on the solidarity of fellow villagers and their mutual support. But the extended power of the landlords and the incursion of market forces that obliged peasants to produce export crops and pay high taxes destroyed the villagers' solidarity, turned land itself into a marketable commodity, and thus eroded the security of village life. This process was most apparent and most advanced in the more developed peripheral societies—for example, Mexico and Cuba; but even in Africa, colonial powers took strong measures to force peasants out of their old patterns. Cash taxes were imposed, and this made it necessary for peasants to grow cash crops or migrate to cities and plantations in order to earn cash incomes. The French and Belgians in Africa used forced peasant labor in mines and plantations and to build roads, and forced labor was utilized as well in Vietnam's major rice fields and rubber plantations. In Indonesia also, a combination of taxes and concentrated landownership forced peasants into tenancy relations or onto plantations. In many parts of Eastern Europe, similar patterns had developed as early as the sixteenth century, when Poland, Hungary, and the Baltic areas were absorbed into the growing capitalist world economy. These patterns continued to prevail in the first decades of the twentieth century; and while legal serfdom had generally been abolished, the big landowners could impose very disadvantageous tenancy contracts on the peasants. In other words, in most of the peripheral world of the early 1900s, coerced peasant labor produced the key export crops.[15]

Now, it cannot be demonstrated that this pattern of coerced labor actually made the peasants any poorer than they had been. But it can be demonstrated that the new demands of the capitalist world system increased the economic insecurity of the peasants by subjecting them to uncertain and fluctuating market conditions, brought them humiliating new forms of subjection, and ultimately uprooted them in vast numbers.[16] While many traditional forms of social organization had been extremely inegalitarian, at the village level, precapitalist peasant society had at least provided its members with a protective environment. That protection was destroyed by the intrusion of the world system, and one consequence of the displacement was the outbreak of numerous peasant rebellions throughout the peripheral world. The targets of these rebellions were the comprador and pariah capitalists, the landowners, and of course, the representatives of core powers. But almost everywhere such uprisings failed because the peasantry was not sufficiently coordinated, and because it had only the most rudimentary of weapons.

When the partially Westernized middle class began to organize the peasants and to coordinate their activities, the situation in peripheral societies changed very dramatically. It was at that point that worldwide revolution began to topple the prevailing capitalist world system. The first such event in the twentieth century, that is, the outbreak of the first effectively organized anti-core revolt of peasants and members of the new middle class, occurred in Mexico in 1910. However the story of the Mexican revolution, and the similar revolts that followed it, is best told in later chapters of the book; for this upheaval was only the beginning of a long war that still rages in many portions of the peripheral world.

The strange case of South Africa

South Africa was at once the most extreme, and in many ways, the most successful peripheral society of the early twentieth century. Today, socially frozen, it remains a testament to the inequalities of colonial development. The discussion of it here reflects the fact that it is also very rich, important to core capitalist economies because of its mineral wealth, and peculiar among the former colonies in having a large European minority that has managed to hang on to absolute power. While its very survival and extremism may, in some respects, make South Africa a poor example of an early twentieth-century peripheral society, much of what has happened there is the direct result of forces that were powerful throughout the periphery. But its economic importance and archaic social structure make it a target for anticolonial sentiment in the late twentieth century, and the probable site of a future terrible race war, so that a brief explanation of its unique situation is necessary. Other, predominantly European peripheral societies like Canada and Australia have moved into the ranks of the core. Colonies with substantial non-European majorities have gradually become independent, and destroyed the old colonial social structures. South Africa lies in between these two common patterns of change. It is rich and industrialized, but has a poor and exploited non-European majority.

By 1911, South Africa contained 6 million people, 21.4 percent of whom were white—either English or Dutch. (The English and the Dutch were political enemies in South Africa, and did not reconcile their differences there until about 1950—and then only in order to keep down the African majority.) These Europeans were the masters and owners of South Africa's key economic enterprises, and they drew on the African population (67.3 percent of the country's total) for cheap labor. The population also included a substantial number of Asians (about 2.5 percent of the population), most of whom were from India. Originally imported as coolies, members of this group were now gradually forming an intermediary mercantile class, between the Europeans and the Africans. An even larger number of people (8.8 percent of the population) were of mixed heritage, that is, European-African; known as "Coloureds," they also served as a buffer between the whites and the blacks. Asians and Coloureds had more rights than Africans, but less than whites, and were also in an intermediary position in terms of wealth.

Since 1911 the large but minority white population has maintained its rule and increased racial segregation through strict laws and coercion to maintain races apart from each other. Undoubtedly the separation of races (the Africans themselves are divided into various nations and tribes) has helped the whites to keep power, but it has not prevented the development of severe racial tensions and resentments and the gradual rise of an African political movement hostile to the whites. The natural wealth of South Africa (primarily gold and diamonds, but many other products as well) has made it a very popular choice among investors from core societies, particularly the United Kingdom and the United States. In turn the large profit from mineral exports has enabled South Africa's whites to maintain a high standard of living and a large modern army to defend their privileges. It has also attracted Africans into the country's mines and industries despite the political and cultural humiliation involved. Thus the world's most rigorous system of discriminatory racial laws has not only survived but grown more rigorous over time.[17]

Ultimately, South Africa's success will backfire and work against the present interests of core economies and the ruling South African whites. Gandhi, who began his professional career as a lawyer in South Africa's Indian community, formulated his anticolonial ideology with a mind to the injustices he saw there early in the century.[18] Today, South Africa still serves as a reminder of the grievous tendencies of unrestrained imperialism, tendencies that have been thwarted in other peripheral societies only by means of anticolonial uprisings.

The Dangerous Middle:
Semi-peripheral Class-Structures and Politics

The discussion of class structures and politics in peripheral societies has emphasized that various classes in these societies had mutually antagonistic interests, particularly with respect to dealings within the capitalist world system. Specifically, the controllers of the land and certain members of the middle classes were allies of that world system, while other classes were either hostile or at least potentially hostile to it. The discussion has also suggested that as the twentieth century advanced, and as the new civil servants and intellectual middle class became more nationalistic, revolutionary movements broke out, movements opposed to core domination and the capitalist world system.

The key difference between peripheral societies and semi-peripheral societies at the start of the twentieth century was that while in the former this revolutionary process was barely beginning, in the latter it was already well under way. Thus, while the class structures of semi-peripheral societies were quite similar to those of some peripheral societies (the most highly developed ones), semi-peripheral elites were already much more nationalistic than peripheral elites. The semi-peripheral middle classes, though still split between the "new" and the "old," were no longer dominated by comprador or pariah capitalists. These individuals were being replaced by a native, modern commercial middle class with a distinct interest in domestic economic independence. The civil service elite, in control of fully independent state structures, was better developed and much stronger than its counterpart in peripheral societies. And the workers, and even the peasants, were also somewhat better organized and, on the whole, more literate than in peripheral societies.

Thus, while the same basic class divisions and grievances existed in all non-core societies, outright violent conflict was more likely in semi-peripherals than in peripherals, since in the former the classes were better organized and more conscious of their interests. Moreover, in the semi-peripheral society the middle classes and the elite actually controlled powerful state structures, and their nationalistic goals called for strengthening their society's international position vis-à-vis the core. This made the politics of semi-peripheral societies particularly unstable. Their governments participated in the expensive and dangerous international power game against other members of the semi-periphery and against the core societies. But national solidarity was weaker throughout the semi-periphery than in core societies, and a semi-peripheral government found it relatively much more expensive to maintain internal order and much more difficult to raise the taxes necessary for participation in the international power contest. Consequently, while they did not suffer nearly as much as peripheral societies from direct exploitation and disruption by the core economies, semi-peripheral societies were more exposed to internal disorder and to the danger inherent in active participation in the struggle over world resources and markets. This danger became particularly apparent in the three main semi-peripheral societies, Russia, Japan, and Austria-Hungary.

Russia

The class composition of Russia according to the national census of 1897 shows a pattern very similar to the divisions by class in a fairly developed peripheral society of the same period. Except for the fact that there were relatively more peasants, and relatively fewer

TABLE 16

Russian Class-Structure in 1897

Elite and Upper-Middle Class	2% of the population and their dependents (about half government officials, and half professionals, owners of larger enterprises, and large landowners)
Other Middle Classes	6% of the population and their dependents
Working and Lower Service Class	11% of the population and their dependents
Peasants	78% of the population and their dependents
Soldiers and Police (not counting officers)	1% of the population and their dependents
In custody, criminals, beggars, prostitutes, etc.	1% of the population

SOURCE   V. I. Lenin, *The Development of Capitalism in Russia* (Moscow: Foreign Language Publishing House, 1956), pp. 549–555.

members of the working class, this breakdown of classes is similar to that which existed in Mexico in 1900 (See Table 15.)

Culturally, Russia was very divided. The subject European population (Finns, Lithuanians, Estonians, Poles, a large proportion of the 3 million or so Jews, and a number of others) did not accept the legitimacy of Russian rule and remained linguistically and ethnically non-Russian. Ukrainians formed at least 20 percent of the population, and while they were close to the Russians both in terms of language and in terms of perceived ethnic identity, there is some question as to how loyal they were to the Russian state. The Georgians and Armenians in the Caucasus were non-Russians, and from the Crimea to the Pacific there were large numbers of Tartars, Mongols, Turks, and many other non-European, non-Christian populations. In all, the dominant Russians made up only about half the empire's population; nor were they the sole members of the empire's elite, for it was also culturally divided and contained some regional elites that were only ambiguously loyal to the empire. The elite in the Baltic countries, for example, was neither Russian nor Balt, but German. Even in the two leading cities, Saint Petersburg and Moscow, French, English, and German fashions and tastes were dominant among the elite and the upper-middle class, and French, not Russian, was the preferred language of the administrative elite.[19]

Russia's economy was, in some respects, typically peripheral.

Wheat was the major export, and the economy imported large quantities of manufactured goods. Foreign (chiefly French) capital played a major role in railway construction.

In all these respects, Russian society was distinctly peripheral. Yet, in 1900, Russia was not peripheral within the world system. In terms of international politics, it was at the very center of important power conflicts in Europe and Asia. This was so because, for all its relative backwardness and poverty, the Russian state was immense, relatively united, and in possession of a large and effective army. And because of pressure from the core countries, Russia was in the process of deep change by 1900.

From the 1850s to the 1880s, Russia suffered a series of international reverses that made it clear that a state's effectiveness in international actions depended on a strong industrial economy. The price of economic backwardness was political weakness. Economist Alexander Gerschenkron has observed that "there is little doubt that" in the 1890s:

> military considerations had a good deal to do with the Russian government's conversion to a policy of rapid industrialization . . . . the government turned toward the goal of a drastic increase in the economic potential of the country.[20]

Because its military goals were primary after 1890, the Russian government concentrated on stimulating railway. construction, iron and steel production, and a machine industry. The government, rather than society at large, was both the main source of demand for industrial products and the main organizer of industrial production.

But from where could the government draw the funds necessary for importing foreign technology and machinery?: from increased agricultural exports, and from higher taxes squeezed out of the peasantry, the overwhelming majority of the population. In order to permit rapid economic growth, and in order to create an environment conducive to foreign investment, social order also had to be maintained—and at the very time that the population was being squeezed harder economically. As Gerschenkron has put it: "Industrialization required political stability, but industrialization, the cost of which was largely defrayed by the peasantry, was itself a threat to stability."[21]

The program worked. From 1890 to 1900, Russian industrial output grew, on the average, by 8 percent a year, a considerably more rapid rate of increase than was shown in the industrial sector of any Western country during the same period (8 percent growth per year means a doubling every 9 years). The structure of the Russian economy was drastically transformed during this decade, but it was also a time of great stress within the society, particularly among the peasants. Gerschenkron points out that in the 1890s Russian agriculture produced less bread grain (the basic peasant food) per capita than it had three decades earlier. This squeeze on the peasantry was translated into growing peasant unrest. Had the Russian state not been relatively strong even at the beginning of the country's industrialization, this process might have collapsed at its very start. As it was, despite all the ethnic and class divisions within Russia in the late nineteenth century, the Imperial army and police maintained order. Still, by the first years of the twentieth century, the degree of unrest had risen dangerously, and it was in the hope of both distracting the population and scoring a major victory that Russia engaged Japan in a war in 1904 over control of Korea and North China. By early 1905 Russia had lost a series of decisive battles. Frustration, loss of confidence in the government, and, most important, years of accumulated grievances (increased by high taxes to pay for the war) combined to provoke a major revolution. That 1905 revolution was crushed.

From 1906 to 1914 major social and economic reforms were carried out to reduce peasant grievances. But the basic transformation of the Russian economy was so well under way that industrial growth continued at a rapid rate, averaging about 6 percent per year during this period. Such continued growth meant, however, that the middle and working classes also grew in number and organization. As long as industrial growth proceeded smoothly, and as long as the state machinery and police remained strong, this change in the class structure did not present much of a problem. But circumstances became different in 1914, when Germany invaded Russia and destroyed its state machinery. Thereupon the suffering of total war combined with the unrest provoked by 25 years of rapid change, and in 1917 this combination set off a peasant and working-class revolution. By then the army and police had abandoned the government because of extremely severe war losses, and most members of the middle class or the elite had also lost faith in the government's ability to survive. As a result, this time, the disgruntled workers and peasants rather easily overthrew the government.[22]

At least three general conclusions are suggested by this account of Russia's early industrialization. First, semi-peripheral societies trying to become core economies but lacking the necessary social and economic structures must have strong state machines. The state must be the primary mover in the process of industrialization. But the process has high costs, at least in the short run. This is particularly true for the peasantry which must bear the burden of providing the necessary surplus for investment. The state will have to repress peasant protest in order to keep consumption down and investment high. If the state is successful in this, and if industrialization advances, the working class will grow as well and present an increasingly greater demand for higher consumption. Since the state's short-term economic goal is to maximize investment while keeping costs down, the demands of a growing working class will also be repressed.

Second, the state's new despotic rule is also not likely to please the middle class—even if it does not suffer directly from the economic strain of state-sponsored industrialization. As the middle class of the industrializing society grows, it will also demand effective political representation (using as its model the Western European middle class). By the start of the twentieth century, the small but growing Russian middle class was demanding political reforms (similar to those achieved earlier by middle classes in Western Europe) that would give it a greater share of power. The slowness of these reforms alienated many members of the class, among them the highly educated, politically dangerous intellectuals who became leaders and organizers of the workers and the peasants.

Third, the very success of the semi-peripheral state trying to industrialize creates not only internal dangers but grave external dangers as well. Along with domestic unrest, economic success brings the state into increasingly severe conflict with its neighbors. With large parts of the home population hostile to the government, a military disaster tends to break the coercive power of the state and promote revolution. In other words, an industrializing semi-peripheral power is likely to get involved in severe international conflicts, and it must win (despite fragile circumstances) or face drastic consequences at home.

The Russian revolution of 1917, then, was caused not by economic stagnation but by great economic success followed by military defeat at the hands of more advanced states in the world system.

Japan

Japan, like Russia, was a relatively poor society at the start of the twentieth century; and again like Russia, it was a society well on the way to industrialization. Here, too, the push had been started because of a perceived weakness in the international arena rather than because of any purely domestic economic developments. In the 1860s it seemed that Japan was fated to become another China, a peripheral colonial society dominated by the core states. Japan escaped that fate, mainly because it had the great advantage of being far more unified culturally than any other peripheral society.

In 1868 there was a revolution in Japan. Known as the Meiji Restoration, it was not a "left-wing" uprising but a revolt led by members of the lower nobility. Their aim was to preserve as much as possible of traditional Japanese ways, but also to industrialize the economy, create a large and modern armed force, and prevent Japan from becoming subordinate to the Westerners. Because Japan started early enough, before the debilitating effects of peripherality could take hold (until the 1850s Japan had been too isolated from the world system to suffer from peripherality) and because Japan started off with the obvious advantage of being a unified nation-state, the revolutionists of 1868 succeeded brilliantly. Japan never went through a strictly peripheral stage. Rather, it entered the world system as a semi-peripheral society.

It is important to note that the Meiji Restoration was neither democratic nor gentle. As in Russia twenty years later, the only source of income for the needed investments was the peasants; and they were drastically taxed. Numerous peasant uprisings occurred, but these were put down. The state became an absolutist, tyrannical instrument of economic and military growth. At first, almost all the key industries were developed by the government rather than by private capitalists. Later, the government gave up many of the enterprises it owned to private capitalists. From the 1880s to 1945, Japan was dominated by a small elite of high government officials, military leaders, and the controllers of the large industrial firms developed and fostered by the government.

In the 1880s, as economic transformation began to give it substantial military strength, Japan began to play with vigor the imperialistic game already in progress among the great powers. It developed a "need" for colonies—for raw materials, for markets, and for growing room—and it began to acquire colonies, first Taiwan, taken from China, then Korea, and eventually various parts of China. Japanese nationalism and involvement in the international competition for territory led Japan to war with Russia in 1904, and quick success in that war marked Japan as a potentially successful challenger to core domination. It was this "need" to play the imperialist role in the world system that dominated Japan's drive to further economic progress and military expansion. The general welfare of the population of Japan was not at stake. Quite the contrary, in order to fuel rapid economic growth and great military power the elite kept down wages and consumption for the Japanese masses; and it was not until after 1945 that the standard of living for the average Japanese rose to a level consistent with Japan's great economic progress. Until then, the benefits of industrialization had been applied to the conduct of foreign affairs.[23]

Japan, like Russia, exemplifies three generalizations. First, in semi-peripheral societies, the state must be prime mover if peripherality is to be avoided. This means taxing the population, particularly the peasants, to the utmost, in order to obtain investments and maintain social stability during the painful early stages of industrialization.

Second, the industrializing semi-peripheral state cannot be democratic. Rather, to enforce the necessary policies, it must be absolutist. The true elite in this situation is the government administration (civil and military), not the controllers of private capital. Third, foreign policy is crucial. Japan won all of its colonial expansionist wars until it was defeated by the United States in 1945. By then, Japan had been so transformed by seventy-five years of industrial success that it was no longer in any danger of reverting to peripheral status. Its economic structure was so similar to that of core societies that military disaster could no longer have the impact it had on Russia in 1917.

Austria-Hungary

Austria-Hungary stood in marked contrast to both Japan and Russia. It was certainly richer than either of the two other major semi-peripheral societies, and at least in the Austrian half, considerably more democratic. But the Austro-Hungarian state was very weak, primarily because power was shared between the Austrian and Hungarian halves of the empire. Every step taken by the state to strengthen itself was met with serious resistance, usually a reflection of the society's great cultural division. Along with the two main groups, Austrian Germans and Hungarians, there were Czechs, Slovaks, Slovenes, Croats, Serbs, Italians, Romanians, Poles, Jews, and several smaller groups; none of these minorities fully accepted Austrian or Hungarian rule. In addition, while certain parts of the empire were substantially industrialized, other parts were very rural. And everywhere the army was badly organized and ineffective, especially compared to West European armies.

But while there were complex domestic ethnic and class divisions within the Austro-Hungarian Empire, it was the empire's international position that determined its ultimate fate. Austria-Hungary, like the other semi-peripheral states, was deeply involved in the great power game, at least in Eastern Europe. It had its own colonies in Eastern Europe, and was expansionist, like other great powers at the start of the twentieth century. Its "need to expand" placed the country in potentially serious conflict with Russia (and, to a lesser extent, Italy) which sought to expand into the same area. But because it was so weak, and so internally divided, the Austro-Hungarian Empire was not a viable competitor in the world system. Rather than succeeding in the early 1900s, as did Japan, Austria-Hungary was destroyed during World War I (a war it had helped to provoke) and vanished from among the world's independent states.[24]

It is important to note that, despite its fate, Austria-Hungary in 1900 was in many ways more developed economically than either

Russia or Japan. Its weakness rested not as much in economic backwardness as in the fact that it was not a nation-state, and states that are as internally divided as Austria-Hungary was cannot participate in the twentieth-century competition for world power and hope to succeed. The competition requires too great an effort to allow serious internal division in its winners.

A Note on Democracy

In the early twentieth century three of the four major core societies were political democracies. In these three the large majority of the male adult population had the right to vote, and elections were both relatively free and relatively meaningful in that elected officials had real power. In the fourth core society, Germany, democracy was less well established; but the parliament and party system were strong enough, and becoming stronger at a rapid rate, suggesting that a greater degree of democracy was likely in the near future. In the minor core societies, the same pattern prevailed. Politics were either substantially democratic, or at least seemed on the way to becoming democratic.

Among the semi-peripheral societies, the pattern was rather different. Parliaments tended to be weaker (in the case of Japan and Russia, very weak) and less representative of the general population.

Among peripheral societies, only the very richest, namely the English overseas societies, had attained a level of democratic politics. In the three richest Latin American societies, Chile, Uruguay, and Argentina, the first decade of the century saw considerable progress toward the establishment of democratic parliamentary systems; throughout the rest of the peripheral world, stable parliamentary democracy was virtually absent. In direct colonies, of course, foreigners ruled; and even in most independent peripheral societies, democracy did not prevail.

The main reason is that democracy developed where there was a strong capitalist middle class. This middle class did not have to be entirely urban; indeed, the landowning rural middle class did very well in pushing for democratic reforms. Urban or rural, most members of the middle class opposed oligarchic rule and authoritarianism, largely because these infringed on their personal liberties. Furthermore, in any society in which a substantial minority of people had property and wealth, that large minority was likely to resist domination by any small elite which would restrict enjoyment of rights over private property. Since most of the middle class tended to be well educated, politically aware, and easily organized, there were, in the most advanced societies, powerful movements for the democratization of national politics. In semi-peripheral and peripheral societies (with the exceptions noted above) this was not the case.

It is particularly interesting to look at a part of a core society which had many peripheral characteristics, namely the Southern United States, to confirm this point. After the Civil War, the South retained an economic and class structure that was more characteristic of primary exporting peripheral economies than of industrialized core economies. Agriculture remained more important than in the rest of the United States, cultural divisions (based, in this case, on race) were deep, and controllers of the land and foreign (that is, Yankee) investors wielded disproportionate influence on the regional economy and politics. Not surprisingly the South had a weaker middle class than the rest of the United States, and it was by far the least democratic part of the country. Not only a very large proportion of blacks but also many poor whites did not have the right to vote. In many ways, political, economic, and social structures in the South were quite similar to those in the peripheral world, except that the external domination did not come from a foreign core state but from within the United States itself.[25]

But when a peripheral society moves toward semi-peripherality, or when a semi-peripheral society seriously attempts to attain core status, lack of democracy is not a disadvantage. On the contrary, non-democratic governments tend to fare better than democracies in leading their societies to rapid industrial and military advances: they are more likely to keep down consumption (thus freeing funds for investment), and they are also more likely to repress discontent powerfully and ruthlessly.

As subsequent chapters will show, the role of democracy became much more complicated as the twentieth century progressed. In part, this was because, as the working classes in industrial societies became stronger, the middle classes became fearful and turned at least partially antidemocratic. Also, dramatic political failure, particularly in the international power game, seriously weakened the legitimacy of certain governments, and several democratic governments collapsed because of international failure. Third, middle classes that grew from the ranks of purely administrative, civil or military service groups tended to be less democratic than middle classes that were composed of private entrepreneurs; this difference is understandable, since the administrative middle classes developed within centralized, bureaucratic systems rather than within economically decentralized systems that promoted individual action and independence.

These and other influences on democracy in the world system will be broached more fully in later sections of the book.[26] At this point, it seems sufficient to say that in the early twentieth century, the existence of political democracy in the core societies possibly (but not certainly) made life more pleasant for the middle classes than it would otherwise have been. Certainly (and more important) the working classes in these societies found it easier to organize than they would have under more authoritarian political systems. But nevertheless, in the early 1900s the presence or absence of democracy had little impact on international politics or the workings of the world system. Later, this was to change.

Pressures for Change

The capitalist world system seemed secure in the early twentieth century, and the core societies appeared to be in firm control of the system. These very successes, however, were creating strong destabilizing pressures.

The first destabilizing element was the intense expansionist rivalry within the core and semi-periphery. Because the world was, in a sense, "filled up" by 1910, further territorial expansion pitted core powers, and semi-peripheral powers, against each other and generally required war. Such expansion may not have been necessary to core states; but the major powers believed that it was, and the consequences of that belief were undeniably real.

The second, severely destabilizing element was that, soon after a peripheral society was brought into the world system, certain natives, notably members of the Western-educated elites, began to formulate nationalist, anti-core ideologies, and to use their skills in order to organize the classes that had serious grievances against the world system. Since the large majority of the peripheral world consisted of peasants who were oppressed by the expansion of the world system, once organization began to spread into rural areas, the entire structure of world control by a few core societies began to be in doubt. In other words, the more a peripheral area was developed, the more likely it became that some kind of reaction would take place there against the obvious disadvantages of peripherality. In 1910, this response to peripherality was still not a worldwide phenomenon. But the forces that were to make it worldwide were active everywhere, and the very nature of the world economy insured the continuation and growth of these forces.

Third, by 1910, several semi-peripheral societies, notably Russia and Japan, were partially successful in developing economies and state machineries that could challenge the core's domination of the world. The number of participants in the world power game was bound to grow as other societies with plentiful resources and populations made the transition from peripheral to semi-peripheral status. Thus, the competition for control of the world system, already very strong in 1910, was bound to grow more acute.

Fourth, class structures within the core were also changing. As the working class became better organized, and as the middle class continued to grow, the balance of political forces changed. The domination of the small capitalist elite began to weaken, a trend that would have a particularly strong effect in times of crisis, when discontent was most likely to surface. In the international crises that developed as the century progressed, the increased organization of the middle and working classes produced certain important changes in the behavior of core powers in the world system.

Fifth, in the early twentieth century, there were many people who were culturally distinct from those who ruled the state in which they lived. As nationalism spread, and as a series of periodic crises shook the entire world, these nonruling peoples developed ethnic, religious, linguistic, or regional nationalisms that challenged the growth and success of their nation-states. This change was to be evident among various cultural minorities in many of the core societies, but it was to be more apparent in non-core societies, where the majority of culturally distinct groups opposed to each other and to the state often comprised a majority of the population. Culturally based differences would not have become increasingly acute, however, if it had not been for the continuous growth of economies and the growth of nationalism which characterized the capitalist world system.

In the end, the major destabilizing element in the capitalist world system, the element that stood at the heart of the five elements already outlined, involved the very nature of capitalism itself. The rationality of capitalism, its search for constantly increasing profits, and its continuously successful expansion of scientific and technological knowledge had pushed the Western societies into a preeminent position throughout the world. The internal pressures for constant growth that had caused this rise could not stop in 1910. The competition within the core became greater than ever. Growth continued, encouraging ever greater scientific and technological advances, and prompting economic expansion and, thereby, the acceleration of all the destabilizing elements that accompany growth. Not only did growth continue in the core, but as the core's influence spread throughout the periphery, the same elements spread throughout the world. The process was an old one, and in a way, it had been going on since 1500. But the early twentieth century marked an important turning point, because until then the powers in the world system had had continued room for growth into new areas. After 1900, only a few isolated areas remained outside the system; and the growth of any power thus had to involve areas already within the system. Internal growth, spawned by success, was the capitalist world system's major destabilizing element.

IV

Struggle in the Core
and Semi-periphery
(1914–1945)

World War I, 1914–1918

In August 1914, war broke out between the United Kingdom, France, and Russia on one side, and Germany and Austria-Hungary on the other. The leaders of these states, and probably a substantial portion of public opinion, particularly in the core states, felt that at stake was nothing less than control of the entire world system.

The pretext for the war was a dispute between Austria-Hungary and Serbia over a political assassination. But the cause of the war was the pattern established during several decades of frenetic competition between the main powers over the division of the world. The Balkans and the Ottoman Empire were a main field for the struggle because they were still "undivided" peripheral areas.

Gradually, as the war proceeded, Italy and Japan joined the British-French side,, and the Ottoman Empire joined the Germans. A number of other peripheral states joined in the struggle, and in 1917 the United States entered on the British-French side. It was the fact that the large powers controlled such a large proportion of the world's population and economy that made it a world war.

The extraordinary fact of World War I was the ability of the main participants to mobilize so large a proportion of their total human power and production. Everyone seemed directly or indirectly involved. Among the participating states in Europe, virtually all men of military age went into the army; enormous numbers of them would die before the conflict was over. To make up for the domestic losses in manpower, women were brought into the labor force in large numbers.

In France, to take the most extreme example, some 7.8 million men were called to arms during the four years of war. In 1911, the total male population of France between the ages of 10 and 34 (that is, males who would be of military age at any time between 1914 and 1918) had amounted to just that, 7.8 million; thus, in effect, there was close to total mobilization for the war. Of France's 7.8 million soldiers, 1.4 million were killed in combat or died under other circumstances while in the army, that is, 18 percent of the total. With another 3.6

TABLE 17

Military Deaths as a Proportion of Military Aged Males, 1914–1918

	Males of Military Age, 1914–1918*	Military Deaths	Percentage of Total (col. 2/col. 1)
France	7,785,000	1,400,000	18%
Germany	14,341,000	1,800,000	13%
Austria-Hungary	10,415,000	1,290,000	12%
Italy (entered in 1915)	6,969,000	600,000	9%
Bulgaria (on German side)	878,000	90,000	10%
United States (entered in 1917)	21,610,000	116,000	0.5%

SOURCE Henri Bunle, *Le Mouvement naturel de la population daus le monde de 1906 à 1936* (Paris: Institut national d'études démographiques, 1954), pp. 110–12; Martin Gilbert, *First World War Altas* (New York: Macmillan, 1970), p. 158.
* All those no older than 38 at the start of the war and no older than 42 at the end, and all those at least 18 by the last year of the war.

million wounded or captured, there were about 5 million total "casualties" of one sort or another among French soldiers. (Multiple casualties inflate the number somewhat.) This represented 64 percent of the country's total male population of military age during the war![1]

While the relative casualty rates were not quite so high in the other participating countries, the totals were still staggering.

The British Empire lost about 1 million men, Russia probably close to 2 million, and the Ottoman Empire approximately 500 thousand. The small participants (particularly Serbia, Romania, and Belgium on the British-French side) lost close to another 500 thousand. In all, in the four years of the war about nine to ten million soldiers died.[2] Food shortages and the resulting diseases killed millions of civilians, particularly in Eastern Europe, where relatively backward economies and transportation networks broke down completely by the end of the war. Of the major participating powers, only the United States sustained minor losses. (Japan did also, but it was virtually inactive in the fighting.) In terms of numbers of soldiers killed out of the total contributed to the pool, France's losses were about 36 times as high as those of the United States.

The war was devastating for two reasons. First, it was the world's first fully industrialized war, for in its course much modern technology was brought to bear. Second, military strategy was still based largely on outdated conceptions, and even against machine guns and heavy artillery, emphasized personal bravery and massed charges.[3]

To add to the suffering, a naval blockade of Germany and a submarine blockade of import-dependent Great Britain produced serious shortages for the civilian populations of these states; in the other participating societies, economic disorganization also resulted in serious sacrifices. By 1918, the peripheral and semi-peripheral societies most actively engaged in the war were on the verge of total internal collapse. The Communist Revolution of November 1917 had put Russia out of the war, and in Austria-Hungary the long-brewing revolt of various national minorities finally occurred and caused the state to vanish in 1918. The Ottoman Empire also disintegrated.

It is a measure of the degree of nationalism within the core societies, and of the enormous resources they could mobilize and organize, that the war continued so long. There were serious military mutinies in France in 1917, and strikes against the war in Germany. But the war continued until the United States began to contribute enough fresh troops to tip the balance. In 1918, after a last offensive, the German army collapsed, and strikes and mutinies in Germany led to the overthrow of the government. The war ended in November 1918.

An immediate result of the war was the creation in Eastern Europe of a number of newly independent peripheral states carved out of the ruins of the German, Austrian, and Russian empires. This large belt of small states—Finland, Estonia, Latvia, Lithuania, Poland, Czechoslovakia, Austria, Hungary, and the previously independent Balkan states (Yugoslavia and Romania took large parts of the former Austrian and Russian empires)—created a new peripheral zone that was "up for grabs." Twenty years later, as a recovered Germany launched a new challenge for control of the world system, conflict over this particular part of the world would start the European part of World War II.

In the rest of the world there was little outward political change. Germany's African colonies were divided between France, Britain, and Belgium, and Japan and Britain took over the small German possessions in Asia and the Pacific. The Arab portions of the Ottoman Empire were divided between Britain, France, and some Arab states.[4]

The social and economic strains of the war produced more important results than the changes in boundaries. As a reaction against the brutality and waste of the war, the working class and peasants in large portions of peripheral and semi-peripheral Europe moved sharply to the left politically and increasingly threatened the old social order. Even in the core societies, the working class made a push for more power; and in the immediate postwar years, it seemed as if the entire capitalist world system was on the verge of collapse because of socialist revolutions and increased working-class political activity. But aside from Russia, where the new Communist regime managed to hang on to power despite military intervention by the main capitalist powers, the Left was defeated everywhere, and the capitalist system survived relatively intact.

Nationalist Reactions against the Left

The strikes and working-class protests that broke out in core societies in the final stage and aftermath of the war were not produced entirely by the war itself. The numerical growth of working-class organizations and their increased political and strike activity against the capitalist system had begun in the nineteenth century, and the early twentieth century had witnessed severe conflict between the working class and the middle and upper capitalist classes. But during the opening years of World War I, the nationalism of the masses (along with government measures taken to curb working-class organizations) had eased this domestic conflict. As disillusionment grew during the war, and as the strains of accelerated industrial production for war purposes began to have an effect, the level of strike activity grew. The end of the war let loose a storm of strikes in Europe. In reaction, strong repressive actions were taken by the middle and upper classes in an effort to preserve the capitalist system. In the United Kingdom, special laws were passed to repress strikers; in Germany the government used the remnants of the army and right-wing veterans' groups to crush revolutionary activity; in Italy the government and middle classes brought Mussolini's fascists to power in order to curb the workers and peasants by violent means.[5] The fear of socialism also produced a severe reaction in the United States, where many working-class organizations were repressed and their leaders deported or arrested.[6]

Combining with repression to ease the pressure of working-class militancy was the greater economic prosperity of the 1920s. Indeed, throughout most of the industrialized world, the 1920s were a period of relative labor peace. A lingering depression in the United Kingdom, produced largely by its desperate attempts to maintain the international strength of its currency, probably explains a major exception, the British general strike of 1926.[7]

The figures in Table 18 on strike activity in the major capitalist core societies show the rise of working-class militancy in the early twentieth century, the peak being reached in the late 1910s, and the decline in the 1920s. Even in the United States, which avoided the suffering experienced by Europe during the war, accelerated produc-

TABLE 18

Strikes Per Year in the Major Core Societies, 1880–1929

	France	*United Kingdom*	*United States*
1880–1889	187	no data	863°
1890–1899	442	816	1419
1900–1909	942	475	2507†
1910–1914	1188	932	no data
1915	98	672	1593
1916	312	532	3789
1917	686	730	4450
1918	496	1165	3353
1919	2047	1352	3630
1920	1879	1607	3411
1921	565	763	2385
1922–1929	972	485	1060

SOURCE   For France: Edward Shorter and Charles Tilly, *Strikes in France 1830–1968* (London: Cambridge University Press, 1974), pp. 361–364; for the United Kingdom: B. R. Mitchell and Phyllis Deane, *Abstract of British Historical Statistics* (Cambridge: Cambridge University Press, 1971), p. 71; for the United States: U.S. Bureau of the Census, *Historical Statistics of the United States Colonial Times to 1957* (Washington: U.S. Government Printing Office, 1960), p. 99.
° Average for years 1881–1889
† Average for years 1900–1905 and 1914. No data are available for 1906–1913.

tion for the war was accompanied by a rising number of strikes. As in Europe, a large decline in strike activity followed the climax of the late 1910s.

The huge strikes that took place in the cities of Italy in 1919 and 1920 soon spread to the countryside, where the peasants tried to take over the land from large landowners. There were attempted communist revolutions in various parts of Germany in 1919, notably in Berlin and in Bavaria; and in the same year Hungary briefly became a communist country. In the United Kingdom, the simmering Irish revolt broke out in 1916, was repressed, and then broke out again in 1919. In 1921 Ireland became independent. Everywhere, the Left seemed to be on the rise. But everywhere, including Ireland, which became a fairly conservative republic once it had broken away from Britain, the Left was crushed.[8] For much of Europe (and indeed the world) during these years, the Russian Revolution served as a model of future trends. But the same revolution that served as a positive example for left-wing militancy served equally as a spur to antileft activities among those who feared communism. Throughout Europe and the United States, one of the most powerful tools at the disposal of the antileft forces was nationalism—the fear of foreign ideologies and foreign domination. The middle and upper classes were the most fearful of change, and, as World War I had shown, in the more developed countries even the working class could be counted on to support nationalism.

In the victorious core societies, the appeal to nationalism, fear of communism, the relatively large number of middle-class voters, and the prosperity of the 1920s allowed conservative forces to triumph through a democratic electoral process. In the peripheral and semi-peripheral societies, where economic conditions were far poorer, where the middle classes were numerically weaker, and where poor peasants presented a potential threat to social order, harsher methods were used to put down the Left. Landowners and the frightened middle classes used military force. Extreme nationalism, violent antisocialist and anticommunist measures, and rule by military and police might (with the consent of the middle and upper classes) is what came to be called fascism.

Not surprisingly, fascism first developed in the semi-peripheral societies of Europe. These were the societies under the greatest strain in the world system because they were at once less developed than the core societies and yet involved in the same power struggle. They were also societies that had relatively strong nationalist elites. Italy became the first major fascist society in 1922, and gradually, fascism spread throughout Eastern Europe (except, of course, for Russia), to Japan, and to Germany. How fascism spread, and why, in the 1930s, Germany became a fascist state, can only be explained in light of the second catastrophe that hit the capitalist world system in the twentieth century, the Depression of 1929 to 1939.

The Great Depression

For all the destruction of World War I, the fundamental economic trends of the prewar period continued after the peace. Technological progress in the core continued at a very rapid pace. Automobile production, in its infancy before the war, grew far more rapidly after the war; and communications also kept on improving. Medical advances multiplied, and death rates in the industrialized societies continued to fall. The movement of people from rural areas to the cities also continued. The United Kingdom, which had been losing its dominant position in the world economy throughout the late nineteenth century, slipped further, while the United States extended its lead as the main industrial economy. Industrialization increased as well in semi-peripheral societies, and even in the rich peripheral societies. (Canada, for example, became a highly developed industrial economy during this period.) In contrast, the mass of poor peripheral societies remained as dependent as ever on the capitalist core.

The United States, however, did not assume the former role of the United Kingdom in the world system. The resulting disequilibrium was probably the main reason for the depression that struck the system after 1929. While this catastrophe cannot be explained definitively here (economists continue to debate its complex causes), three sets of facts regarding its origins should be incorporated into the discussion.

First, World War I created serious financial strains in the European core. To finance war expenditures, all the core societies (except the United States) and the semi-peripheral participants borrowed heavily, depleted their assets, and rapidly inflated their currencies. Efforts to return to prewar financial stability after 1918 seriously injured the British economy, which simply could not recoup its losses. The attempt contributed heavily to an enduring economic slump which persisted in the United Kingdom throughout the 1920s. In Germany, heavy war debts were augmented by steep reparations set down by the victorious Allies. Unable to pay, Germany printed worthless paper money, and there resulted an inflation which wiped out the savings of many middle-class Germans in 1923. The new political entities created in Eastern Europe from the fallen Austro-Hungarian Empire also had weak economies and inadequate credit structures, and their involvement in the world banking system ultimately destroyed its balance. Even though the late 1920s were a period of relative stability and prosperity, the fundamental weaknesses of the world credit and banking structure, and the economic difficulties they caused were not resolved.

Second, the preceding financial situation was intensified because, as the United Kingdom lost its dominant economic position, the United States remained unwilling to take over financial leadership of the world system. The world was effectively without a central banker (a role filled by the British before the war), and this void contributed heavily to the chaos of the 1930s. As economist Charles Kindleberger has put it, "The world economic system was unstable unless some country stabilized it, as Britain had done in the nineteenth century and up to 1913. In 1929, the British couldn't and the United States wouldn't."[9]

Third, the dominant economy in the 1920s and 1930s, the United States, was largely self-sufficient, quite unlike the United Kingdom during the nineteenth century. The relative decline of the United Kingdom, the withdrawal of Russia from the world system during the twenties (to be discussed in a later section of this chapter), and the fact that the new dominant core power was relatively inactive in world trade led to a glut of manufactured goods. Lenin had predicted that without peripheral outlets, the capitalist core would overproduce and sink into depression. Had the United States' share in world trade increased as quickly as the country's total productivity, the Depression probably would not have occurred. The extraordinary strength of the United States economy in the early decades of the twentieth century is suggested by the comparison of manufacturing productions provided in Table 19.

Manufacturing grew rapidly throughout the postwar world, but in the United States it grew so fast that by 1929 the American economy was producing almost one-half of all the world's manufactured goods. Yet, in 1929 the United Kingdom and Germany were still exporting more manufactured goods than the United States.[10] This can be explained by the larger internal market of the United States, and by the fact that its people failed to see their stake in maintaining the world capitalist trading network. Although American investments abroad expanded quickly in the 1920s (from about 3.5 billion dollars in 1913 to 17 billion in 1929), they remained smaller than British foreign investments and were too heavily concentrated in short-term loans.[11] But the underfinanced and relatively disorganized condition of the world trading network hurt the United States as much as it hurt other core economies, and it was the inability to unload the country's agricultural production and excess industrial production that set off the stock-market crash of 1929 in the United States. In Europe, a series of bank failures related to the problematic credit structure produced that crisis.[12] In short, exceedingly complex transactions within the entire world economic network were more responsible for the crisis than events within individual national economies.

TABLE 19

Core Portions of World Manufacturing Output

	1900	1913	1929	*Percentage of World Population in 1929*
United States	30%	36%	43%	6%
United Kingdom	20%	14%	9%	2%
Germany	17%	16%	11%	3%
France	7%	6%	7%	2%
Total "Old Core"	74%	72%	70%	13%

SOURCE R. A. C. Parker, *Europe 1919–1945* (New York: Delacorte, 1970), p. 102; Richard B. Morris and Graham W. Irwin, eds., *Harper Encyclopedia of the Modern World* (New York: Harper & Row, 1970), p. 707. For population: W. S. and E. S. Woytinsky, *World Population and Production: Trends and Outlooks* (New York: The Twentieth Century Fund, 1953), pp. 36–44.

This is indicated by the rapid spread of the effects of the New York stock collapse of 1929. Soon the entire world (except the Soviet Union) was plunged into crisis.

It is well known that the United States partially withdrew from international political affairs during the 1920s and 1930s because of domestic political considerations. This political withdrawal, in effect, doomed the postwar international arrangement to failure, although the unwillingness of the United States to assume a hegemonic role in the world economy was probably an even more important factor (but since international economics and international politics are so inseparable, it would be somewhat pointless to analyze the one without the other). This isolationism stands in marked contrast to the economic and political role the United States would assume during and after World War II. Then, with the United States well involved, the capitalist world system would experience a sustained period of economic prosperity rather than financial chaos and depression.

The economic consequences of the Depression were extremely serious. In the United States the GNP fell from 104 billion dollars in 1929 to 56 billion in 1933, and unemployment rose from 3 percent of the labor force to 25 percent. In Germany and the United Kingdom, unemployment rose to 16 percent of the labor force and 20 percent of the labor force, respectively, by 1933.[13] Nor were the core societies the only ones affected. The peripheral primary exporting economies were particularly hard hit as slack demand for their products caused sharp drops in the level of prices. From 1926–30 to 1936–38 the price of manufactured goods in world trade fell about 17 percent; but since the price of primary products fell even more (27 percent), the over-specialized peripheral economies wound up paying relatively more for their imports.[14]

Aside from the economic hardships, the Depression caused severe political turmoil and a resurgence of both right-wing and left-wing extremism. Such political and social consequences set the stage for World War II.

The Social Roots of Fascism

Broadly speaking, there were two types of reactions to the Depression. In the core societies, there was a process of democratic adaptation: that is, the creation of social security systems, insurance schemes to protect both working and middle classes, acceptance of many working-class demands, particularly with respect to the right of unions to strike and bargain collectively, and generally greater government involvement in economic support of the population. These measures preserved the capitalist system by defusing the political discontent aroused by the Depression. Extremist protest activity grew, but remained under control.

The economies of semi-peripheral and European peripheral societies were not rich enough to afford such meliorative measures. In these societies the nationalist upper classes and the civil-service middle class turned to authoritarian conservative solutions to maintain social order. The working class was too small to organize effective resistance, and the peasantry was neither sufficiently well organized nor sufficiently united to stop this trend. Between 1920 and 1939 almost all of Southern and Eastern Europe became fascist. Japan followed the same pattern.

The puzzle is that in 1933 Germany, a powerful industrial state, also became fascist. The rise of Nazism in Germany was instrumental in pushing peripheral Europe deeper toward fascism, and it ultimately polarized the world into two antagonistic sides—the fascists and the antifascists. Why was it that such an advanced society failed to adopt the kind of moderate, centrist reforms accepted in all the other highly developed core states? This question has an importance beyond strict historical interest, for an answer to it might resolve whether or not the transformation that occurred in Germany in the 1930s could reoccur again, in one or more of today's highly advanced capitalist societies.

The Marxist explanation of fascism considers it a final stage of capitalist imperialism. Assuming that capitalist economies need to grow, and that they need to expand their areas of colonial domination in order to acquire ever greater sources of cheap raw materials and new markets for their surplus goods, the Marxist concludes that a capitalist economy cut off from colonial expansion collapses on itself; the working class reacts against the weakened social order and revolution occurs. A suggestion of this theory is that in order to ward off their fate, capitalist economies must embark on a more determined push for colonial areas. In a closed world system (where the colonial spoils have been divided or where resistance from peripheral areas no longer permits easy domination) the only means of colonization are hypermilitarization and wars of conquest. These solutions have the great advantage of allowing thorough control of the working class by internal military force and stimulation of the economy by large military expenditures. How are these costs paid? By depressing wages and preventing working-class protest. How is national morale maintained in such difficult circumstances? By fervent nationalism, persecution of supposedly threatening minority groups, and the creation of a national war psychosis that accepts sacrifice in order to defeat internal and external threats to prosperity and national grandeur. The middle and upper classes retain their economic privileges in this system and thus support the regime. In sum, in a closed world system, a country is bound to be pushed into war as it tries to expand its colonial domain.[15]

This theory fits the Leninist interpretation of imperialism, but it presents only the external reasons for aggressive imperialism. Fascism was also the product of a deep fear that working-class socialism had inspired among capitalist elites and the middle classes. To people reacting to the uncertainties and financial collapse of the Depression, fascism had greater appeal than old-fashioned imperialism. Widespread middle-class support gave fascism a mass component that right-wing movements had previously lacked, a difference not accounted for in Leninist theory.

Two types of fascism developed in the 1930s—industrial fascism and agrarian fascism. Germany, the great loser of World War I, became the prime example of industrial fascism. Internationally, if not in terms of its domestic structure, this former core society had been relegated to semi-peripheral status since the end of the war. The German capitalist elite and middle classes believed that this demotion was largely responsible for Germany's economic disasters. The German fascist movement, the Nazi Party, offered a road back to international political strength, core status, economic stability, and control of working-class, socialist protest. The rise of fascism in Japan can be explained in the same way, since Japan's rapid industrialization and semi-peripheral status combined to create the most volatile kind of domestic political situation. Italy had become fascist in the 1920s for similar reasons.[16]

The other type of fascism, agrarian fascism, was less dangerous than Germany's because it occurred in smaller, less-developed societies. Those in which it took hold were Portugal, Hungary, Poland, Romania, Bulgaria, Yugoslavia, Greece, the Baltic states, and several Latin American ones. In some ways these fascist governments resembled the old-fashioned authoritarian regimes that had long prevailed in independent, peripheral societies, for within each landowners and the small civil-service elite joined together against lower classes protesting the effects of the Depression. Ideologically, agrarian fascism was as fiercely nationalistic and antisocialist as industrial fascism; but because the middle classes were far smaller in the more backward, primarily agrarian societies, the mass component of fascism was less there than in the industrial fascist states. In any case, the small fascist societies had much less scope for imperialistic ambition than relatively powerful Germany or Japan; thus the international consequences of agrarian fascism remained more limited than those of German, Japanese, or Italian fascism.[17]

The United States, the United Kingdom, and France escaped fascism because, unlike postwar Germany, they still controlled large parts of the world, and because there pressures for drastic solutions to the Depression were much less intense. The remainder of northern Europe escaped as well. Like the major Allies, Belgium and the Netherlands had substantial colonial empires, and the relatively prosperous Scandinavian countries and Switzerland were not participants in the world power competition (though in 1938 Switzerland had much larger total foreign investments than Germany, and Sweden also had considerable foreign holdings).[18]

Is the Marxist-Leninist theory of fascism correct? Final proof is not possible, but the outcome of the first fascist experiment suggests that the theory is not a correct view of the economic problems faced by Germany, Japan, and Italy in the 1920s and early 1930s. After being defeated during World War II, and losing their international power, all three of these societies came to prosper greatly as capitalist economies, particularly Germany and Japan. But in the years between the wars, substantial portions of the upper and middle classes in these three states still believed that colonial expansion and great-power status were necessary for economic survival. As it happens, however, during the 1930s it seemed that the theory was correct. The German and Japanese economies advanced more quickly in the late 1930s than the democratic capitalist societies, which were still floundering in economic depression. Here, again, one must invoke the "Thomas theorem"—"If men define situations as real, they are real in their consequences." In a time of economic collapse, political turmoil, and social upheaval, elites and large portions of the middle class in the semi-periphery (and Germany was temporarily semi-peripheral) adopted a logical and consistent view of the world that promised them relief from trouble. If the Marxist-Leninist theory is correct, or if substantial portions of the elites and middle classes in capitalist societies come to accept it as correct, fascism may occur again in capitalist societies that fall into deep economic trouble.

The fascist view of the international economic and political situation was almost identical to the Marxist-Leninist explanation. Fascists and Marxist-Leninists hoped for different outcomes, of course, but their fundamental analyses were similar. As in the period that preceded World War I, the "Leninist" behavior of several great powers led to a predictable outcome—world war.

Consequences of Fascism

The political history of Germany from 1924 to 1933 shows how the Depression eroded support for democratic, moderate government. After World War I, Germany overthrew its monarchy and established a parliamentary government. By the late 1920s, a period of prosperity (which followed the recovery from the inflation of 1923) produced large electoral majorities for the German democratic parties (those of the Center and the democratic socialists). With the Depression the democratic socialists lost much working-class support to the Communists (revolutionary socialists), while the middle classes abandoned the parties of the center in large numbers and moved to the far right. Large German corporations began to finance Nazi activities in order to suppress Communist and socialist demands, and large numbers of small-business owners, farmers, and unemployed members of the middle class provided the mass of activists for the party. Mass support came from those afraid of communism, and those who could be persuaded that the root of all evil lay in foreign, particularly Jewish, conspiracies.

TABLE 20
Voting Patterns in Germany, 1924–1932

		Dec. 1924	*May 1928*	*Sept. 1930*	*July 1932*	*Nov. 1932*
*	Nazis	3% ⎫ 25%	3% ⎫ 21%	18% ⎫ 32%	37% ⎫ 44%	33% ⎫ 43%
	Other Far Right	22% ⎭	18% ⎭	14% ⎭	7% ⎭	10% ⎭
†	Center Parties	36% ⎫ 62%	33% ⎫ 63%	27% ⎫ 52%	18% ⎫ 40%	18% ⎫ 38%
	Democratic Socialists	26% ⎭	30% ⎭	25% ⎭	22% ⎭	20% ⎭
	Communists‡	9%	11%	13%	14%	17%
	Others	4%	6%	3%	1%	2%

SOURCE   R. A. C. Parker, *Europe 1919–1945* (New York: Delacorte, 1970), p. 222.

* = antidemocratic right;
† = democratic center;
‡ = antidemocratic left.

In 1933 Hitler and his Nazi Party took power, helped by other far-right allies and tacit acceptance by some of the Center parties. The opposition Socialists and Communists were outlawed, anti-Jewish legislation was passed, and the economy was rapidly geared to rearmament (thus solving the unemployment problem). An aggressive foreign policy soon allowed Germany to dominate Eastern Europe, which, by the late 1930s, was being turned into a series of German economic colonies geared to German economic needs. The threat this posed to France and the United Kingdom finally provoked a belated reaction. Germany had already annexed Austria and Czechoslovakia; when it invaded Poland in 1939, World War II broke out.[19]

Despite the great historical and cultural differences between Germany and Japan the two societies wound up in rather similar situations in the 1930s. From the very start of Japan's push toward major core status, a major component of Japanese policy had been its imperialism abroad and heavy industrialization for military purposes at home. Before World War I, Japan had taken pieces of China, conquered Korea, and defeated Russian expansionism in the Far East. After the war, growing prosperity and the influence of the urban middle class liberalized Japanese politics. The Depression reversed this process of liberalization. Japan had become dependent on its export trade to finance the import of vital raw materials, and the Depression in the capitalist world system resulted in steep tariff walls raised by the core powers to protect their economies. (The United States, the United Kingdom, and France all followed very protectionist policies after 1929). Edwin Reischauer, America's foremost expert on Japan, has observed:

> The businessman's program of continued economic expansion and prosperity through a growing export trade was suddenly revealed to be dangerously dependent on the good will and tolerance of foreign powers. Huge political units like Russia, the United States, and the British Empire could ride the storm of world depression, for they had their own sources of supply for most raw materials and their own consuming markets. But a smaller unit like Japan, which depended on other lands for much of its raw materials, and on China, India, and the Occident for a vital part of its consuming market, seemed entirely at the mercy of the tariff policies of other nations.[20]

The Japanese military and the large corporations which dominated the economy combined in the late 1920s to return Japan to authoritarian nationalism at home and vigorous expansionist imperialism abroad, much as the same forces combined in Germany to install a fascist regime. The economic statistics in Tables 21–23 suggest the trends of the Japanese economy in the early twentieth century. Between 1929 and 1938, the only major industrial powers that increased their share of world manufacturing output were Germany and Japan (along with the Soviet Union, which will be discussed later in this chapter). German and Japanese fascist policies certainly seemed to pay off in terms of expanding the national share of world trade. In

TABLE 21
Percentage Increase in Per Capita GNP from 1900 to 1929

United States	16.5%
France	16.1%
United Kingdom	
(excluding Ireland)	5.2%
Germany	7.3%
Japan	32.8%

SOURCE   Simon Kuznets, *Economic Growth of Nations: Total Output and Production Structure* (Cambridge: The Belknap Press of Harvard University, 1971), pp. 38–40.

TABLE 22
**Japanese Percentage
of Total World Manufacturing Produce, 1900–1939**

1900	0.6%
1913	1.2%
1929	3.5%
1939	3.8%

SOURCE   Richard B. Morris and Graham W. Irwin, eds., *Harper Encyclopedia of the Modern World* (New York: Harper & Row, 1970), 723; R. A. C. Parker, Europe 1919–1945 (New York: Delacorte, 1970), p. 102.

TABLE 23
Source of World Total Manufactured Exports

	1899	*1913*	*1929*	*1937*
United Kingdom	33.8%	30.6%	23.8%	22.4%
United States	11.5%	13.0%	21.4%	20.3%
France	15.1%	12.7%	11.1%	6.1%
Germany	23.2%	27.5%	21.9%	23.4%
Japan	1.6%	2.5%	4.1%	7.5%

SOURCE   William Woodruff, *Impact of Western Man: A Study of Europe's Role in the World Economy 1750–1960* (New York: St. Martin's Press, 1966), 274.

short, while the Depression clearly weakened the capitalist core, the fascist societies of the semi-periphery that were the main challengers of the core societies grew stronger.

In 1931, Japan officially annexed the northern Chinese province of Manchuria. In 1932, the military effectively took over the Japanese government. It gradually strengthened its position, and in 1937 launched a full-scale invasion of China. In 1941, in order to take over the rich oil, rubber, and other mineral and agricultural riches of Southeast Asia (then controlled by the British, French, Dutch, and Americans) the Japanese tried to destroy the only military force capable of resisting them, the American Pacific fleet stationed at Pearl Harbor. By this act, Japan signalled its full entry into the core of the capitalist world system as a challenger of the old core.[21]

A list of political and economic events in Germany and Japan in the 1930s barely indicates the magnitude of the social changes that accompanied these events. Strict antilabor laws, hysterical xenophobia, militarization of every aspect of civilian life, extreme police repression, and the glorification of war turned these two societies into fiercely imperial machines. At a more mundane level, change was equally dramatic. In the capitalist core, the 1920s and 1930s saw an improvement in the status of women (who had gained the right to vote in Britain and Germany in 1918, and in the United States in 1920), an improvement in the lives of the working classes, and a great outpouring of literary and artistic work. The same trends prevailed in Germany and Japan in the 1920s. In the 1930s they were reversed. German and Japanese women were supposed to go back to their homes and breed new soldiers for the empire, literature and the arts were censored and suppressed, working-class wages were frozen, and democratic practices eliminated.[22]

The New Deal Alternative to Fascism

In the United States and the United Kingdom of the 1930s, fascism was never a serious threat. In France, which was economically weaker and politically less stable, the decade was marked by the electoral triumph of the left rather than the right, even though a number of fascist movements did develop. In none of the core societies was frustrated nationalism nearly as strong as in Germany or Japan. The Depression consequently produced a rather different reaction in these societies.

The main example of the moderate democratic reformism that prevailed in core societies was the American government's New Deal. Franklin Roosevelt and the Democratic Party won overwhelming electoral control of the United States in 1932, and there followed a dramatic series of federal reforms designed to alleviate the Depression. Banking, corporation law, and the stock exchange were reformed. Social security and numerous public welfare schemes went into effect. The rights of labor unions to strike and bargain collectively were strongly affirmed by law. Although these acts did not end the Depression, they made the government both popular and stable; and extremist challenges from both the far right and the left were easily pushed aside.

The New Deal did not end capitalism or bring about economic and social equality between classes (this was not Roosevelt's intent); but it did lessen inequality a bit, and more importantly, it created the impression of greater equality. Income distribution figures for the United States during this period show the small but significant extent of the redistribution (see Table 24). The index of inequality decreased steadily from 1929 to 1944, and was then to remain pretty much unchanged into the 1960s.

Another aspect of the New Deal was that it marked the first time in the United States that the federal government became a major force in the peacetime economy. This does not signify that the government ended private enterprise (though right-wing criticism of the New Deal has often declared so), or that the government took over a significant portion of the means of production, but, rather, that it became a major spender in the economy as well as an increasingly important regulator of private enterprise. The growth of government spending is indicated in Table 25, which lists the percentages of the

TABLE 24
Percentage Distribution of Family Personal Income in the United States, 1929–1941

Consumer Units		1929	1935–1936	1941	Percentage of Change 1929–1941
Lowest	20%	3.5%	4.1%	4.1%	+17%
Second	20%	9.0%	9.2%	9.5%	+ 6%
Third	20%	13.8%	14.1%	15.3%	+11%
Fourth	20%	19.3%	20.9%	22.3%	+16%
Top	20%	54.4%	51.7%	48.8%	−10%
Top	5%	30.0%	26.5%	24.0%	−20%

SOURCE Edward C. Budd, "Inequality in Income and Taxes," in Maurice Zeitlin, ed., *American Society, Inc.: Studies of the Social Structure and Political Economy of the United States* (Chicago: Markham, 1970), p. 144.

TABLE 25
GNP and Government Spending

	GNP (*in $ billions*)	*Federal Government Spending* (*in $ billions*)	*Spending* *as Percentage* *of GNP*
1900	17	0.5	2.9%
1910	31	0.7	2.3%
1920	89	6.4 (remnant of wartime spending)	7.2%
1929	104	3.3	3.2%
1933	56	4.6	8.2%
1937	91	7.8	8.6%
1941	126	13.3 (start of wartime spending)	10.6%

SOURCE   U.S. Bureau of the Census, *Historical Statistics of the United States Colonial Times to 1957* (Washington: U.S. Government Printing Office, 1960), pp. 139 and 718.

GNP spent by the federal government in years between 1900 and 1941.

Just as the political right has criticized the New Deal for being too socialist (a criticism with no basis if socialism is to mean government seizure of the key means of production, that is, of key businesses), the left has criticized it for not being socialist enough. Since the reformers wanted to save the capitalist system by defusing discontent and shoring up a shaky financial system, the New Deal was actually quite successful—even if it did not end the Depression.

But the New Deal cannot be analyzed in purely local, that is, national terms, because similar measures were taken in other core societies as well and because these measures were all responses to changes that had occurred in industrialized societies quite independently of their political ideology. These effects of industrialization can be summarized in six main points.

1. Industrialization had shifted the distribution of population. Ever larger proportions of the population lived in cities rather than in small towns or villages. In such small settlements, in times of economic depression, people relied on help from relatives and neighbors, and tried to survive by simply growing more of their own food. The residents of large cities were usually somewhat more cut off from their relatives, particularly if they had moved to the city quite recently, and neighbors were not as likely to help each other. More importantly, city people were firmly in the cash economy and could not, like peasants, get by on local production. The city dweller without a job

was helpless. The depression of the 1930s finally brought home the point that some kinds of social insurance were absolutely necessary.[23]

2. Increasing competition in the world system required much greater government participation and protection. Governments had always participated in helping certain sectors of the economy; but as the world system grew tighter, such government help became more important. This was particularly true in the semi-peripheral economies, which probably explains why their governments took over more of their national economies than governments did in core societies. But even in the core, the electorate finally accepted the idea that the government had to play a major role in the economy.

3. The rise of working-class, egalitarian ideologies, and the dangerous example of the Soviet Union set the ideological tone during the interwar period. Capitalist elites rejected and feared socialism, but there was little doubt that the challenge had to be met one way or another. The fascist response, of course, was one possibility. The only other possible response (except for socialism itself) was to give in to certain working-class demands, and to create somewhat greater equality and government action simply to save the system.

4. The spread of egalitarian ideals was particularly important because continued economic growth for a long period of time had accustomed populations in core societies (and this, for the first time in world history) to a continually rising standard of living. Since rising standards of living had become normal, falling standards were even more threatening during the Great Depression than they had been in previous economic depressions.

5. World communications and domestic communications in each core society were far more developed in the 1930s than ever before. Radio, movies, the spread of literacy, improvements in railroads and automobiles, as well as the concentration of people into cities made core populations more aware of what was going on nationally and internationally than they ever had been in the past. The spread of egalitarian ideals was more rapid, and the awareness of falling standards of living was more thorough.

6. Finally, the main capitalist economies had experienced a great concentration of businesses. A few giant corporations had acquired a disproportionate amount of power, and the electorate demanded that governments step in as regulators. Business had become so concentrated that the private interests of the corporation could set economic policy, and free market forces were becoming less important. By 1929 the largest 100 manufacturing corporations in the United States, for example, owned 40 percent of all assets in manufacturing.[24] The onset of the Depression convinced the middle classes that some form of government participation in economic decisions was obligatory.

TABLE 26
**Decrease or Increase in Income Shares
of Top 5 Percent of Consuming Units, 1920s to 1930s**

United Kingdom (1929–1938)	− 6%
United States (1929–1941)	−20%
Sweden (1930–1935)	− 7%
Denmark (1925–1939)	− 6%
Germany (1928–1936)	+15%

SOURCE Simon Kuznets, "Quantitative Aspects of the Economic Growth of Nations," Part VIII, *Economic Development and Cultural Change,* Vol. XI, No. 2, part II (January 1963), pp. 60–62.

Placed in a world context, then, events in the United States were neither unique nor based purely on the vagaries of Roosevelt's actions. Other core societies experienced similar, moderate declines of gross inequality because of reforms like the New Deal. Among the most advanced industrial societies, only Germany had a different pattern during the 1930s (see Table 26). There, the degree of concentration of wealth at the top increased somewhat rather than decreasing. This, of course, reflects the fascist "solution" to the Depression.

There had already been a noticeable decrease in economic inequality in industrial societies during and immediately after World War I; social insurance, recognition of unions, and government participation in the economy were not entirely inventions of the thirties. The New Deal and similar reforms merely accelerated existing trends and certified transformations that had been occurring for many decades. In the fascist societies, particularly Germany, this was not the case; there the thirties marked a reversal of some of these older trends. (That, in a few words, was the essence of the right-wing solution to the Depression. Rather than being accelerated, egalitarian trends were reversed.)

The Soviet Union: Opting Out of the World System

After the Revolution of 1917, Russia (which changed its name to the Union of Soviet Socialist Republics) took a radically different course in its development. There was a period during which the Soviets beat back attempts at foreign interference and invasion as well as a series of attempted counterrevolutions. By 1921, Soviet power was fairly well consolidated. There followed a period of economic normalization and a return to the more stable conditions that had preceded the start of World War I. This relative calm was a prerequisite to repairing some of the damage done by seven years of foreign and civil war. Finally, in 1928, the Soviet Union launched on a program of massive industrialization in order to catch up to the industrial core. In effect, at that point, the Soviet Union also withdrew from the capitalist world system and chose (or was forced) to rely on its own enormous resources in order to advance.[25]

Recently, a number of former peripheral societies have tried to accomplish the same program by also withdrawing from the world system, closing off the outside world in order to stimulate internal development and prevent core control and exploitation of the economy. Developments in the Soviet Union illustrate the possibilities of this approach as well as its limitations and severe negative side effects. The Soviet Union also had two traits that gave it an advantage.

First, it was huge. In 1920 the Soviet Union was the world's largest country in terms of area and was inhabited by 134 million people, or about 7 percent of the world's population. The country had immense, largely untapped natural resources, and in this respect was much like the United States.

Second, the Soviet Union did not start its industrialization program from scratch. Poor as it was in 1920, it had the advantage of an intense prewar Russian industrialization (from about 1890 to 1913). It also had a substantial body of trained personnel, fine universities, and a nationalistic civil service. As a result of World War I, the Soviet Union lost many of its most rebellious non-Russian provinces in Europe (Poland, Finland, the Baltic countries, and a part of Romania) while it kept its entire, sparsely populated, Asiatic Empire (Siberia) and most of the valuable Ukraine. In 1926, 53 percent of the population was Russian, 21 percent was Ukrainian, and 3 percent were other Slavs. Only 23 percent of the population was non-Slavic.[26]

The Soviet Union also had several major disadvantages. First, there was the hostility of the dominant capitalist world system, which feared communist ideology because it might serve as an example for domestic revolution. Second, there had been enormous destruction within the country during the world war and the civil war. Finally, and in some ways most dangerously, there was the fact that the land area of the Soviet Union made it ideally suited for domination by the core or by growing semi-peripheral economies. Before World War I, the economy, even while industrializing, had been a major exporter of agricultural products. There were extensive unused resources and huge empty spaces suited for colonization and exploitation. As it happened, the United Kingdom and France were too exhausted to undertake a search for new empires. The United States was not sufficiently interested to mount anything but a few desultory military expeditions, all of them short lived. Japan, though strengthening, was still too weak to undertake to conquer Siberia, especially when easier and more immediately lucrative profits seemed available in China. Germany, which aimed at a colonization of Eastern Europe and large parts of Russia during World War I, was a defeated power, and not until the revival in the 1930s would a threat from this source become severe.

The economic backwardness and consequent military and political weakness of the Soviet Union were the major considerations that led to the closure (or withdrawal from the world system) of the Soviet economy after 1928. Stalin, the successor of Lenin as head of the Soviet Union, launched a massive industrialization program and set up an authoritarian, extremely repressive police state to maintain order during the difficult push toward self-sufficiency.

In retrospect, the direction taken by the Soviet Union after 1928 strangely resembles some aspects of Japanese policy in the last quarter of the nineteenth century; and it resembles many aspects of prerevolutionary Russian industrialization as well. First, Soviet industrialization was clearly aimed at strengthening the military position of the state. Heavy industry was emphasized over consumer goods and light industry. The main goal was independence in a hostile world system. Second, the investment for industrialization had to be squeezed out of the peasantry. Third, economic progress was accompanied by strong nationalism and policies aimed at preventing the economy from slipping into peripheral status. That was the whole point of the closure: to prevent the kind of economic and cultural integration into the world system that characterized the relations between weak peripheral societies and strong core ones. As in Japan after 1868, or Russia in the late nineteenth century, foreign investment was allowed only under special circumstances—and then it was tightly controlled by the government. Finally, as in previous semi-peripheral efforts at industrialization, the main agent of change was the state rather than the private sector and private capitalist entrepreneurs. These tendencies were even stronger in the Soviet Union than they had been in Russia before 1913 or Japan after the Meiji Restoration. This suggests that while it is important to remember that the Soviet Union claimed to be guided by Marxist ideology, and in certain respects it was, in many other respects its policies after 1928 were more than anything else the product of a nationalistic effort at development in the context of the existing world system.

Based as it was on intense domestic effort, the Soviet Union's developmental effort squeezed the population very hard. In the short run, heavy industry produced no consumer goods; but a growing industrial labor force had to be fed. With few consumer goods to exchange, it was difficult to get rural producers of food to sell their produce; in essence, they received too little in return. Furthermore, the industrial workers themselves could hardly be rewarded with more than the bare necessities. All surplus production had to go to building more industries. In this stage of the process, the very success of industrialization increased social tensions. Workers, both rural and industrial, were being severely deprived for the sake of increased production. The only solution was repression.

Soviet industrialization was very rapid in the 1930s. The Soviet Union went from producing 5 percent of the world's manufacturing goods in 1929 to producing 18 percent in 1938. (During that time, the share of the United States, the United Kingdom, and France fell from 59 to 52 percent of the total.)[27] From 1929 to 1940 Soviet industrial production tripled, and it may have risen even faster.[28]

The dramatic increase in industrial production involved a big shift in the labor force. In 1926, of 85.5 million people in the civilian labor force, 81 percent worked in agriculture. By 1940, the civilian labor force had grown to 97.8 million, of which only 59 percent were in agriculture.[29] This change involved large movements of population from rural to urban areas and important changes in life style. At the same time the Soviet school system was vastly expanded, allowing large numbers to be educated, and new public health measures greatly reduced mortality. Although the progress in these areas was part of a long-term transformation occurring throughout the world, and one which had already occurred to a significant extent in industrialized societies, the fact that the Soviet Union made significant advances, even during the hardest periods of its forced industrialization, shows that, judged by these criterion, the developmental program was successful.[30]

However, the forced industrialization of the Soviet Union was extremely costly in terms of human lives and freedoms. In order to ensure needed deliveries of food, the Communist Party of the Soviet Union (C.P.S.U.) collectivized the country's agriculture. In theory, this was done as part of the transformation from capitalism to socialism, but, in effect, it was a way to police the peasantry and squeeze a surplus out of agriculture. The peasants resisted, and some 5 million of them were shot or deported to Siberia.[31] By 1940, nearly 97 percent of all peasants had been forced into collectives, but, as political scientist Merle Fainsod has written:

> The collectivization crisis of the early thirties exacted a terrible price . . . [it] involved the uprooting and exile of millions of peasants and robbed the countryside of its most efficient and enterprising element. The slaughter of livestock and draft animals [by the resisting peasants] inflicted a wound on the Soviet economy from which it took nearly a decade to recover. The disorganization of work in the new collective farms contributed to the disastrous harvest of 1931 and 1932. Despite

the drastic decline in crop yields, the authorities were ruthless in enforcing their demands on the countryside, and near-famine conditions prevailed in many rural areas. . . . An unknown number of peasants, variously estimated at from one to several million, died of starvation. . . .[32]

As a result, Soviet agricultural production was probably no higher in 1940 than it had been in 1913; and meat production fell considerably from the levels reached in 1928, before the start of massive collectivization.[33] In addition, during the interval, the population had risen by about 20 percent. The average Russian was thus less well-fed in 1940 than before World War I. This pattern contrasted markedly with the pattern of industrialization in Western Europe and the United States, where agriculture had improved its productivity as quickly as, or even more quickly than industry. To this day, Soviet agriculture remains peculiarly backward, a burden that continues to cause severe imbalances in an otherwise advanced economy.

It was not only the peasantry which suffered, though as a class it was the most exploited group in the Soviet Union. The standard of living in the cities (measured in terms of housing) was no higher in 1938 than it had been in 1913.[34] (This estimate, just as the one on agricultural production, is based on official Soviet statistics.) Such lack of movement is to be expected in view of the rapid growth of cities and the de-emphasis on consumer goods. But the climate of fear and repression imposed on the population by the secret police was certainly worse in the 1930s than in prerevolutionary Russia.

The estimated number of people killed, deported, and jailed by the police during the 1930s (not even counting the legions of peasants) is almost unbelievable. Soviet historian Roy A. Medvedev has estimated that of the top 134 officials of the C.P.S.U. in 1934, 110 had been arrested by 1939, and many, if not most, of them were shot. Possibly up to 90 percent of all local Party officials suffered the same fate, as did many scientists, artists, military officers, and thousands upon thousands of civil servants and quite ordinary people.

Medvedev believes that in 1936–39 four or five million Soviet citizens were arrested and that at least 500 thousand were shot. He writes:

In 1937–38 there were days when up to a thousand people were shot in Moscow alone . . . The simple truth must be stated: not one of the tyrants and despots of the past persecuted and destroyed so many of his compatriots.[35]

Nor did this repression stop in the 1930s; it continued through the 1940s and early 1950s. Counting all arrests and executions, probably over ten million individuals were victims of the purges.

Why they occurred remains hotly debated. Was Stalin mad? Every modernizing revolution, from at least the French Revolution of 1789, has involved political terror and repression. But the scale of repression within the Soviet Union was so unprecedented that people living outside the country did not believe that such excesses were possible. Was it, perhaps, the extraordinarily rapid pace of the Soviet transformation that provoked such massive terror? Did it seem the only way to keep the population under control during the period of change? Did a feeling of extreme vulnerability to outside interference motivate Stalin? How could the very officials who were next in line for execution continue to carry out orders? Was revolutionary ideology so strongly ingrained? Was it all a question of nationalism? These questions, vital as they are, have not been fully answered. All that can be said, and it is a sobering conclusion, is that all of this "worked." In about 25 years, the Soviet Union raised itself from the position of a relatively vulnerable, backward semi-peripheral society to a position as the world's second strongest power, an advance even more dramatic than the rise of Japan after 1868. The cost was enormous, and the effects of the Stalinist method of industrialization continue to be felt in the Soviet Union. The repressive apparatus established during the 1930s remains in place, even though it is used more sparingly than it was in the traumatic early stages of Soviet progress.

World War II, 1939–1945

By the late 1930s the capitalist world system seemed to be approaching collapse. Measures on the order of the New Deal had maintained political stability in the democratic core, but the Depression had not been cured. From Germany, Italy, and Japan, fascism was expanding. By 1939, large parts of China had fallen to the Japanese; Italy had conquered Ethiopia and incorporated Albania; and Germany had taken over Austria and Czechoslovakia, and was rapidly taking over the economies of other Eastern European states. In a bitter civil war in Spain (1936–1939), Germany and Italy had provided the help necessary for a fascist victory against the left. By the end of that war, in any case, it was no longer a matter of fascism against democratic forces, because the Spanish left had been abandoned by the democratic core and was being sustained almost entirely by Soviet support.[36] The Soviet Union, despite the massive purges, seemed successful beyond all expectations, and also seemed to be the only power able or at least willing to resist fascism. But, despite its partial re-entry into world politics, the Soviet Union was still relatively isolated. *International conflict in the late 1930s was not primarily ideo-*

logical (even though it was described in those terms) but based on a struggle to control and alter the capitalist world system. The semiperipheral states (that is, Germany, Italy, the Soviet Union, and Japan —the civil war in Spain had exhausted it and it dropped out of the world conflict) all faced the same competitors, the rich capitalist core states which still dominated the world economy. On August 23, 1939, the Soviet Union and Germany signed a treaty of nonaggression in which they agreed to divide Eastern Europe and keep out of each other's way.[37] One week later, Germany invaded Poland, and the British and French declared war to save what could be saved of Europe.

George Kennan, historian and diplomat, has pointed out a fact which, even today, is not widely recognized:

> Before the war began, the overwhelming portion of the world's armed strength in land forces and air forces had accumulated in the hands of three political entities—Nazi Germany, Soviet Russia, and Imperial Japan. All these entities were deeply and dangerously hostile to the Western democracies. As things stood in the late thirties, if these three powers were to combine their efforts and stick together in a military enterprise, the remaining Western nations plainly had no hope of defeating them on the land mass of Europe and Asia, with the armaments at hand or even those in prospect. In Europe and Asia, Western democracy had become militarily outclassed. The world balance of power had turned decisively against it.[38]

By mid-1941, Germany (and its junior partners, Italy and several East European satellites) had conquered all of Europe except the United Kingdom, the Soviet Union, and the neutral countries, Sweden, Switzerland, Portugal, and Spain (an unofficial German ally). At that point, it was the logic of German imperialism, and possibly the Nazi's racist theories about the inherent superiority of Germans over Slavs, that changed the outcome. Germany invaded the Soviet Union in order to gain the country's rich resources and to secure land for colonization. By the end of 1941, large parts of the Soviet Union had fallen to Germany, and Japan had invaded Southeast Asia and attacked the United States. By mid-1942, Japan, too, had added enormous territories to its empire. A new world system seemed to have replaced the old one.

As the Germans conquered Europe, the full consequences of the years of Nazi racist nationalism revealed themselves. A systematic campaign of extermination was begun against Jews and Gypsies, and the "inferior" Slavs were consigned to serfdom and slow extermination. France, Belgium, the Netherlands, Norway, and Denmark were squeezed dry to feed Germany and to supply its industries. People

TABLE 27
Deaths During World War II

Country	Population in 1939 (in millions)	Military Deaths	Civilian Deaths	Deaths as Percentage Total 1939 Population
Western Europe	113.6	610,000	692,000	1.1%
United Kingdom†	47.8	326,000	62,000	0.8%
France*†	41.7	250,000	350,000	1.4%
Belgium[1] & Lux.*	8.7	16,000	77,000	1.1%
Netherlands*	8.7	12,000	198,000	2.4%
Denmark*	3.8	400	1,000	less than 0.
Norway*‡	2.9	6,300	3,900	0.4%
Occupied Eastern Europe	72.8	570,000	5,975,000	9.0%
Poland*†‡	34.8	100,000	4,220,000	12.4%
Czechoslovakia*†	15.3	150,000	215,000	2.4%
Yugoslavia*‡	15.5	300,000	1,400,000	11.0%
Greece*	7.2	20,000	140,000	2.2%
German Allies in Europe	159.3	4,492,000	1,436,000	3.7%
Germany†	69.7	3,500,000	700,000	6.0%
Austria†	6.7	230,000	104,000	5.0%
Italy	43.8	330,000	80,000	0.9%
Finland	3.7	82,000	2,000	2.3%
Hungary†	9.2	140,000	280,000	4.6%
Bulgaria	6.3	10,000	10,000	0.3%
Romania†	19.9	200,000	260,000	2.3%
Others				
United States†	131.4	460,000	–	0.3%
Japan	72.5	1,200,000	260,000	2.0%
Soviet Union*†‡	172.0	6,500,000	About 10,000,000	9.6
China‡	about 450.0	—unknown millions died—		?

SOURCE   W. S. Woytinsky and E. S. Woytinsky, *World Population and Production: Trends and Outlo* (New York: The Twentieth Century Fund, 1953), pp. 44 and 47; R. A. C. Parker, *Europe 1919–1945* (N York: Delacorte, 1970), p. 354; U.S. Bureau of the Census, *Historical Statistics of the United States Co nial Times to 1957* (Washington: U.S. Government Printing Office, 1960), p. 735.

* Countries occupied or partially occupied by Germans.
† Countries where, in 1938, there were many Jews. The United States contained 4.8 million, Sov Union 3 million, Poland 3 million, Romania 850,000, Hungary 400,000, Czechoslovakia 360,000, United Kingdom 300,000, France 300,000, Germany 200,000 and Austria 200,000. Of the five to six mill killed, about half were Polish Jews.
‡ Countries occupied or partially occupied by Germans and having strong resistance movements. All occupied countries mounted some kind of resistance. China had a very strong Communist guerrilla movem against the Japanese.

from all the occupied European countries were enslaved and removed to Germany as replacements for German laborers gone to war. Nazi Germany was pursuing the old policy of imperialism that had been practiced by core states in peripheral areas for over a century. But the Germans would carry cultural arrogance and the economic exploitation of labor and primary resources in conquered areas to an extent never reached by the old core.

Estimates of deaths in Europe during the war show the extent to which the Germans practiced their racist policies (see Table 27). Civilian death rates in Slavic countries, particularly those with strong resistance movements, and among European Jews were incomparably higher than those of other conquered populations—and they were high everywhere.

At least 35 million people, and possibly more than 40 million, died. Of this number, some five to six million were European Jews murdered by the Germans, mostly in Eastern Europe where the Jewish population had been concentrated. (There were about nine million Jews in Europe in 1939.)

World War II was, in the end, a highly mechanized war, and after the entry of the United States and the Soviet Union against the Germans, there was little doubt about the outcome. Industrial production determined the victors, and, by 1943, it was clear that the Germans and Japanese had lost. The figures in Table 28 on military production more or less explain the defeat.

In 1945, the war ended with the complete victory of the United States, the United Kingdom, and the Soviet Union against Germany and Japan.

The Postwar Arrangement

There were some major political changes following the war. These can be briefly summarized.

Germany and Japan were defeated and lost their colonial territories, in Eastern Europe and East Asia. The Soviet Union took over Germany's Eastern European economic empire, and the United States, the Netherlands, France, and the United Kingdom reclaimed their Asian empires from Japan. China, about which more in the next chapter, achieved effective independence.

The boundary changes in Eastern Europe entailed large-scale human migrations, putting a finishing touch on the terrible disruption and misery caused by the war. Some 14 million Germans left Eastern Europe for Germany, and some 7 million Slavs were moved into areas left by the Germans.[39] In Asia, millions of Japanese returned to Japan from the lost Empire; the war and its aftermath also caused millions of Chinese to migrate within China. In terms of social disruption, the immediate effects of World War II continued to be felt into the early 1950s.

The end of the war marked the end of the great twentieth-century conflict over control of the capitalist world system. The United States had won and was the primary core power. France and Britain, which kept their overseas empires (in any event, for a few years), were nevertheless economically ruined. The German and Japanese challenges had failed. Western Europe (and soon, Japan) took on roles formerly filled only by the minor core powers, such as Belgium or the Netherlands; that is, they became subsidiary members of the core, profiting from the world system, but neither controlling nor maintaining it. After 1945 the capitalist world system held together, but primarily because the United States took over most of the costs of maintaining that system. The willingness of the United States to take on this imperial burden contrasted with the aftermath of World War I. The result within the capitalist system was a prolonged period of success and economic expansion rather than financial and economic chaos. The political and economic hegemony of the United States prevented the emergence of any challenge within the core.

The other major development of this postwar period was the emergence, for the first time, of a dynamic, industrial, powerful, yet fundamentally anticapitalist society. (Although one might argue, with good reason, that Germany and Japan in the 1930s were just as strongly anticapitalist, these societies being very strongly dominated by authoritarian state structures.) The Soviet Union had existed since late in 1917, but not until World War II did it emerge as a great world power. After the war, the Soviet Union, in effect, created its own "socialist" world system by taking over Eastern Europe and East

TABLE 28
Tank and Airplane Production, 1939–1944

	Germany	Japan	United Kingdom	United States	Soviet Union
Tanks (1940–1944)	23,000	?	27,000	72,000	(More than Germany
Airplanes (1939–1944)	112,000	61,000	119,000	258,000	(40,000 in 1944, probably as many Germany in total)

SOURCE R. A. C. Parker, *Europe 1919–1945* (New York: Delacorte, 1970), p. 347.

Germany. This presented a serious challenge to the world system now dominated by the United States.

For some years, it seemed that the two world systems would quickly come to war. That they did not can be attributed to three main factors. First, neither side needed conquests in the other's domain. Both the Soviet Union and the United States were absorbing vast new areas and burdens and creating imperial structures to rule their new empires. Secondly, both sides were war weary, particularly the Soviet Union. Public opinion in the United States was also not ready for a new war, and in Western Europe there was enough sympathy for communist ideas and for the Soviet Union that an aroused United States would have had to fight such a war pretty much alone. Third, and possibly most importantly, by 1950, when both sides seemed ready to take up war again, they both had nuclear fission weapons, and after 1954, fusion weapons. War would then have meant an unacceptable scale of destruction.

In any case, after 1945 the main drama in the world began to occur in places other than the old core and semi-periphery. A number of peripheral societies revolted against the core and created a new semi-periphery hostile to the core. This produced a new threat to the capitalist world system, possibly an even greater one than the emergence of the Soviet Union. Why and how, and with what social effects, are questions that will take up the remainder of this book.

V

Revolutions in the Periphery
(1910–1950)

The roots of instability in peripheral societies, touched upon in Chapter III, will be more systematically discussed in this chapter. Three trends of the early twentieth century will form the basis of this discussion: first, the increasing commercialization of agriculture, which created a set of problems that made the entire economic and political structure in the periphery unstable; second, because of contact with the West, rapid population growth and pressures for economic change; and third, the appearance of a new, highly nationalistic elite that could channel the mass discontent created by the development of peripheral economies.

The review of these topics will be followed by a close look at Mexico and China, two examples of the revolutionary process in peripheral societies. This process, which began in the early part of the century, has spread and created a large number of new societies hostile to core domination. The revolutionary new semi-periphery that has taken shape ultimately presented the core with a severe challenge, one that core societies still have not met successfully.

Commercialization of Agriculture and its Consequences

Commercialization of agriculture in peripheral societies turned former village-based landholding arrangements into money-based private-property systems. Powerful controllers of the land (usually, but not always, direct landowners) appropriated the profits of commercial agriculture which was in turn based on exports to the world economy. The relative security of old village social arrangements was destroyed and replaced by more demanding and less secure market pressures. This process actually began long before the twentieth century, but in the years that preceded World War I, the change accelerated and absorbed large portions of the peripheral world that had not yet been fully transformed.

One typical example, Mexico, has already been mentioned. Egyptian economic integration into the world system exhibits a similar pattern—rapid growth in the production of cash crops and in foreign trade. In the first half of the nineteenth century Egypt became an important cotton exporter. From 1848–1852 to 1908–1912 the amount of cotton (by weight) exported yearly increased about 19 times, and by World War I cotton made up about 87 percent of all Egyptian exports.[1] As it happens, in Egypt (as in Mexico) there had been large landed estates long before the nineteenth-century growth of modern capitalist market forces. But the system of land tenure was totally overhauled in the first half of the 1800s. New landholding patterns emphasized private rather than communal property and initiated schemes for irrigation and development that were designed to increase cotton production. By 1896, 44 percent of Egypt's cultivated land was owned by 12,000 landlords (no more than 2 percent of all owners). The huge majority of peasants held increasingly fragmented small plots, and therefore had to lease land from landowners in order to ensure survival. After World War I the spectacular growth of cotton production ceased, and production grew slowly until about 1950. But the basic landholding pattern remained unchanged. In 1952, 0.1 percent of all Egyptian landowners held 20 percent of the cultivated land; the top 6 percent held 65 percent; and the millions of peasants shared the rest.[2]

Inequality in landholding does not necessarily produce unrest. But combined with other aspects of peripheral economies, it is an important destabilizing force. Those other aspects, in Egypt, were rapid population increase, great poverty, stagnation of economic opportunities and relative neglect of all aspects of the economy that were not related to cotton production, and finally, a large degree of foreign control over the Egyptian political system and economy. From 1895–1899 to 1945–1949, the per capita GNP in Egypt declined from a meager $131 per year to $117 (measured in 1965 U.S. dollars),[3] while the economy of the core capitalist societies and the successful semi-peripheral societies made great advances. (Population growth will be examined below.) After World War I, some industry developed, but slowly, and only in those areas where the supply of local cheap labor made it economical to substitute domestic production for imports. By 1937, 70 percent of the working population was still involved in agriculture, and by 1950 that proportion had fallen only to 60 percent,[4] a figure that seems quite high when compared to the proportion of the population in agriculture in core societies even at the start of the twentieth century, and very high when compared to the figures for core societies in the middle of the century.

Even within this stagnant, poor economy, there was the example of the few very rich landowners and, perhaps more bothersome, the example of the Europeans who gave orders to the Egyptian government, lived in what appeared to be splendid luxury, and whose own economies were constantly growing.

Much the same story can be told about India, where in the nine-teenth century, British colonial policy systematically favored the land-owners and the growth of commercial agriculture. Barrington Moore has observed:

> In addition to law and order, the British introduced into Indian society in the nineteenth century railroads and a substantial amount of irrigation. The most important prerequisites for com-mercial agriculture and industrial growth would seem to have been present. Yet what growth there was turned out to be abor-tive and sickly. Why? A decisive part of the answer, I think, is that *pax Britannica* simply enabled the landlord and now also the moneylender to pocket the economic surplus generated in the countryside. . . .

Moore adds:

> To lay all the blame on British shoulders is obviously absurd. There is much evidence . . . to demonstrate that this blight was inherent in India's own social structure and traditions. Two centuries of British occupation merely allowed it to spread and root more deeply throughout Indian society.[5]

The transformation to a commercial agricultural system was probably less thorough in India than in many other colonial societies, and India's middle peasant class survived the experience without being expropriated by landowners. Yet, from the 1890s to the 1940s, the production of food crops in India declined by 7 percent (while population rose by almost 40 percent) and commercial crop produc-tion (mainly of cotton, jute, tea, peanuts, and sugar cane) grew by 85 percent.[6] Furthermore, British colonial policy leaned on the very rich Indian landowners for support; and the lavish style of life of this small segment of the population contrasted sharply with the stagnat-ing, or possibly even declining, standard of living of the average peas-ant. From the 1880s to the early 1900s India's per capita GNP de-clined by about 5 percent, and by the middle 1950s, it had risen only slightly, to $77 (in 1965 U.S. dollars) per year (compared to $60 in the 1880s).[7] As in Egypt, industrial growth was not great enough to absorb very much of the poor rural work force. And the privileges, powers, and arrogance of the British colonial population could hardly fail to arouse discontent.

India and Egypt were not unique. China, Vietnam, Indonesia, and other societies went through similar experiences—growth of a com-mercial agricultural sector, concentration of landownership, Western domination, economic stagnation or decline for the bulk of the peas-ant population, and ultimately, extreme resentment against the do-mestic and foreign elite that profited from this pattern.[8]

Here one should not lose sight of an important point: while the activities of the imperialist powers may invite the conclusion that the main force leading to subjection of peripheral masses was willful and carefully planned colonialism, and while willfulness was a factor in some measure, total responsibility for that subjection cannot be assigned so easily. The impersonal power of the market, combined with the military and political power of the capitalist core, generally acted as the main agent of peripheral change. This can be seen by examining the case of Turkey, which never became a European colony.

The declining Ottoman Empire began to reform itself as early as the late eighteenth century. The obvious approach to reform was to imitate the West, since the West seemed to be getting stronger while the Turks were becoming weaker. In the nineteenth century the empire's landholding laws were reformed, and private property was assured by the state. At the same time, Western demand for agricultural goods was growing. As historian Bernard Lewis has written:

> The commercial and financial developments of the time, including the expansion of Turkish agricultural exports, brought a flow of steady money, and created a class of persons with sufficient cash to bid for leases, buy estates, and lend money on land. The new laws gave them legal powers to enforce contracts of debt and sale; the new police protected them from the hazards which formerly attended such enforcements.[9]

Why was there a "new police"? In order to strengthen the state, the Turkish government had created a modern police and military apparatus based on the Western model. This innovation was essential in order to collect taxes and build a structure that might resist foreign military intervention. The very attempt to strengthen the state created the possibility of extending commercial agriculture. But the Turks did not take the next step, heavy taxation of agriculture in order to yield a surplus that might be invested in industry. Rather, the partial modernization of the Turkish administrative system helped duplicate the kind of condition that typified colonial societies. A new landowning class came into existence. Lewis observes:

> In the Balkan provinces this gave rise to bitter social struggles. . . . In western and central Anatolia it produced the familiar figures of the Aga, the rich peasant or landlord, dominating and often owning the village, and of his still more powerful protector, the merchant landowner residing in the town. The position of the peasant was much worsened by these changes.[10]

Economic opportunities for Western Europeans were created by these changes, and European finance, through loans, railway construction, and investment in agriculture, penetrated Turkey. By 1914 Europeans owned the railways, tramways, key port operations, electricity, gas, and water utilities in the cities, and most of the country's few operating mines and factories. Native handicrafts were ruined by European imports, and a new comprador class came into being, serving as the agents of the Europeans.[11]

The Turkish experience was particularly tragic because a large portion of the compradors were "pariah capitalists." Greeks and Armenian Christians were especially prominent in this class, and while they had always been present in the Ottoman Empire, in the nineteenth century their situation became precarious. For one thing, they were the agents of foreign penetration. Second, the Turks were trying to revive their state by creating a sense of nationalism, and in return, the Greeks and Armenians, who felt no sense of shared nationalism with the Turks, were becoming nationalistic in their own right. The Turkish state was deeply split on cultural as well as economic grounds, and this produced a series of bloody massacres and wars between the Turks and various Christian populations in the Ottoman Empire. There were many Turkish massacres of Christians, which culminated during World War I in the killing of over one million Armenians. To the West, this was only one more example of barbarism, for which the Turks were supposedly well known. But like many of the tragedies that have afflicted the modern world, it was nothing of the sort. In the early 1800s the Armenians were considered among the most loyal minorities in the Ottoman Empire, and far from being persecuted, they were allowed their own laws and institutions. It was the economic and political changes of the nineteenth century that changed all this.[12] Rising nationalism, the attempt to create a strong nation-state, the intensification of a cultural division of labor based on growing commerce, and finally, the outbreak of World War I and the violent xenophobia it bred everywhere produced this tragedy. Paradoxically, it was the very progress of the world system that created the conditions for supposedly "traditional" barbarism. The Middle East, knocked about by progress and foreign intervention, has remained a fertile ground for nationalistic hatreds to this day. With the experiences of world wars I and II, and with the other slaughter that has accompanied modern social change, today's Westerners can perhaps understand such events somewhat better than the smug Europeans of the early twentieth century.

Population Problems and the Need for Economic Change

A second, critical problem in the peripheral world in the first half of the twentieth century was rapid population growth. Alluded to in the preceding section, it now requires a more detailed examination.

In Western Europe in the eighteenth and nineteenth centuries the introduction of at least minimal scientific health care and control of epidemics, the extension of cropland in response to market forces, and the improvement of transportation (thus allowing either the shipment of food to areas of temporary shortage or outmigration from famine areas) caused death rates to fall. In the nineteenth and twentieth centuries these beneficial effects of the world economy spread to peripheral societies.

In largely rural societies, birth rates had always been high. Faced with high infant mortality, peasants gave birth to many children in order to assure themselves of at least a few adolescents. The motivation is clear enough. Children provided essential agricultural labor, labor especially required by the extended cultivation of relatively high labor-demanding cash-crops. Children were also the only existing form of old-age insurance. As death rates fell, these concerns did not change. Individual peasants were probably not aware of the rapid decline in mortality, and in any case, the need for old-age insurance and extra labor did not diminish. It probably increased. A pattern of population growth is evident when one examines the demographic history of several peripheral societies. (See Table 29.)

The rapid rate of increase was not much greater than that in the industrial core during the nineteenth century. From 1800 to 1900, for example, the population of England, Wales, and Scotland went from 10.5 million to 37 million, a 252 percent increase. From 1800 to 1950 the British population increased about 365 percent. Because of immigration, as well as because of high birth rates and low death rates, the population of the United States grew from 5.3 million in 1800 to 151.7 million in 1950, an increase of 2760 percent.[13] The United States may not be a good basis of comparison because so much unsettled land was available there; but European populations also grew very rapidly in the 1800s, and in some relatively crowded countries, like the Netherlands, the rates of population growth from 1800 to 1950 were about the same as those in some of the overcrowded peripheral societies. However, the industrialized societies easily absorbed their growing labor force through industry. As the economy progressed, and as the population migrated from rural to urban areas, the incentives to having many children changed, and birth rates began to fall. By the mid-twentieth century population growth rates in highly industrialized societies had slowed, and now their populations are almost stable. This reaction contrasts with the trend in peasant societies of the periphery. There, as death rates continued to fall in the twentieth century, birth rates remained high, and the rate of population growth increased. The population problem in peripheral societies has been directly related to their lack of industrialization. After almost two centuries of rapid population growth, contemporary industrial soci-

TABLE 29
Peripheral Populations, 1800–1950

	1800	*1850*	*1900*	*1950*	*Percentage Increase 1800–1950*
India (including Pakistan and Bangladesh)	125	255*	285	437	+250%
Indonesia	8.5	16	39	76.5	+800%
Indochina	about 7	8	16	29.8	+325%
Egypt	about 2.5	6.8†	9.7‡	19§	+660%
Mexico	6.5	7‖	13.6	25.4	+290%

SOURCE   For India, Indonesia, Indochina: Gunnar Myrdal, *Asian Drama: An Inquiry into the Poverty of Nations* (New York: Pantheon, 1968), p. 1396; for Egypt: Abdel R. Omran, "The Population of Egypt, Past and Present," in Omran, ed., *Egypt: Population Problems and Prospects* (Chapel Hill: University of North Carolina Population Center, 1973), p. 13; for Mexico: W. S. Woytinsky and E. S. Woytinsky, *World Population and Production: Trends and Outlook* (New York: The Twentieth Century Fund, 1953), p. 44.

* for 1871   ‡ for 1897   ‖ for 1840
† for 1882   § for 1947

eties are not overpopulated; they are also no longer experiencing rapid increases in population.

In societies composed largely of peasants, overpopulation is severely felt in the form of an agricultural land shortage. The scarcity of arable land lowers the standard of living among the peasants and creates a strong migratory pressure—some farmers simply have to leave the land for the city. But if the cities do not afford these migrants real employment opportunities, a floating, unemployed or underemployed population is created; meanwhile the rural villages remain economically overcrowded. This process explains the stagnation of per capita GNP in such societies as Egypt and India during this century, as well as the volatile nature of urban masses in the peripheral world. The only possible solutions are rapid industrialization, which creates a new demand for labor, and provision of new land for the growing rural population.

The solution of industrialization

Unfortunately, the more advanced the technological level of the world system, the more difficult it is to find a solution to the population problem through industrialization. In the early period of industrialization, when manufacturing was growing rapidly in the Western core societies, the state of technology was not advanced, and new factories required large new labor forces. Increasingly, however, mechanization and progress have diminished the labor demand of new industry. Industry is now capital or machine intensive, and it takes huge new investments to create significant increases in the demand for labor.

India is an excellent example of this problem because, while it is still struggling to become industrial, in some ways it actually began to industrialize in the late nineteenth century. Its abundance of cheap labor and cotton and jute, as well as the large demand for textiles within the large Indian population meant that some form of import substitution (in this case, the manufacturing of domestic textiles to replace British imports) was more or less inevitable despite the anti-industrial policies that Britain set down for its colonies. Modern textile mills developed in India in the 1880s, and by 1914 the country had the world's fourth largest textile industry. Jute mills, and eventually a small iron and coal industry (to service India's railroads), were developed. But by 1911, only 1.1 percent of the labor force was employed in modern industry, while about 9 percent of the labor force was still employed in traditional handicraft activity. Industrial output grew much more rapidly than industrial employment.[14] Throughout the next decades the same pattern persisted, and even by 1951 only 11 percent of India's labor force was employed in manufacturing, mining, or construction (including traditional handicrafts). Industrial growth had hardly absorbed the surplus rural population, since by 1951 the same total percentage of the labor force was involved in industry and crafts as in 1911.[15] The inability of Indian industrialization to provide adequate employment has continued into the second half of the century. Although it was able to develop a sophisticated nuclear industry in the early 1970s, and a considerable steel industry along with its large textile industry, India still cannot employ its growing population. Large portions of the peasantry remain very poor and underemployed.

The Indian situation shows the effects of peripherality, but these are somewhat more subtle than the discussion has indicated. Peripheral status does not mean that industrial growth is entirely prevented (at least, it need not in the twentieth century), but that it is slowed down at a critical juncture and tends to be too specialized to be of much assistance when a serious peasant-population problem begins to develop. Why does this incapacity happen? In India, inadequate industrialization resulted from the joint influences of the social structure, which was dominated by the controllers of the land, and of the colonial state. Along with maintaining a colonial class structure, the British also prevented the imposition of protective tariffs which

would have helped Indian industry compete against the more advanced British industries. As it was, import substitution could occur
in the few areas in which India's comparative advantage was overwhelming (like textiles), but not over the broad range of industrial
areas that are necessary to a balanced economy. Again, it was a case
of overspecialization rather than absolute lack of development. There
was slow industrial growth instead of rapid and broadly based
growth. By the time India escaped from British colonial rule in 1947,
it was, in a sense, too late, at least for an easy solution. By then the
country's overpopulation problem was quite severe, and world technology still more advanced and capital intensive than in the early
1900s.

This indicates that if Japan had not undergone an economic
revolution in the late 1800s, after the Meiji Restoration, it would have
been in serious economic trouble by the mid-twentieth century, much
as India is today. Immense as Japan's effort may have been in the
nineteenth century, it would have had to be even greater to achieve
comparable results in the twentieth. The pattern is somewhat suggestive. Japan suffered while it industrialized, and in the 1930s and
1940s the Soviet Union suffered much more. Still, in terms of national
economic development, these have been the major success stories of
the last 100 years; and aside from Japan, no Asian, African, or Latin
American society has successfully industrialized (with a few peculiar
exceptions, such as Singapore and South Africa). A theory cannot be
strictly tested with a few cases, but the observed pattern is clear.
The later the start of industrialization, the more difficult, and the less
potential for solution of the overpopulation problem. Delaying the
kind of anti-core revolution that Japan experienced after 1860 mag-
nifies the social and economic problems of peripherality.

Land reform as a solution

Another possible solution to peripheral overpopulation is the
acceptance of agricultural reforms that give more land to the
peasants. As with industrialization, this solution has temporal limitations. The longer the reforms are delayed, the harder they are to
carry out successfully.

One possible reform is the development of new land—by extending irrigation, draining land, or clearing previously forested
areas. However, land is finite, and while much of Latin America still
has unused land, the crowded peripheral societies, like India and
Egypt, do not. Moreover, the development of new land is expensive,
and another problem of these poor economies is their lack of capi-

tal. This insufficiency keeps down both their rate of technological progress in agriculture and their development of new land.

Another possible reform is the confiscation and division of large estates for redistribution to the peasants. Done early enough, or in a society in which there are good credit facilities for peasants (to allow them to purchase the machines and fertilizer needed to cultivate their land efficiently), land reform can boost agricultural production and reduce agricultural problems. In a poor society, without adequate credit facilities, without enough industry to absorb the growing population, and where the land is already seriously overcrowded, land reform has only marginal effects. Peasants may gain title to the land they are cultivating, but they do not gain access to new land as such. By breaking up large estates, some land reforms have actually eliminated an area's only source of capital for a mechanization of agriculture (the big landowners), and have thus caused regression rather than progress. (A good example is Romania, where there was a land reform in 1917, and where average crop yields returned to pre–World War I levels only in the late 1950s and early 1960s.) In Egypt and India, when land-reform laws were finally passed in the 1950s, there was little positive effect. The population was already too large, and the land was already as intensively cultivated as possible, given the poverty and inability of the peasants to use modern machinery.[16]

A further disadvantage of land reform is that it almost always entails a bitter political fight against the controllers of the land. This fight must be undertaken if a society is to remedy the root problems of its peripherality, but if the land-controlling elite is supported by a core power (as it was in India, Indochina, and Egypt), the struggle is particularly difficult and costly.

Despite the uncertain nature of land reform, the pressure for such action is strong. The peasants want more land in order to survive, and big landowners, particularly if they are foreigners or foreign supported, are a natural target for discontent.

It is not likely that many peasants in peripheral societies of the twentieth century have formulated all their land problems in such explicit terms. But it is no exaggeration to say that peasants have felt the consequences of these problems—subjugation to landowners or their agents, land shortage and poverty, and disintegration of traditional forms of social protection. Certainly it is clear that the Westernized intellectuals in peripheral societies have grasped the nature of these problems. For that reason, when organizing people for anti-core revolts, they have almost invariably centered their economic programs on the twin promises of land reform and industrialization.

Nationalist Intellectuals: Civilian and Military

Peasant discontent, economic hardships, subjection to foreign rule, direct or indirect—all were important sources of instability and revolution in the periphery. But discontent was not translated into revolution easily or quickly. The opposition to change was strong, both because the entrenched elites opposed it, and primarily because the world system, that is, the interests of the core powers, resisted. To overcome that resistance took considerable organization. As described previously, the early revolts against the economic and political transformations imposed by the core invariably failed, except in the unusual case of Japan. Starting in the twentieth century, this pattern of failure was slowly reversed as a new group of leaders emerged to challenge the preeminence of the core and its local allies. This group consisted of intellectuals, both civilian and military.

The new intellectuals in peripheral societies were "all persons with an *advanced modern education*"[17]—the word *modern* should probably be replaced here by *Western*. This category must be distinguished from the "traditional intellectuals," the bearers of traditional learning and religion, for it has not been the fact of being "learned" that has made the modern intellectuals a powerful revolutionary force. Rather, it has been their understanding of Western ideology and Western organizational techniques that has made them so important.

In the early stages of contact between the periphery and the modern world system, those peripheral citizens who acquired a Western education tended to be admirers, and even servile imitators, of the West. As such, they supported the extension of core influence. But with time, disillusion inevitably set in. First, there was the increasingly evident fact that Western influence was clearly intended to dominate peripheral societies for the advantage of the core, not of the local populations. Secondly, and this was particularly important in the direct colonies of the West, "natives," even if they had an advanced Western education, were still treated as inferiors. The dawning realization of permanent inferiority in the world system, both for themselves and for their societies, pushed the intellectuals into opposition. Finally, there was the circumstance that in peripheral societies, what native elites there were tended to be the major controllers of the land and traditional aristocrats who collaborated with the core, but who did not accept Westernized native intellectuals as members of the local elite. A revolt against the core also meant a revolt against the collaborationist controllers of the land, and *vice versa.*

The prime ideological aim of the intellectuals was to "catch up" with the core. Whether one speaks of the "conservative" Japanese elite after 1868, the "radical" Chinese Communist leadership in the mid-twentieth century, or the military dictatorship of Kemal Ataturk in Turkey in the 1920s and 1930s, all the leaders of strongly nationalist movements in peripheral societies (and in semi-peripheral ones as well) have been obsessed with this need to catch up, to raise their own societies to a higher level in the world system so that they would no longer suffer the economic and emotional consequences of being subjected peripherals. In that sense, all nationalistic movements in the periphery have been "revolutionary," for their aim has been to change the world system. The success of revolutionary movements led by modern intellectuals has been the result of their decision to "catch up" by adapting Western techniques and ideas. It is in this respect that the new intellectuals differed greatly from the original anti-core movements, which simply tried to keep the core out in order to preserve traditional societies.

An ideological commitment to modernizing revolutionary change is not, however, the same thing as actual power. In order to carry out their programs, the intellectuals needed to seize control, which meant ousting domestic and core elites. Here, one should distinguish between states that were legally independent (even if their economies were heavily influenced by the world system and dominated by core interests) and those that were direct colonies.

Formally independent peripheral states in the twentieth century have all had armies in which the officer corps was heavily influenced by Western ideas and technology. As historian Harry Benda has observed:

> Westernization—thinking and acting in western, rather than traditionally indigenous ways—can extend to types of social activity that in the west have not, as a rule, formed part of intellectual activity as such. The most common, and historically the most significant, representative of this category is the new military group, the "Young Turks" so to speak, of the non-western world. Nor is this at all surprising, since one of the prime contacts between west and non-west during the past century-and-a-half has been military in nature. As a result, the desire to attain equality with the west has often found expression in terms of military equality, and officers were often the first social group to receive western training.

Further:

> Wherever . . . the impact of the west did not lead to outright political domination . . . there the officer has almost invariably

emerged as the modern political non-western leader. Since he
as a rule possesses a monopoly of physical power, he can fairly
easily grasp control in a society where he represents the most
powerful—even if numerically weak—social group with a vested
interest in modernization and change.[18]

The career of Kemal Ataturk, a member of the "Young Turks"
who sought to modernize the Ottoman Empire at the end of the
nineteenth century and in the first decade of the twentieth, is a perfect example of this kind of Westernizing, nation-building officer.
After the defeat of the Ottomans and the disintegration of the Empire in 1918, it seemed that Turkey would be divided among the
European powers. Ataturk, a successful World War I general, re-
treated into the interior, organized a powerful army, and drove the
foreigners out (primarily the Greek army, which was being encouraged to invade Turkey by Great Britain). Ataturk himself was an
almost fanatical Westernizer who felt that Turkey's only hope was
to adopt a Western way of life. He abolished Islam as the state
religion, prohibited the wearing of traditional clothes, changed the
Turkish alphabet from Arabic to Latin script, reformed the language,
and established a Western legal system. In the process, he created
modern Turkey.[19]

Chiang Kai-shek, first a follower and then a leader of the revolutionary movement that overthrew the Chinese Empire (1911), replaced it with a more modern republic. He also derived his power
from his military command and influence with the modernized segment of the officer corps. Like Ataturk, it was his ambition to create
a modern China, independent of Western and Japanese control. That
he failed, while Ataturk succeeded, does not negate the example,
for in the 1920s and early 1930s, his failure was not a foregone conclusion.[20]

Gamal Nasser, a colonel in the Egyptian army, carried out a
revolution in 1952 similar to Ataturk's revolution.

The movements led by Ataturk, Chiang Kai-shek, and Nasser
all had this in common: they were based on control of the military,
and sought to impose modernizing change from above. They did not
require long periods of organization among the masses, particularly
among the peasants.

In colonial societies, however, there were no armies, at least
not native ones, since the occupying colonial power had its own
local army. While many of the soldiers, and even noncommissioned
officers in colonial armies were natives, the officers were Europeans.
But local intellectuals, particularly those who had attended Western
universities, were almost inevitably drawn into revolutionary activity. For one thing, they could not find employment commensurate
with their education. Top positions were monopolized by colonizers,

and the overspecialized, relatively-stagnant colonial economies afforded few opportunities. Intellectuals could become school teachers or clerks in the colonial governments or European commercial enterprises, scarcely the sort of thing to satisfy their ambitions. Those who became inspired by the revolutionary cause found themselves in need of an army. In order to carry out a revolution, they would have to organize the masses, their only source of enough force to counteract the military superiority of the colonizers.

The wave of decolonization that occurred in the 1960s has created an impression that the British and French generally gave up their colonies peacefully; but when one's perspective includes the first half of the twentieth century and the 1950s, this is seen to be a false impression. Early nationalist movements were repressed, usually with much bloodshed, and it was only after the main colonies had forcefully ejected the West that the core gave up what remained in order to avoid an endless series of colonial wars. In such colonies as India, Indochina, Indonesia, and Algeria, Europeans were ejected by force, not withdrawn in kindness. This meant long organizational campaigns, and particularly the mobilization of the peasants into revolutionary armies capable of wearing out and defeating the West. Success went to those intellectual leaders who combined Western knowledge with extensive efforts in their own rural hinterlands.

Although their tactics and policies were quite different, Gandhi and Ho Chi Minh were the colonial world's most successful intellectual organizers of the masses before 1950.

Gandhi was trained as a lawyer in England, and in 1914, after practicing law in South Africa and being horrified by the naked racial injustices in that society, he returned to India to organize a revolution. Combining British ideas with an extraordinary ability to promote pride in Indian culture (by using Indian languages rather than English, by dressing like an Indian, not like an Englishman), he organized a host of strikes, protest movements, and ostensibly passive actions designed to paralyze the colonial government. After years of activity, the climax came during World War II when in 1942–1943 the "Quit India" movement led to violence, and the British realized that the only way to maintain their control was through constant repressive war. For this they did not have the strength, and shortly after the war, in 1947, India became independent. What made Gandhi's movement so effective was the threat of mass violence, and particularly, the actual violence of 1942–1943. Gandhi's organization had spread so thoroughly across India that the threat of even greater violence impressed the British.[21]

The revolutionary career of Ho Chi Minh was also a combination of Western training, nationalism, and extraordinary organizational effort. Educated in Vietnam in a school that offered what the Franco-American journalist Bernard Fall has called a "blend" of all

that was best in French education with a solid anchoring in Vietnamese culture," he travelled widely in Europe, America, and Asia,
and became a communist in France in 1920 because of the anti-
imperialist platform of the new French Communist Party.[22] There followed long years of undercover organizational work, and in the early
1940s, while French Indochina was occupied by the Japanese, he
formed a guerrilla army, relying on support from discontented
peasants. After World War II, rejecting the "British" solution to
colonial unrest, the French launched a war of reconquest to reverse
the Vietnamese Revolution. In 1954 the Vietnamese Communist
army destroyed a French army and Ho became the leader of an independent North Vietnam.[23]

In both India and Vietnam the main nationalist leaders were
intellectuals. Nehru, Gandhi's chief disciple, also received a British
education, as did hundreds of the organizers of the Indian independence movement. General Giap, Ho's main military leader, and Pham
Van Dong, long the Prime Minister of North Vietnam, attended the
same school as Ho. In both the Indian and Vietnamese cases, the
struggle of the intellectuals would have come to naught without
support from the countryside. As a result of that support, when the
nationalist parties came to power, they had far deeper roots within
the society than did the military regimes of Turkey, Egypt, or
China, which built their support from the top down instead of from
the bottom up. Because India gained its independence more through
the threat of violence than because of a protracted war, however,
India's independent regime did not develop as thorough an organization, particularly in the countryside, as did the Vietnamese Communist Party. This ultimately made an important difference in the
degree of social change in the two countries; the Vietnamese were
able to carry out a much more rapid and total social and economic
transformation than the Indians.

This last point reflects a basic one. Although the motivation for
nationalist anti-core revolts has been quite similar throughout the
peripheral world, and although the successful leadership has tended
to come from the ranks of Westernized intellectuals, the particular
circumstances of the struggle, and the different types of organizations that characterized the revolutionary movements have resulted
in disparate rates of social change.

The Class Basis of Revolutions—Two Examples

Knowing that peasant unrest, slow industrialization, an overspecialized economy, and discontented intellectuals constitute basic
causal forces in the revolutions of peripheral societies does not

really explain the varied development of these revolutions. There have been hundreds, if not thousands, of revolutionary movements in the peripheral world during the past century, and while most have failed, there have been major variations even among the successful ones. A look at two major cases between 1910 and 1950 may begin to explain why some peripheral revolutions have produced more radical outcomes than others.

Mexico, 1910–1950

In the decades preceding the outbreak of revolution in 1910, Mexico underwent rapid, peripheral economic development (that is, development oriented to the export of primary products). By 1910 land had become concentrated in a very few hands (1 percent of the population owned 85 percent of the land, and 95 percent of the peasants had no land).[24] The Revolution broke out unexpectedly, rather than being planned. A strong peasant component emerged, led primarily by the peasant leader Zapata, but though this movement was somewhat inspired by what Eric Wolf calls "disaffected intellectuals with urban ties," it remained too local and insufficiently organized to take over the country.[25] The way was thus left open to more moderate middle-class forces which gained control of the Revolution. The Revolution as such was a failure, and the civil war, which lasted into the early 1920s, involved the deaths of a million or more people. In all these years, no revolutionary organization developed capable of seizing the state and carrying out a radical social and economic transformation.[26] Nevertheless, the Revolution accomplished several important objectives. First, it created a much more integrated national culture in which Indian and peasant rights were at least accorded legitimacy, and in which efforts were made to create a nation-state rather than continue with the culturally malintegrated state in existence before 1910. Second, and partly as a result of the first change, the Revolution created an embryonic state machine dedicated, at least in principle, to the goals of economic improvement and active government participation in that process. While little was actually done before the 1930s, the institutional basis of revolutionary change was established.

In 1934, Lazaro Cardenas, a military general, became President of Mexico. Using the state machinery created by the Revolution, he carried out a massive land reform, took over many foreign-owned interests (particularly oil companies), and had the government invest large sums in economic development.[27] It was under Cardenas (who was President until 1940) that the Revolution really took place, a quarter of a century after the outbreak of civil war.

But even under Cardenas, and especially under the presidents who followed him in power, change has been only *somewhat* radical, and Mexico has neither experienced the kind of overwhelming change that occurred in Russia, nor has it ever left the world system. Since, in fact, the kind of total revolution experienced by the Soviet Union has been the exception rather than the rule, the reasons for frequent moderation such as this must be considered.

First, the largest of the revolutionary armies were composed of peasants (Zapata at his strongest had 70 thousand men, while the moderate army that ultimately won the civil war had only 26 thousand). But such revolutionary armies tend to fall apart rather easily unless they are tightly organized and led by intellectuals with a coherent economic and social plan. Zapata and the cowboy revolutionary leader, Pancho Villa (who mobilized some 40 thousand men), lacked the necessary sophistication. Their followers, essentially rural anarchists, had no program beyond immediate land reform.[28]

Second, even if unsuccessful in the short run, peasant violence frightens moderates, who try to temper the process of change. The threat of renewed violence remains real, but latent, and encourages moderates to carry out partial reforms to head off greater turmoil.

Third, revolutionary change requires a strong state. But by the time the real social and economic revolution began in Mexico in the 1930s, a new class structure had developed. Primarily, the new state had created a bureaucratic machine which, while concerned with social and economic progress, was conservative in wishing to preserve its own privileges and position. It was the government bureaucracy, acting as a distinct class, that carried out Mexico's reforms and moderated the extent of change. Had a peasant-intellectual alliance won the Revolution in the 1910s, Mexico would have experienced much more rapid and extreme change.

Fourth, the kind of partial revolution experienced by Mexico was hardly a failure for being moderate. Mexico emerged in the 1940s as an industrializing, progressive society. Even while it continued to permit foreign investment, it did not fall back into the extreme overspecialization and dependence from which it had suffered before 1910. The Revolution moved Mexico into the ranks of the semi-periphery. In many ways, this was similar to the results of other "revolutions from above," namely those of Turkey and Egypt.

The extent of the change brought by the Mexican Revolution can be seen by looking at Table 30 and its national statistics for several years between 1910 and 1950.

Though Mexico's revolution was limited, it was certainly the first Latin American revolution to achieve any success. Was the rate of change of Mexico after 1910 faster than in the rest of Latin America? Unfortunately, this question cannot be answered without

TABLE 30
Social and Economic Changes in Mexico, 1910–1950

	1910	1921	1930	1940	1950
Illiterate population	77%	71%	67%	58%	43%
Change by decade*		−8%	−6%	−13%	−26%
Poor population (according to Wilkie's poverty index)	57%	53%	50%	46%	39%
Change by decade*		−7%	−6%	−8%	−15%
Growth by decade* of per capita GNP		3.3%	12.0%	23.2%	43.3%
Manufacturing index (1910 = 100) by value	100	123	242	466	1066 (for 1945)
Change by decade*		23%	96%	93%	129% (for half decade)

SOURCE James W. Wilkie, *The Mexican Revolution: Federal Expenditure and Social Change Since 1910* (Berkeley: University of California Press, 1970), pp. 208, 236, 262, 264.

* Year indicates end of decade.

also having statistics on other countries, and for most cases, these are not available. Yet it is at least suggestive that by 1969, Mexico, the second most populous society in Latin America, had a per capita GNP that was exceeded only by those in Argentina (which was almost three times as rich as Mexico in 1910 but less than twice as rich in 1969) and Venezuela (which has a much smaller population and immense oil resources).[29] (Other exceptions are not meaningful because they relate to small societies with highly unusual attributes. Panama's statistics are distorted by the presence of the Canal Zone, Puerto Rico is part of the United States, and the small islands of Martinique, Tobago, and Trinidad have few residents and many tourists.) What makes Mexico's progress striking is that at the start of the century, a number of other Latin American societies were no poorer than Mexico and several were richer. Of the Latin American societies with large numbers of Indians (who have always been at the bottom of the social scale), Mexico has made the most progress by far.[30] Finally, Mexico's political life since the late 1930s has been unusually stable, and compared to other major Latin American societies, it has been relatively free of violence. This is the case even though Mexico is not a democracy, but rather a fairly mild one-party dictatorship where the ruling party allows elections but always wins.

China, 1910–1950

The revolt that overthrew the Chinese Empire in 1911 had been brewing for a long time. In the middle of the nineteenth century, a largely peasant uprising, the Taiping Rebellion, almost succeeded in overthrowing the reigning dynasty. By 1900 the old regime was in a state of virtual collapse. Foreigners controlled the main ports, dramatic changes had occurred in the coastal economy, and the outdated institutions of China could no longer cope with either foreign intervention or domestic discontent. But the 1911 change did not produce a revolutionary government. Rather, the country fell into many pieces, each province governed by this or that general, governor, or warlord. By the early 1920s, a nationalist government had been established under Sun Yat-sen, but it was not until his party, the Kuomintang, built up an army under Chiang Kai-shek that the central government gained a real measure of power over much, if hardly all, of China.

From the very start, however, the Kuomintang was based on urban, largely middle-class support, on the army, and on an alliance with the landed gentry in rural areas. The Kuomintang was nationalistic. It was led by men familiar with Western ideas, imbued with a sense of humiliation because of China's subjection, and at least among its urban supporters, eager to strengthen China through industrialization and legal reform. The alliance with controllers of the land (either gentry or local warlords) was more tactical than ideological. Yet because of the support he received from the gentry, Chiang (who became the leader of the Kuomintang after Sun Yat-sen) never pushed a program of rural reform. Because the overwhelming majority of China's population consisted of poor peasants, the Kuomintang never received the support of the majority of the population. Political scientist Chalmers Johnson has noted:

> The National Movement . . . that began with Sun Yat-sen and developed among the students and educators in Peking after May 4, 1919, was not a mass movement; it was confined almost entirely to the socially mobilized but unassimilated intelligentsia and to the small middle classes that grew up in the treaty ports.[31]

The Chinese masses were more or less indifferent to the Kuomintang, which based its efforts to control the countryside on "opportunistic alliances among military leaders" and sheer military force rather than mass organization and support.[32] In that sense, the Kuomintang was "a head without a body" (just as, in a sense, Zapata's movement in Mexico was a body without a head).

Had China isolated itself from a hostile world, this nonsupport might not have made a decisive difference. In 1927 Chiang succeeded in crushing the Communist Party which had based its support on the urban working class. The working class was too small to mount a revolution, and what was left of the Communist movement barely escaped extermination. This failure of the Communists provoked a drastic shift in strategy, and in the 1930s, under Mao Tse-tung, the Communists began to organize the peasants.[33] Still, the Kuomintang succeeded in extending its control over most of China until the Japanese invasion of 1937. It was then that the failure of mass support for Chiang did prove decisive.

Because the basically conservative Chiang regime had not modernized China sufficiently by 1937, the Japanese quickly conquered most of the coastal cities, thus eliminating the only progressive base of Kuomintang support, the small but growing class of urban industrialists. The gentry and the warlords were left, and the Kuomintang, feebly resisting from the interior, became yet another corrupt, landlord-controlled regime. The Communists, on the other hand, stepped into the rural vacuum and organized an effective anti-Japanese effort among the peasants, particularly in northern China. A decade of patient organization, of promoting rural security, and of uniting the peasants against the Japanese yielded impressive results. Johnson observes:

> The devastation and exploitation that accompanied the Japanese invasion produced a radical change in the political attitude of the northern Chinese. The peasants of north China gave very strong support to Communist organizational initiatives during the war, and the largest number of Communist guerrilla bases was located in the rural areas of the north.[34]

By 1945 when the Japanese were defeated by the United States in the Pacific War and were forced to evacuate China, Chiang had no mass support, only a loose alliance of local controllers of the land, and the financial and material aid of the United States. This proved to be insufficient against the Communist mass organization, which finally took complete control in 1949.

Because of the nature of the revolutionary struggle in China, the Communist Party came to power as a radical movement deeply committed to massive land reform, industrialization, and the creation of a strong Chinese nation-state. Backed by its grass-roots organization, it set out to accomplish these tasks, and within a decade had made very substantial progress in eliminating the terrible rural poverty that had characterized China throughout the twentieth century.

Interestingly, several aspects of the Chinese Revolution strengthen the theory that a successful revolution in a peripheral society requires a combination of Westernized intellectual leadership and mass peasant support. Comparing the revolutionary program of the Communist Party to the conservative, anti–land-reform program of the Kuomintang, one might suppose that the social origins of the Communist and Kuomintang leadership were quite different. In fact, this was not the case, since both were led by similar types of people. The main difference was in their organizational strategies and political programs. Because China has turned so deeply inward since the Communist Revolution, and severed so many of its ties with the world system (as did the Soviet Union after 1928), one might suppose that the leadership of the Communist movement was more "native" than that of the Kuomintang. Again, this was not the case, and if anything, the Communist leaders had been more exposed to Western ideas than the leaders of the Kuomintang. While Chiang's ideology stressed old-fashioned Confucian loyalty, the Communists stressed their version of Western Marxism.[35] Although in both parties a majority of the elite had foreign educational experience, the Communists had a larger proportion of members with such experience (see Tables 31 and 32).

The leadership of the two movements, then, did not differ much

TABLE 31
Education of Chinese Revolutionary Elites, 1920s–1940s

	Kuomintang Executive Committee	Communist Politburo
No higher education	2 (1%)	2 (7%)
Chinese higher education only	123 (47%)	2 (7%)
Foreign education	136 (52%)	25 (86%)
Total known	261 (100%)	29 (100%)
Unknown	26 —	13 —

SOURCE Robert C. North and Ithiel de Sola Pool, "Kuomintang and Chinese Communist Elites," in Harold D. Lasswell and Daniel Lerner, eds., *World Revolutionary Elites: Studies in Coercive Ideological Movements* (Cambridge: M. I. T. Press, 1966), p. 381–82.

TABLE 32
Class Background of Chinese Revolutionary Elites
(Determined by Father's Occupation)

	Kuomintang Executive Committee 1929, 1926, 1924	Communist Executive Committee, 1945
Wealthy landlord, traditional scholar-official	34%	33%
Wealthy merchant and other upper class	15%	7%
Small landlord, merchant, wealthy peasant, or other middle class	45%	37%
Other peasant	6%	17%
Worker	0%	7%

SOURCE Robert C. North and Ithiel de Sola Pool, "Kuomintang and Chinese Communist Elites," in Harold D. Lasswell and Daniel Lerner, eds., *World Revolutionary Elites: Studies in Coercive Ideological Movements* (Cambridge: M. I. T. Press, 1966), p. 378.

in their social origins. The Communists, to be sure, had more lower-class representation in their leadership, but like the Kuomintang, the overwhelming majority of its leaders came from the upper and middle classes. Like other successful mass revolutionary movements in peripheral societies, the Chinese Communists were led by intellectuals from the upper strata of society, but succeeded in combining their ideological and organizational talents with the resentments and needs of the peasantry. What effects this had on China after 1950 will be discussed in a later chapter.

Conclusion: the New Semi-periphery

This brief summary of revolution in peripheral societies in the first half of the twentieth century allows certain general conclusions.

First, while the causes of the revolutionary situation throughout peripheral areas tended to be the same, the nature of the various revolutions that took place varied considerably. The major basis of difference was the degree to which various classes were mobilized in the struggle. The more strongly the mass of peasants were organized, the more radical the outcome was likely to be.

Second, while the intellectuals who led the major revolutions had many programs in common (strengthening the state, encouraging economic diversification and growth, asserting national independence against the world system), there were major differences of opinion about how to carry out these reforms. The Chinese Communist Party had a vastly different program than the Kuomintang, just as the various factions in the Mexican Revolution had different programs. But it was perhaps not so much ideological differences but the source of support of the various revolutionary movements that produced different outcomes. Leaders have certainly been important, but their sources of support have been more important. The conservative basis of the Kuomintang was far more responsible for Chiang Kai-shek's failures than any personal shortcomings he might have had.

The relative influences of support and leadership are illustrated as well by India's nationalist movement. Rarely, if ever, has any new state had as dedicated, intelligent, and humane a set of leaders as India in 1947. Yet, because the independence movement was heavily based on support from prosperous (rather than poor) peasants in the countryside and on the urban commercial and industrial middle class, the radical components of the movement were submerged, and independent India did not carry out a policy of revolutionary social and economic change. Consequently, many of India's colonial problems have remained, and the pace of economic growth has been slow.[36] This slowness has perpetuated the poverty, divisiveness, and terrible social inequality which characterized preindependence India. Compared to China's, India's revolution has been a failure, even if, in the short run, it was both more gentle and much more demo-cratic.[37]

Third, the major common outcome of every peripheral revo-lutionary movement has been the creation of a new kind of elite. Control of the state machinery has been crucial in determining the rapidity of change. The key question about peripheral revolutions is, what social groups take control, and how solidly do they establish their power? The more solidly the state controls its population (that is, the better and more thorough its organizational base), the more likely it is that revolutionary policies will be carried out effectively.

This last conclusion provides a direct link to Chapter III on the nature of change in semi-peripheral societies. In effect, success-ful anti-core revolts in peripheral societies created a new set of semi-peripheral societies. By 1950, China, Mexico, India, and Turkey were all semi-peripheral. By 1955, Egypt and North Vietnam had also achieved this status. All were striving to change. All had powerful governments that were the main agents of change. Semi-peripheral societies in the 1950s faced many of the same problems and tensions as semi-peripheral societies at the start of the twentieth century. Not the least of these problems was the continuing supremacy and hos-tility of the capitalist core.

VI

The American World System
(1945–1975)

The postwar capitalist system differed from the pre-1939 world system in several important respects. Most of the changes were the result of continuing, long-term processes, rather than immediate effects of the war, but the war itself accelerated these changes and revealed some that had not yet been manifest. There were five basic changes.

First, the United States emerged as the unrivaled core capitalist state. The rest of the core, soon joined by Germany, Italy, and Japan, became secondary.

Second, the United States assumed the financial, economic, and military-political burdens of maintaining the capitalist world system —burdens it had rejected after the end of World War I. This acceptance was decisive in preventing the kind of chaos that disrupted capitalist societies immediately after 1918. Not only did the capitalist system survive, but it entered a period of unparalleled prosperity and economic growth.

Third, prosperity increased generally, but economic growth, while rapid, was unevenly distributed. This had always been the case, and while post-1945 trends do not mark a change in this respect, the fact that the core experienced more rapid and more consistent economic growth than the periphery became more of an issue than ever before. The differential growth rates widened the gap between the rich core and the poor non-core.

Fourth, nationalist, anti-core revolutionary movements spread throughout the periphery and became virtually universal even though they did not succeed everywhere. In effect, this meant that by the early 1970s there were far fewer old-fashioned, totally-dependent peripheral societies than there had been in 1945. Instead, a growing number of semi-peripheral societies and a large number of contentious, often virulently nationalistic, anti-core societies came to challenge the prosperity and success of the rich capitalist core.

Much of the political history of the 1945–1975 period comprises a series of wars between the core and the revolutionary periphery. The major though not the only such wars were the first Indochinese (1946–1954), the Algerian (1954–1962), and the second Indochinese (1963–1975) wars. The core, led by the United States, and secondarily by the United Kingdom and France, defined these wars primarily in terms of capitalist versus communist struggles. In fact, they were merely an extension of the fight begun in about 1910 between the core and periphery. The core lost these wars. But while the major Communist states, the Soviet Union and China, provided substantial aid to the revolutionary periphery, they neither controlled nor in any direct way profited from peripheral revolutionary movements.

The fifth change (to be treated at length in a later chapter) was the emergence of a large communist world system between 1945 and 1950. By 1950, about one-third of the people in the world lived in a withdrawn, self-sufficient communist system that hardly interacted with the capitalist world system except on its margins. Since 1960, some parts of the communist world have greatly increased their interaction with capitalist societies, but the semi-seclusion of this large portion of the world for at least a decade, if not more, justifies its being treated as a distinct world system.

The first four major aspects of the post–World War II capitalist world system will be treated in this chapter. It will first examine the dominant position of the United States in the world system, and then the reaction of the periphery.

The Dominance of the United States

Even before the end of the World War, the United States began to give substantial amounts of economic aid to its allies. After the end of the war, this aid continued, and the United States helped the secondary core powers rebuild their economies.

The most striking, because it was unprecedented, aspect of this policy was that the defeated powers were not treated as enemies. Though there were some policy makers who felt that Germany and Japan ought to be turned into agrarian, peripheral societies, this was not done.

The wisdom of America's aid policy saved the shaken capitalist system in Western Europe and Japan. Since the West European societies and Japan were highly industrialized, their ultimate recovery was, in any case, inevitable. But an actively colonial, exploitative policy on the part of the United States would have produced many more anticapitalist, anti-core revolts. A ruthlessly exploited Germany or Japan would have turned into fiercely nationalistic, dangerous semi-peripheral powers, as they did in the 1930s. Without the stabilizing effect of American aid and trade, it is likely that France and Italy would have become communist in the late 1940s. These considerations determined American policy. The outcome was that Germany and Japan, despite their failure to gain hegemonic power, reentered the core. Their postwar recoveries gave them the benefits of core status, and in fact, within two decades, they were the second and third most powerful capitalist economies.

At first, American aid was concentrated in Western Europe. The aid program of the immediate postwar years (largely, but not entirely administered through the Marshall Plan) was substantial and effective.

If anything, American aid of the 1945–1955 period was too successful. It fully accomplished its aim of preserving the world capitalist core from communism and from a relapse into the aggressive, dangerous nationalist excesses of the 1930s. At least, core nationalism no longer threatened the unity of the core. An illusion was created that massive aid could work under different circumstances, outside the core as well as in it.

Indeed, it did, but a quick examination of the social and economic structures of the heavily aided core shows why it was that aid worked so well. Western Europe and Japan were already in-

TABLE 33
American Foreign Aid, Grants, and Credits,
Nonmilitary, 1945–1955

	Millions of $s	*Percentage of Total*
Western Europe	24,767	65.1%
Eastern Europe	1,097	2.9%
Near East and South Asia (minus Greece)	1,840	4.8%
Greece	1,324	3.5%
Africa	143	0.4%
Far East and Pacific (minus Japan, Republic of China, Taiwan, South Korea)	1,837	4.8%
Japan	2,302	6.0%
Republic of China-Taiwan	1,257	3.3%
South Korea	1,358	3.6%
Americas	1,151	3.0%
International Agencies	976	2.6%
[Western Europe, Japan, plus the main clients of the United States, i.e., Greece, Taiwan, South Korea	31,008	81.5%]
Total	38,052	100.0%

SOURCE   U.S. Bureau of the Census, *Statistical Abstract of the United States: 1974* (Washington: U.S. Government Printing Office, 1974), pp. 784–85.

dustrialized and urbanized. They contained highly literate, skilled populations. Their governments ruled highly integrated nation-states with a high degree of cultural unity and a strong sense of the value of their own cultures. In 1945, their diversified, productive economies were depressed by war and destruction, but the only shortages were material, not social, organizational, or even political. Political turmoil in the core, like the turmoil after World War I, was the product of the war and the artificially depressed economies. But in this case it was no longer part of a long-term revolutionary trend. Since the working classes had gained a substantial share of power in the 1930s in the democracies, and gained such powers in the defeated fascist states after the war as a result of the democratization enforced by the Americans, the key social conflict of the early part of the century was contained and rendered nonrevolutionary. In these conditions, the success of the aid program was assured since all that was missing was capital for reconstruction and a guarantee of security.

The stabilization of the capitalist core was followed by rapid economic growth, increased international trade, and the spread of American private capital into other core economies. Because the other core societies were highly diversified and already very advanced, American capital did not turn them into colonial, dependent peripheral states. This is a well-known story, and an important one. It serves to emphasize the limits of the theory proposed in earlier chapters about the nature of the capitalist world system. Foreign investment is neither necessarily exploitative nor harmful if it goes into strong nation-states with skilled populations and strong, diversified economies. Essentially, American investment in other core economies after 1945 was quite similar (in result if not in terms of the specific kinds of investments) to West European investment in the United States in the late nineteenth century, or to core investments in Canada and Australia. Such investment certainly produced some resentment in the countries, but the benefit to them clearly outweighed the disadvantage; for the economic stimulation this investment provided helped them experience general, long-term balanced growth. By the 1970s, Western Europe, Canada, and Australia are not much poorer than the United States; and some parts of Western Europe have not only narrowed the gap which was still quite substantial in 1950, but become richer than the United States.

The domination of the United States outside the core

The continuing rise of nationalistic, anti-core revolutions in peripheral areas ultimately produced a large-scale American aid program whose main purpose was to contain the rise of such movements and to make the peripheral world safer for American investment and security interests. This program was based, at least superficially, on the successful Marshall Plan. There had been increasing American investment outside the core since the early 1900s, and after 1945 this type of investment increased. In the 1950s, as aid to the core was phased out, a massive American aid program to non-core areas was initiated.

Neither aid nor private investment could conceivably have the same effect outside the core as inside the core. While Western Europe and Japan had had their "modernizing revolutions" by 1945, most of the peripheral world had not gone through this experience. American private investment in the periphery, therefore, tended to concentrate in certain extractive, colonial endeavors. (More recently, it has also flowed into a particular kind of industry based on the exploitation of cheap labor. This more recent development will be discussed later in the chapter.) Such investment did not make the host economies poorer in any absolute sense, just the opposite, but it did reinforce the tendency toward unbalanced growth and toward the kind of overspecialization that characterizes peripheral economies. It also strengthened the "enclave" elites and neither satisfied rising nationalist aspirations nor reduced internal inequality in peripheral economies. Nor did such investments reduce the gap in wealth between the core and the periphery. Finally, the terms of exchange between the United States and the periphery were quite different from those between the United States and other core societies. American investment in the periphery not only went into different sectors of the economy than had American investment in the core, it was also much more profitable. It produced larger amounts of exportable (that is, back-to-the-United States) profit and was more markedly *extractive* rather than *constructive*, at least in terms of creating balanced economic growth. Against these tendencies, aid programs were not likely to make much difference. In fact, many have accused the American aid programs in the periphery of being directed toward perpetuating colonial or "enclave" economies.[1] Although it is difficult to prove or disprove this accusation (intention is never easily proved), the results of such programs have strengthened the argument of those who claim that balanced development in the periphery was never the American intention.

Tables 34, 35, and 36 contain statistics that suggest the dualities of American private investment abroad.

There is no way of mistaking the difference between American investments in the core and those outside it. Investments inside the core were substantially higher, but profits from outside the core were much higher. In 1972, 27 percent of American investment abroad was outside the core, but 54 percent of all profits, precisely

TABLE 34
**American Private Overseas Long-Term Investment
and Profits, by Area**

Area	Investment		1972 Profits* as percentage of total world profits	1972 Profits† as percentage return on value of investment
	1960	1972		
Canada	35%	27%	12%	4%
West Europe	21%	33%	23%	6%
Japan	1%	2%	2%	7%
Australia, New Zealand, South Africa	4%	6%	4%	6%
Core (plus South Africa)	61%	68%	41%	5%
Venezuela	8%	3%	4%	12%
Rest of Americas	18%	15%	8%	14%
Middle East	4%	2%	31%	120%
Rest of World	5%	7%	11%	14%
Non-Core	35%	27%	54%	17%
International (Shipping)	4%	5%	5%	8%
World Total	$31.865 billion = 100%	$94.031 billion = 100%	$8.004 billion = 100%	8.5%

SOURCE   U.S. Bureau of the Census, *Statistical Abstract of the United States: 1974* (Washington: U.S. Government Printing Office, 1974), pp. 781–82.

* Profit is defined as total interest, dividends, and branch earnings as reported to the United States government. It is likely that these figures understate both assets and profits.
† Profits in 1960 were $2.355 billion, equal to 7.4 percent of investment.

twice as large a percentage, came from that area. The *rate* of return was more than three times as large outside the core as within the core. To be sure, much of this disproportion was due to the enormous profitability of American oil companies in the Middle East which returned, in 1972, more profit than the total stated value of invest-

TABLE 35
American Foreign Investment in 1972 by Industry and Area

Area	Mining and Smelting	Petroleum*	Manufacturing	Other
Canada	14%	21%	45%	21%
West Europe	less than 1%	23%	57%	20%
Japan	0	36%	53%	11%
Australia, New Zealand, South Africa	16%	20%	48%	16%
Core (plus South Africa)	7%	22%	51%	20%
Venezuela	with "other"	58%	20%	22%
Rest of Americas	15%	20%	37%	29%
Middle East	less than 1%	88%	5%	7%
Rest of World	10%	59%	15%	17%
Non-Core	11%	39%	26%	24%
International (Shipping)	0	49%†	0	51%‡
World Total	8%	28%	42%	22%

SOURCE   U.S. Bureau of the Census, *Statistical Abstract of the United States: 1974* (Washington: U.S. Government Printing Office, 1974), pp. 781–782.

* Petroleum includes refining and distribution. In the core, particularly in Europe and Japan, almost all 1972 petroleum investment was in these areas rather than in resource extraction. The reverse is true outside the core, particularly in the Middle East.
† Mostly oil tankers
‡ Mostly other ships

ment, and almost one-third of all American foreign profits. But even leaving this aside, the discrepancy is obvious.

Even though Table 35 conceals much of the discrepancy in foreign investment patterns, the pattern is, nevertheless, as expected. On the average, half of American investment in core economies is in manufacturing, but only one quarter of investment outside the core is in manufacturing. If types of manufacturing, petroleum, and "other" investments could be broken down further, the discrepancy would be greater. Most petroleum investment outside the core is in the extraction of raw materials, while in the core petroleum investment tends to be concentrated in refining and distribution. The category labeled "Other" includes such industries as tourism, retailing, and agriculture, and most peripheral "other" investments tend to be concentrated in tourism and primary production. Even in manufacturing, investments outside the core tend to be concentrated in industries that use relatively unskilled, cheap labor; these industries are not as prevalent in the core, where manufacturing involves more complex and more diversified procedures.

Of all American foreign profits in 1972, 49 percent came from petroleum companies. But even though these companies were heavy investors throughout the world, 86 percent of their profits came from outside the core, that is, primarily from resource extraction. While petroleum was by far the most important foreign investment of American companies in 1972, a similar, if far less extreme, pattern could be demonstrated for a number of other important raw materials.

Playing an ideological game with numbers is always risky. But in this case, the conclusion is more or less unavoidable. American investors abroad received considerably more profit from investments outside the core, and in extractive, primary producing industries, than they did from investments in other core economies. But they received these benefits in return for considerably lower investments, and for considerably less diversified investments than they placed in the core (see Table 36).

A similar pattern could be demonstrated for the investments of other core economies in the periphery and semi-periphery, although on this point it is sufficient to understand the pattern of American investment since the United States has been the overwhelmingly dominant overseas investor since 1945. In 1960, for example, the United Kingdom, the world's second biggest foreign investor, held a portfolio worth only some $6 billion compared to American investments of $32 billion.[2] European and Japanese foreign investment grew even faster than that of the United States after 1960, but the American total remains predominant.

Here it seems necessary to stress that this pattern cannot be explained by resorting to stories about dark and secret plots by core investors in peripheral areas, even though some news stories about American companies abroad sometimes give that impression. Rather, this pattern has been the result of natural capital flows in response to economic oportunities. Yet the very market conditions that make investment in manufacturing less profitable than investment in primary extraction, and which make it undesirable to invest in anything but primary extractive industries in the periphery have increased the

TABLE 36
**Rate of Return on American Foreign Investment,
by Industry, Core–Non-Core, as Percentage of Investment**

Industry	*1970*		*1971*		*1972*	
	Core	*Non-Core*	*Core*	*Non-Core*	*Core*	*Non-Core*
Mining and Smelting	7.8	13.0	6.1	8.9	4.8	6.9
Petroleum	2.2	26.0	2.5	31.5	1.8	34.4
Manufacturing	5.6	6.0	5.5	5.4	5.5	5.2
Other	6.2	5.6	7.8	5.4	8.1	6.6
Total	5.1	14.4	5.3	16.0	5.1	17.1

SOURCE   U.S. Bureau of the Census, *Statistical Abstract of the United States: 1974* (Washington: U.S. Government Printing Office, 1974), p. 781; *Statistical Abstract of the United States: 1973*, p. 769; *Statistical Abstract of the United States: 1972*, p. 767.

discrepancy in wealth between core and non-core. This, in brief, is the heart of the problem. Sinister plots can always be exposed and stopped, while impersonal market factors, at least in the capitalist world order, are difficult, if not impossible to reverse. A simple conspiratorial theory of economic imperialism will not work.

Economic growth in the modern world

Before returning to the question of aid, there is reason to consider the patterns of economic growth since 1945. It is difficult to find accurate figures for the rate of economic growth in most of the world's peripheral societies, but Nobel laureate Simon Kuznets has studied a number of economies with great care, and his results can be used as indicative, if not totally conclusive, findings. Some other statistical estimates can be consulted as well to determine whether or not the economic gap between core and non-core economies is closing or increasing.

Table 37 must be interpreted cautiously. For one thing, the list of non-core societies included in Kuznets' studies was not drawn randomly; and his cases are not exactly "typical" precisely because they are bound to be those that kept somewhat better records than most peripheral economies. They do, however, give an idea of trends, and represent important cases; moreover, more recent research on

TABLE 37
Economic Growth Rates (GNP per capita)
for Selected Core and Non-Core Cases (percentage per decade)

Capitalist Core	*Growth per decade, about 1860–1965*	*Growth per decade, about 1950–1965*	*1965 GNP per capita in U.S. dollars*
United Kingdom	13.4	27.8	1870
France	17.0	44.1	2047
Netherlands	12.6	38.9	1609
Germany-West Germany	18.3	63.3	1939
Denmark	20.2	39.0	2238
Sweden	28.9	40.8	2713
Italy (from 1895–1899)	22.9	60.4	1100
Japan (from 1874–1879)	32.3	128.4	876
United States	17.3	20.8	3580
Canada	18.7	21.1	2507
Australia	10.2	23.9	2023
Average (not weighted by population)	19.3	46.2	2046

Non-Core*	*Growth per decade, about 1900–1965*	*Growth per decade, about 1950–1965*	*1965 GNP per capita in U.S. dollars*
Argentina	10.1	8.9 (1925–1929 to 1963–1967)	811
Mexico	18.2	22.3 (1925–1929 to 1963–1967)	461
Ghana	15.6	14.2	312
Philippines	10.3	30.0	255
Egypt	about 5.0	29.8	185
India (from 1861–1869)	6.2	12.2	86
Average (not weighted by population)	10.9	19.6	352

SOURCE Simon Kuznets, *Economic Growth of Nations* (Cambridge: The Belknap Press of Harvard University, 1971), pp. 11–19 and 30–31.

* By way of comparison, Russian/Soviet per capita GNP growth rates since 1910 amount to close to 40 percent per decade, and the Soviet 1965 per capita GNP was about $1200. Precise comparisons with Communist economies are almost impossible because economic statistics are kept somewhat differently, and because many of the most important statistics are either not published or unreliable. The same considerations apply for most peripheral economies, which do not keep reliable statistics or have begun to keep them only in recent years. This is why Kuznets' selection was so restricted outside the core.

growth rates shows that the same pattern of unequal growth has
persisted in the 1970s. Second, many of the poorest contemporary
peripheral economies may not have experienced any growth at all in
the last several decades; thus this particular sample of non-core cases
may be biased on the high side in demonstrating growth. This is not
the case for the core economies, since the main ones are included,
and since their statistics tend to be more reliable. Third, at very low
levels of per capita GNP (such as India's), the meaning of the
numbers is open to debate. Much of the national product is grown
by peasants who consume their product, and is therefore not easily
counted. Whereas $86 per year in a rich, industrial economy amounts
to nothing at all, it may provide sustenance in a very poor economy.
The difference between per capita levels of, say, $80 and $160 is
much harder to interpret than the difference between levels of $1000
and $2000. Finally, the rather low growth rates of the United States,
Canada, and Australia compared to other core societies is somewhat
misleading, because these three economies started off with high per
capita GNP in the nineteenth century, and because they have successfully absorbed enormous population increases. This point is equally
important in considering the relatively low growth rates of some
peripheral societies which have also had large population increases.
As pointed out in the previous chapter, this accounts for much of the
persisting poverty.

When all due caution is taken, it is still possible to draw valid conclusions. The first of these is that the core has experienced relatively
greater economic growth than the periphery. Since 1950, most of the
world has experienced very high rates of economic growth, and many
peripheral economies have experienced growth rates higher than the
historical growth rates in core economies. But at the same time,
since 1950, core societies have also grown faster than in the past;
instead of decreasing since 1950, the gap between the core and the
rest of the world has actually increased. In absolute terms, the gap
has increased very substantially, since, for such economies as Egypt
or India, even high growth rates produce small absolute increases.
In 1965, for example, a 10 percent increase in per capita GNP in the
United States amounted to $360 per year, while a 30 percent growth
in Egypt amounted to $60. This means that even if some very poor
economies experience rapid growth, the rich economies will still be
increasing the absolute gap between rich and poor. An important
fact about all this has been that not only has the gap increased but,
as the world has become increasingly integrated (at least, that part
outside the communist area), the perception of the gap between rich
and poor has grown. Thus the resentment produced by the gap has
grown as well, and it is small satisfaction for peripheral societies to
learn that they have done better, in percentage terms, than, say, the

United Kingdom in the nineteenth century. The fact remains that they are falling farther behind instead of catching up.

Another important observation is that the intensely nationalistic, semi-peripheral and fascist powers of the 1930s have, since 1950, done extraordinarily well in terms of economic development. In the long run, the extreme political dynamism that pushed them into opposition to the capitalist core translated itself into economic dynamism, even though, of course, since 1945 they have evolved as parliamentary democracies and fully accepted members of the core.

A final conclusion is that while it is impossible to make precise comparisons between communist and capitalist economies, it is clear that since 1930 the Soviet Union, and since 1950 other communist economies as well have had very high growth rates, rates probably comparable to those experienced by Japan, or at least West Germany.

Another way of comparing the relative economic strength of various societies is to look at certain other, nonmonetary indicators of industrial development. The best single indicator is probably the amount of energy consumed per capita. Since this can be measured for the entire world, it becomes possible to show what percentage of all energy is consumed by any particular society, and thus to establish a basis for comparison that is less open to questionable interpretations than GNP per capita. In a sense, such a comparison is similar to examinations in earlier chapters of the division of total world manufacturing product. A comparison of energy consumption in 1952 and 1972, for example, can reliably show the relative change between various economies. Even though all societies consumed more energy in 1972 than in 1952, the rate of growth differed significantly.

Table 38 confirms the impression given by the previous table, namely that the rates of growth in the peripheral and semi-peripheral societies of Asia, the Americas, and Africa have been slower than the rates in the core and the communist world. On the whole, most core societies have gained on the United States (with the notable exception of the United Kingdom); and while the capitalist core as a whole has lost a very small bit of its world lead, that bit has gone to the Soviet Union and Communist Eastern Europe. Relative to the core, the per capita energy consumption of the non-core was *lower* in 1972 than in 1952, even though, of course, absolutely it was larger in 1972 than in 1952. Relative to the United States, Japan, the Soviet Union, and Communist Eastern Europe made very significant advances. In this domain, in fact, the Soviet Union and Communist Eastern Europe now compare favorably with Western Europe, reflecting the fact that though their general standard of living remains lower, their industrial strength has grown very rapidly. The picture becomes more vivid when one considers how energy consumption is divided among the world's population. In 1972 the 17 percent that lived in the core consumed almost 60

TABLE 38
**World Energy Consumption, 1952 and 1972,
and World Population, 1972**

Country	Energy: percentage of world total, consumed in 1952	1952 index of per capita energy consumption (U.S. = 100)	Energy: percentage of world total, consumed in 1972	1972 index of per capita energy consumption (U.S. = 100)	Population: percentage of total in world by area, 1972
United States	36	100	32.7	100	5.5
Canada	2.5	76	3.2	93	0.6
United Kingdom	7	59	4.1	46	1.5
West Germany	4.5	41	4.5	46	1.6
France	3	30	2.9	36	1.4
Japan	2	11	4.7	28	2.8
Rest of European core plus Australia, New Zealand, and Israel	6	27	6.0	28	3.6
Total Core	61	—	58.1	—	17.0

Soviet Union	13	26	15.9	41	6.6
Communist Eastern Europe	6	21	6.6	39	2.9
Total Communist Europe	19	—	22.5	—	9.5
Rest of Europe	1	10	1.4	14	1.7
Rest of Asia, Africa, Americas	19	about 5–6	18.0	about 4	71.8
World Total	100	—	100.0	about 17	100.0

SOURCE For 1952: Norton Ginsburg, *Atlas of Economic Development* (Chicago: University of Chicago Press, 1961), pp. 78–81; for 1972: United States Bureau of the Census, *Statistical Abstracts of the United States: 1974* (Washington: U.S. Government Printing Office, 1974), 815–17 and 829–30.

percent of the world's energy, the 10 percent that lived in Communist Europe and the Soviet Union consumed almost one-quarter, and the poorest 70 percent of the world consumed less than one-fifth. The United States alone, with less than 6 percent of the world's population, consumed in 1972, as in 1952, about one-third of all the world's energy.

The issue of foreign aid

These facts about the relative economic growth in the core and periphery and about the nature of core investment in the non-core lead one back to the issue of American foreign aid. To what extent did it contribute to narrowing the gap between rich and poor societies?

The United States gave and lent a great deal of money between 1945 and 1973 (in terms of its 1972 population, some $450 per person in nonmilitary foreign aid), but in most of the world, the actual impact of that aid was small. The billions received by India may seem large in some respects, but they seem to wane when divided by the total Indian population; then it is evident that American aid of $15 per capita could not have the kind of major impact created elsewhere by aid over $100 per capita. The same applies for aid to Africa and Latin America. In fact, since 1955, American foreign aid has had significant impact only in relatively small states that, for one reason or another, were considered politically important. Greece, Turkey, Israel, Jordan, Taiwan, South Korea, and South Vietnam have all been close military allies of the United States. Yugoslavia has been the major counterweight to Soviet power in Eastern Europe ever since 1948 when it became the first communist state to defy the Soviet Union. In some cases, particularly Israel, Jordan, and South Vietnam, truly large amounts of aid were given. The success or failure of this aid can be evaluated only in terms of the donor's long-range political goals. In Taiwan and South Korea, it succeeded, as it had earlier in Western Europe, in establishing firmly anticommunist, relatively prosperous and stable states. In South Vietnam, aid failed altogether, as did the immense military effort that went with it. In the Near East, aid from the United States certainly helped Israel considerably, and probably kept Jordan's pro-American monarchy in power. Beyond these cases, firm conclusions cannot really be made, except to say that while the amounts of aid money may seem huge, they were not, and they were quite unlikely to promote fundamental social and economic change.

Possibly it is more important to point out that American nonmilitary aid, like military aid provided by the United States, had an immediate political goal rather than a goal directed toward fundamental change in poor countries. The goal was to strengthen certain key governments, to gain good will, and to limit first Russian, and later

Chinese influence. The impression received by many Americans that the goal was to help poor economies catch up to rich ones, or to create "democracies," was, from the start, more a matter of public relations than of real purpose. It was not so much that American policy was directly opposed to economic development, since in Western Europe and Japan the United States certainly helped previously industrialized societies regain their prosperity. Nor was it simply a matter of trying to impose a certain kind of social system on those societies that received aid, since Yugoslavia, a communist but anti-Soviet state, received much aid. The realization that the main goal of American foreign aid has always been to gain certain advantages in the international political power struggle clarifies many of these issues and makes it evident that the expectations of its more idealistic supporters as well as the accusations of many of its detractors have more or less missed the point.

On the whole, military aid from the United States has gone to the same strategic countries that have received large amounts of non-military aid. From 1945 to 1973 the American government gave about 59 billion dollars of military aid (compared to about 94 billion of nonmilitary aid). From 1945 to 1955, 58 percent of the military aid went to Western Europe, 13 percent to the Near East and South Asia, and 27 percent to the Far East and Pacific (mostly to South Korea and the Republic of China-Taiwan). As with nonmilitary aid, the pattern shifted after the mid-1950s; and from 1956 to 1973, Western Europe received only 17 percent of all American military aid, while the Far East received 65 percent, and the Near East close to 14 percent. From 1968 to 1973, over 90 percent of the military aid went to the Far East, primarily to South Vietnam, and almost all the rest went to the Near East, primarily Israel.[3] The major recipients of American nonmilitary aid, except India, have also received substantial military aid, and all but India and Yugoslavia have been members of American-led military alliances, either formally or informally.

A last point on aid from the United States should be mentioned. Since about 1960, other rich countries (primarily from Western Europe, but also Japan and Canada, and since the early 1970s, some of the very rich Arab oil states) have also given much aid to poorer societies. The United States has remained the largest donor, but the relative (relative, that is, to their own population and wealth) efforts of several other core societies have been greater. The Soviet Union has also given a great deal of foreign aid, both military and nonmilitary. But most aid, except for that given by a few small, relatively neutral countries (like Sweden), has had the purpose of gaining concrete political advantages. In few cases has the amount of aid provided been large enough to make much of a difference in causing fundamental change. The Soviet Union, like the United States, has concentrated on helping

TABLE 39
American Foreign Aid Grants and Credits (nonmilitary), 1945–1973

Area or Country*	Total in million $s 1945–1973	As percentage of world total by recipient for 1945–1973	Per capita $s (1972 population)	Total in million $s 1956–1973	As percentage of world total by recipient for 1956–1973
Western Europe	23,554	25.1	—	−1,213	negative
Among which:					
France	4,175	4.4	80	−1,302	negative
West Germany	2,865	3.1	47	−1,041	negative
Italy	3,017	3.2	55	+ 222	0.4
United Kingdom	6,092	6.5	108	− 828	negative
Yugoslavia†	1,976	2.1	94	+1,115	2.0
Eastern Europe (includes Soviet Union)	1,984	2.1	6	+ 887	1.6
East Mediterranean‡ and South Asia	25,472	27.1	—	22,308	39.9
Among which:					
India	8,924	9.5	15	8,525	15.3
Israel	2,047	2.2	682	1,657	3.0
Jordan	817	0.9	327	791	1.4
Pakistan§	4,598	4.9	31	4,204	7.4
Greece	1,697	1.8	189	373	0.7
Turkey	2,635	2.8	70	2,250	4.0

Africa (minus Egypt)	4,721	5.0	14	4,578	8.2
Far East and Pacific	22,819	24.3	—	16,065	28.8
Among which:					
Japan	2,066	2.2	19	− 236	negative
Republic of China—Taiwan	2,324	2.5	158	1,067	1.9
South Korea	5,514	5.9	164	4,156	7.4
South Vietnam	5,940	6.3	318	5,695	10.2
Western Hemisphere	10,355	11.0	36	9,204	16.5
International Agencies	4,987	5.3	—	4,011	7.2
World Total	93,891			55,839	

SOURCE   United States Bureau of the Census, *Statistical Abstract of the United States: 1974* (Washington: U.S. Government Printing Office, 1974), pp. 784–785.

* Area division is according to U.S. State Department categories, and may therefore appear confusing.
† Yugoslavia is counted as part of Western Europe.
‡ Including Egypt.
§ Includes Bangladesh.

some of its small clients with important strategic positions (such as Cuba since 1960, which has been kept economically viable by Soviet aid) and also on strengthening its influence in India. France and the United Kingdom have sent most of their help to former colonies in order to try to keep their remaining interests safe. Japan has given aid with an eye to securing sources of natural resources, and West German aid has been given with an eye to markets for German industrial exports.

When compared to other major internal and international forces that have shaped twentieth-century societies, foreign aid has not loomed large. American aid has helped the United States maintain its hegemonic position in the capitalist world system, as it was intended to do. It has not, however, changed any of the major trends of the last twenty years. It has neither caused rapid economic growth in peripheral countries, nor managed to stop the gradual spread of anti-core, nationalistic movements in the periphery.

The Revolt of the Periphery

To what extent has the prosperity of the core depended on exploitation of the periphery? Some large American, European, and Japanese corporations have obviously made large profits from their investments in the periphery, but are these profits vital for the core as a whole? Most world trade, after all, takes place within the core, between the rich economies, not between the rich and the poor. But can it be that some primary products exported from the periphery to the core do play a vital role? Can it be that the political and economic weakness of the periphery keeps the price of these vital products cheap, thus providing a bonus to the core economies? That certainly seems to have been the case with petroleum, the main resource exported from the periphery to the core, at least until the price increases of 1973–1974. But does this mean very much? Can it be, instead, that capitalist economies simply seek the cheapest resources, and that if one resource becomes too expensive, another will replace it, no matter where that resource lies? It may well be that the seeming dependence of the core on a few key exports from peripheral areas is an illusion, since rising prices only trigger the discovery and use of substitutes.

Much has been written about this question, and in many ways, the issue remains the same as when Lenin wrote *Imperialism* in 1916. Does capitalism need to exploit colonial areas? Is the alternative a fall in profits, a bitter struggle between the capitalist core powers for declining resources and markets, and ultimately, domestic class war and revolution? Or is Lenin's theory fundamentally false?

Looking at the world before 1914, earlier chapters concluded that the wild race for new colonies in the late 1800s and early 1900s was probably economically irrational. But since the core states behaved *as if* colonial expansion through conquest were vital for survival, then the consequences were the same *as if* Lenin's theory had been correct. Again, in the 1930s, the pattern was repeated. Germany, Japan, and Italy behaved *as if* colonial expansion were necessary for them to compete against the capitalist core. The results were the same as in 1914, that is, world war, and seeming confirmation of the Leninist theory.

The economic development of the post–World War II world system, however, suggests that Lenin's theory is flawed. The main losers of the war, Germany and Japan, stripped of colonies, and even of significant political influence in the core, became the most dynamic economies of the core. In part, this may have been because they had fairly low military expenses, particularly Japan. On the other hand, the biggest winner of the war, the United States, has assumed the costs of maintaining military order in the world system, and may well have paid a price in slower economic growth.

In any case, since 1945, the main core powers, and since 1960 primarily the United States, have again behaved *as if* they believed the old Leninist theory. The United States has poured huge sums into aid and war in order to contain the major nationalist, anti-core revolutionary movements of the peripheral and semi-peripheral world. Vietnam was only the most extreme case, not an isolated instance of irrationality. Why, if not to protect its interests, has the United States supported counter-revolution so often? The best known examples have been China (1946–1949), Greece (1946–1949), the Philippines (1948–1952), Iran (1952), Guatemala (1954), Cuba (1959–1961), Laos (1959–1975), the Congo (1960–1965), Vietnam (in the form of aid to the French until 1954, and then independently until 1975), the Dominican Republic (1965), Cambodia (1970–1975), Chile (1971–1973), and Angola (1974–1975), not to mention dozens of other instances of involvement around the world.[4]

The neatness with which the Leninist argument fits events is, in a sense, misleading, because there is no convincing evidence that the United States really did act in all these instances simply, or even primarily in order to preserve access to primary resources or to save some foreign investments. There have been major instances of expropriation of such investments (for example, petroleum in Venezuela) which have not produced a strong counteraction, and there have been cases of major intervention where no obvious investments or resources were involved at all (Laos and Vietnam). It may well be that foreign events are now regulated purely as if a giant, deadly chess game between the United States and the Soviet Union were in progress, and that the moves by the United States have been based on a jockeying for position. Somehow, this analogy seems unlikely to provide the total explanation for international behavior of the last thirty years, although it is as reasonable an explanation of certain American (and Soviet) "moves" as the Leninist theory of imperialism.

There is, however, another variant of the imperialism theory, one more satisfactory than the Leninist version. It is this version, or belief in it, which seems to explain why the United States, and the core in general, support conservative regimes and abhor radical leftist regimes. For present purposes, *left* and *right* can be defined in a simple, one-dimensional way. A leftist regime in a peripheral society is one that wishes to develop that society by withdrawing it from the capitalist world system. That is, a leftist revolutionary regime recognizes the many disavantages of peripherality (as these were spelled out in previous chapters) and believes that the only way to escape is through some form of closure followed by a long period of internal effort. Only in this way can successful economic diversification, industrialization, national unity, and the base for ultimate equality with the core be established. A rightist regime in a peripheral society believes that the national economy should remain in the world system. This position obviously provides many benefits. There are continuing investments from the core, technical and financial aid and advice are available, the core continues to pay for primary exports, and, according to this view, ultimately economic development will occur from prolonged participation in the world system.

The policy of the United States has systematically pushed to keep peripheral economies and societies open to the capitalist world system, both by promising benefits to those that remain open (aid) and threatening or actually carrying out punishment against those that do not (either economic sanctions or military intervention, covert, and sometimes overt). While this is close to saying that American policy seeks to protect cheap natural resources and American investments in the periphery, it is not quite the same thing. Venezuela remains an open economy although it has expropriated local oil companies controlled by citizens of the United States. Iran and Saudi Arabia are in the same position. They therefore continue to receive support, aid, from the United States and they remain "allies." In short, if the "imperialism" theory holds at all, it does so now in a rather more subtle way than in the early part of the century. Direct ownership and control of colonial areas are no longer particularly important. Openness, however, is crucial. Even communist states, if they re-enter the capitalist world system, or make serious moves toward re-entry, become acceptable. Yugoslavia, and today much of Eastern Europe, is no longer seen as a potential threat to the capitalist world system; for the Communist Eastern European economies have become major trading partners with core economies, even while they remain formally enemy.

This does not resolve the argument about whether or not the core really needs to keep large parts of the world "open" and within the world capitalist economic network. But there is little doubt that at least until the mid-1970s, the United States and most of the rest of the core has behaved *as if* that were the case.

Seen in that light, the jockeying for position between the United States and the Soviet Union in various corners of the world takes on added significance. A society closed to the capitalist world system becomes a loss to that system; an open society remains a potentially profitable asset. In time, if enough peripheral societies are closed, the capitalist world system will shrink, and, according to the theory that both the United States and the Soviet Union seem to believe, this shrinkage will reduce prosperity in the core. Whether or not the theory is correct becomes secondary, at least in the short run, if the main international players behave as if it were correct. But keeping the periphery "open" has become costly.

Given all this, how important is core, particularly American investment in the non-core? In 1971 the foreign-held assets of corporations based in the United States amounted to a mere 3 percent of all the country's corporate assets. Profits from the outside, however, were much more important and amounted to between 10 and 15 percent of all profits, depending on how taxes are taken into account.[5]

The foreign trade of the United States in 1973 amounted to 10.9 percent of GNP—though in certain key areas (notably petroleum), foreign trade was much more important than this figure suggests. Of the items traded by the United States in that year, 65 percent of all exports, and 70 percent of all imports were to or from developed, primarily core economies. Although other core economies rely much more heavily on foreign trade than does the United States, much of their trade is also within the core. *The core dominates world trade but trades primarily within itself.*[6]

These statistics cannot settle the issue. It is unclear to what extent certain vital components of world trade would be cut off even if most of the non-core closed itself off to the capitalist system. Communist economies, after all, have traded more and more with the capitalist world in the last decade, and even some of the most closed economies still engage in some foreign trade, though not nearly as much as before closure.

Finally, it is not clear to what extent core economies could develop alternate sources of raw materials if they were obliged to stop trading with the non-core. With respect to energy, for example, there is good evidence that core economies have the technological capacity to become far more self-sufficient, and in general, there is a certain amount of flexibility with respect to resource requirements.[7] No one is quite certain how much flexibility there is.

This does not negate the fact that so far it has been cheaper for the core to rely on relatively cheap imports from outside the core in order to fill certain requirements. Nor does it negate the fact that certain powerful interests in the core profit a great deal from foreign investment, particularly outside the core.

In conclusion, it can be said that world trading and investment patterns support the Leninist position up to a certain point. It seems unlikely that they support it entirely, but then, no one can be absolutely certain about this except the ideologues on either side of the question. Nor is anyone certain at what point the capitalist world will abandon its positions outside the core because of the rising cost of maintaining them; and if this occurs, no one can say whether or not capitalist societies will, in fact, adjust to the inevitable short-term dislocation. There will be occasion to return to these questions several times before the end of this book.

The end of old colonialism

In 1947 India, Europe's largest colony, became independent and split into two hostile states, India and Pakistan (which itself later split into Pakistan and Bangladesh). Burma, another part of the British Indian Empire, became a separate state. The reasons for this independence, the rise of the nationalist movement, the long struggle against the British, and Gandhi's ultimate triumph have already been discussed. Faced by the virtual certainty of a long hopeless war against their rule, the British gave up before that war broke out. The fact that after 1945 the British Labor Party came to power accelerated independence. The British working class, eager to push domestic reform and to recover from the hardship of World War II, and in any case, ideologically opposed to colonialism, was hardly likely to launch a war to keep India British. But even without this change in British public opinion, India would have gained its independence.

France and the Netherlands, facing similar situations in their Asian Empires, in Indochina and Indonesia, resisted, and both became involved in debilitating wars which they could not win. When the costs of maintaining colonies so far exceeded possible gains that the French and Dutch populations refused to fight any longer, the wars ended. A colony is profitable only as long as it does not require immense economic cost to keep it. Since the conditions that lead to colonial revolts cannot be eliminated in a colonial situation, the colonized people will keep on fighting even if they lose their first attempt at liberation. The number of discontented intellectuals, of poor peasants, and of humiliated natives cannot, in the long run, decrease. It can only increase, unless balanced, rapid economic growth is achieved and unless the natives themselves gain power. The old controllers of the land and the comprador middle class, as well as their allies from the core, the colonial rulers, cannot, in the long run, survive against skillfully led mass revolts.

At first, the United States favored decolonization. In a sense, colonialism involved partial closure of the colonies to the trade, investment, and influence of any core economy except the metropole. Liberated colonies became open to wider, that is, American, influence and investment. As the United Kingdom and France were gradually forced to abandon all their colonies, American influence, investment, and trade became freer to move in. As late as 1956, when the United Kingdom and France made a brief, rather desperate, last attempt to retain their empires by invading Egypt, the United States strongly opposed this move. After all, this last effort was directed at the Middle East where American oil companies already had things their own way. At that time, it seemed that the United States could gain from both ends. It could avoid the stigma of old-fashioned imperialism by opposing European military rule, and it could gain the benefits of economic imperialism by investing and trading with the newly liberated colonies.[8]

The short war against Egypt in 1956 ended the British Empire, even though it took a few more years for the remainder of the African and Asian segments to gain full independence. Not only were the British facing determined opposition to their rule from the people in their colonies, as well as opposition from their main ally in the core, the United States, but even within Britain a large portion of the population was unwilling to fight colonial wars that seemed likely to hurt rather than to help the British economy.

France held on a few more years, but its surrender in Algeria ended its empire in 1962. Again, the costs of maintaining colonies had far exceeded the possible benefits. First, the war in Indochina had milked France, and in the late 1950s, war in Algeria did the same. It was not that France could not afford to fight the Algerian war, or even that it was militarily defeated. Rather, the high cost of arms, the drain on manpower (drafted for military service in Algeria), and the consequent political turmoil proved unacceptable. Nor was there any chance that control could be maintained while lowering these costs, since every military defeat suffered by the Algerians merely put off the end without eliminating the root causes of revolution. By the time it gave up Algeria, France had already given up most of its African empire to head off more wars.

In 1960, Belgium, panicked by the thought that it, too, would be drawn into a war in its Congo colony, withdrew.

Only Portugal, Western Europe's poorest society, and among its least democratic, continued to fight to keep its African colonies. If the strain was too great for the British and the French, it was that much greater for smaller, weaker, and poorer Portugal. Only the lack of internal democracy in Portugal prevented popular discontent with the war from ending it sooner. Finally, in 1974, the strains of colonial wars provoked a revolt within Portugal, and by 1975, Portugal had withdrawn from its holdings in Africa, the last European empire on that continent.

Today, there remain two European-dominated societies in Africa, Rhodesia and South Africa. Both are run by permanent white settlers, many of them born in Africa. These settlers presumably have no place to go if their rule is overthrown. Both regimes face eventual extinction at the hands of African revolutions, Rhodesia's in the very near future, and South Africa's (with its 4 million whites, huge natural resources, and a great deal of American and British investment) in the much longer run.

In Asia, aside from Hong Kong (which persists as a British colony because this happens to suit the political and economic needs of China) and a few minor enclaves, there are no more European colonies. In Latin America, with a few minor exceptions, the same is true. The old colonialism, still very much alive in 1945, was dead thirty years later.

Few could have foreseen the rapid demise of European colonialism in 1930, or even in 1945, and yet tensions provoked by the development of colonies could have produced no other result. The seeming paradox is: *Economic development of colonies does not reduce the probability of revolt, it increases it.* Economic development uproots peasants from their land, it throws agriculture into an uncertain, fluctuating world market, it tends to concentrate land ownership into the hands of a relatively small number, it brings to the fore an alien merchant middle class, and it trains potential leaders of rebellion. Economic development instills modern nationalism, teaches Western organizational skills, provides an explicitly anti-colonial, largely Marxist-Leninist revolutionary doctrine (taught, ironically, in European and American universities), and it concentrates the colonials in cities where they can be organized more effectively. *The greater the efforts to develop a colonial economy, the sooner the anticolonial revolution.* This, no doubt, explains why Portugal, the poorest European imperial power, which did the very least to develop its colonies, did not face a successful revolutionary movement until a full ten to fifteen years after the French and British.

The revolt of the European colonies was certainly more than a purely economic movement. It was also a major cultural phenomenon, one that continues, and one that provides much of the ideological base of those forces pushing for rapid social change in the peripheral world.

No people like to be told that they are inferior. In the heyday of early twentieth-century imperialism the Europeans explicitly put forward racist explanations for their domination. Whites were said to be inherently superior to blacks, browns, reds, or yellows, and Christianity was said to be morally superior to other religions. The colonial world was overwhelmingly nonwhite, and outside of Latin America (which was, by and large, only indirectly colonized) over-whelmingly non-Christian. The crusading fervor of Gandhi in India, Sukarno in Indonesia, or Nasser in Egypt, along with many other leaders of anti-core revolutionary movements, expressed more than the discontent of uprooted peasants, poor urban migrants, under-paid workers, or hostile intellectuals. It also expressed pride in local cultures and hatred of the supposedly superior Europeans. In fact, peripheral revolutions began to be successful only when their leaders began to reject the assumed superiority of European ways. Peripheral revolutions, therefore, contained a strongly symbolic aspect as well as being expressions of economic discontent. Since the creation of united national cultures is necessary for the creation of strong nation-states, and strong nation-states are necessary in order to reorder the economies of the former colonial areas, this symbolic content of revo-lution has been a necessary ingredient of peripheral revolutions.

When peripheral intellectuals realized that no matter how West-ernized they might become, Europeans would never accept them as equals, the inevitable seeds of successful revolution were planted. Again, it was not a matter of insufficient education in the colonies. *The more colonial natives were brought to Europe to study, the more likely their revolution.* The British, who educated more natives of their colonies than the French, particularly in India, were the first to suffer the consequences of anticolonial revolt. The French were next. The Belgians and Portuguese, who educated very few Africans in European universities, were faced by revolution even later.

The reactive cultural component of peripheral revolutions is best seen by the intractable issue of Israel. Arab nationalism in the Middle East has been active since the early twentieth century. The French and British were driven out after World War II, but in one part of the Arab world, Palestine, European Jews (joined by Jewish refugees from Muslim countries) established an independent Euro-pean state in 1947–1948. In doing this, they uprooted about 600,000 Palestinian Arabs. Many populations have been driven into exile by political events, both in the twentieth century and before. But in this case, the entire Arab world reacted, not simply the Palestinians. Why was this so? Largely because symbolically the Jewish state became a Western (even if non-Christian) enclave in the Arab world. The continuing bitter hostility of the Arabs to Israel can be explained neither by economic reasons nor by any direct interests of Arab societies. The Arab Palestinians have a direct interest in seeing the Jewish state eliminated, but it is relatively clear that Syria and Egypt have little to gain by establishing an Arab Palestinian state. Iraq, Saudi Arabia, Libya, Algeria, Morocco, Sudan, and Kuwait, much less distant Mauritania, have nothing to gain at all, execept pride. Israel has become, by proxy, the West, the symbol of technological arrogance, material success, and in a strange way, a symbol of the imperialism of the past. Whether Jewish Israel wishes to symbolize all this is another question (clearly it wishes it did not have to bear the resultant burden). The irony of the situation is that a non-Christian, previously persecuted minority in Europe has come to stand for the sins of the Europeans and of Western cultural arrogance. Since Israel has come to symbolize the legacy of the West, it will remain under attack until Arab resentment of the West disappears. The United States, the United Kingdom, and France may try to disavow their legacy, but resentment can end only when Arab countries have become as rich and powerful as the old core. And while a few oil-producing Arab societies have become rich, they constitute a small minority of the Arab world.

Israel has become the key emotional issue on which most peripheral societies have been able to express their hatred of the West, and the Arab cause receives overwhelming support in most of the periphery and former periphery. This should awaken the old core to the fact that there is far more at stake than the fate of the Arab Palestinians. The world is not outraged by equal, or greater, injustice elsewhere because the Palestinian issue has become the symbolic focus of the entire peripheral world's hostility to the capitalist world system. Even if Israel were to vanish, this hostility would remain, and other symbolic issues would come to the fore.

By the 1980s the issue of South Africa is likely to become the central symbolic issue in the antagonism between the core and its former periphery.

Neocolonialism

Against this background, international relations in the 1960s and 1970s begin to make more sense. As the old type of colonialism was crumbling under the pressure of armed revolt combined with Western distaste for expensive, long, and ultimately hopeless colonial wars, a new type of colonialism, truer to capitalism's original spirit, was replacing it. Investment rather than direct political control, business rather than military occupation were taking over numerous non-core economies.

The giant multinational corporations that have increasingly dominated the capitalist world system are complex, and it is sometimes difficult to untangle the location of investments, the distribution of profits, and the extent of power held by these organizations. But in the 1960s and 1970s, a relatively small number of firms (about 300, of whom some 200 are based in the United States) have come to control a significant portion of the world economy. Their primary power lies within the core itself, the United States, Canada, Western Europe, and Japan, but they also have a great deal of economic power in the periphery and certain parts of the new semi-periphery. The major petroleum companies (even after their oil resources have been expropriated, they continue to control transportation, refining, and distribution of this most important raw material) are the undisputed giants. Of the ten largest world corporations, eight are oil companies. One of these is the Iranian government's oil corporation, and the seven others are the notorious "seven sisters," Exxon, Royal Dutch Shell, Texaco, Mobil, British Petroleum (itself largely owned by the British government), Standard Oil of California, and Gulf. The two other major multi-national corporations are General Motors and Ford. Of the next 40 largest multinationals, 17 are based in the United States, 4 in the United Kingdom, 1 in the Netherlands, 4 in Japan, 7 in West Germany, 3 in France, 1 in Switzerland, 2 in Italy, and 1 is the Brazilian state petroleum company. Thus, of the top 50 corporations, 24 are in the United States, and all but two of the remainder are in the core. Only state-owned petroleum companies in Iran and Brazil (to be joined very soon, no doubt, by the state-owned Venezuelan, Saudi Arabian, and Kuwaiti petroleum companies) are exceptions. The total sales of these 50 largest corporations amount to a bit over one-half trillion dollars a year, a sum larger than the GNP of any national economy except the United States, and the Soviet Union.[9]

Do these giant corporations therefore control the world? Despite dire predictions, it is now quite clear that the nation-states of the core *are not controlled* by their large corporations, though these undoubtedly have a great deal of power. It is equally clear that they will not ever gain full control of the core states simply because in these states there are other powerful groups which balance the corporate power. These other groups, organized labor, the politically active middle classes, and government military and civilian bureaucracies, are intertwined with the large corporations to some extent, but are hardly at their beck and call. Nor do these corporations control most of the periphery or new semi-periphery, even though there, too, they are often very powerful. They are one element in the global distribution of power, not the only element.

It is, however, quite correct to say that core power in poorer economies exists primarily in the form of multi-national corporate investments and control of certain key sectors of the economy. Consequently, these corporate giants are one of the main targets of nationalist outrage outside the core, as well as the main instrument through which core societies dominate the world system.

Leaving aside the issue of the power of these corporations within the core itself (a topic to be taken up in the next chapter), how has the core gained from this economic power concentrated in the hands of a few of its largest businesses during the 1960s and early 1970s?

First, and most obviously, the core gained access to a large quantity of raw materials, particularly oil. Direct access to these raw materials kept their price cheaper than it would otherwise have been, not so much because weaker economies received a lower price than the going world price for their resources, but because the larger the available quantity of a resource, the lower its price. The large corporations' control over the world economy placed them (that is, the corporations and the core as a whole) in a better bargaining position than the relatively weak and relatively disunited primary producers. It may be that the events since 1973, in which the major oil-producing peripheral societies banded together to raise the price of their resource, will provide a different pattern in the future, but at least throughout the 1950s and 1960s, this did not happen.

Second, the core gained cheap labor. In some cases—Mexico, Taiwan, South Korea, Hong Kong, Puerto Rico, Singapore, and lately Brazil—core investors set up factories to take advantage of low labor costs. But the parent companies continued to be controlled from the core, and this type of investment led to overspecialization and dependency on the larger world market. The core also gained cheap labor from the periphery and semi-periphery in a more direct way. Western Europe imported cheap labor from the semi-peripheral, southern regions of Europe (Portugal, Spain, Greece, Southern Italy, Yugoslavia) as well as from the Islamic rim of the Mediterranean (Morocco, Algeria, Tunisia, Turkey) and from farther away, sub-Saharan Africa. Britain imported cheap labor from the Caribbean (as well as from India and Pakistan), as did Canada and the United States, which also imported cheap labor from Mexico and from the Philippines. This cheap labor, though not a very large part of the total labor force, allowed core laborers to avoid the worst paid, most menial, and most unpleasant tasks. It therefore reduced internal class tensions, and created an important safety valve for core societies. When a temporary downturn occurred in core economies (for example, the recession of 1974–1976) peripheral workers could be fired first to ease domestic pressure. This labor advantage, of course, had little to do with the specific planned actions of large core investors, but was rather the effect of an open world capitalist labor market which drew workers from poorer to richer economies. But there is little evidence that this made non-core economies any poorer. On the contrary, it eased their poverty.

Third, the core gained a place where investment capital could make enormous profits. The profits of American overseas investors (primarily the large multi-national corporations) has already been discussed and demonstrated in Tables 34, 35, and 36. It would be difficult to prove that the large multi-national corporations absolutely needed the profits they gained outside the core, but there is no doubt that these profits helped keep them rich and powerful, even though the overall advantage to core economies was small.

Fourth, the core gained a market for some of its exports. High technology has always been the virtual monopoly of the capitalist core since the start of the capitalist world system, and this remains as true today as ever. Airplanes, automobiles, computers, machinery of all types, particularly heavy machinery, and chemicals continue to be produced primarily in the core. In the 1970s, production of food grains has come to be a high-technology industry increasingly dominated by the United States and Canada. This has meant that technological dynamism, inventions, improvements, and future increases in productivity have continued to come from the core, while the rest of the capitalist world economy has continued to lag. Technological and scientific dynamism does not remain a monopoly of the core because of the core's greater political power. The actual reason is that highly literate, skilled, advanced societies have much greater scientific and research capacities than the periphery. But as long as innovation and research remain in the hands of the core, the rest of the world is not likely to catch up economically. Also, control of much of the world's economy by a few large-core corporations has slowed the emergence of an independent research capacity outside the core for simple economic reasons. Since the advanced economies can conduct research more efficiently, large corporations will continue to conduct their research in the core, and export products rather than the capacity to improve products. As part of the capitalist world economy, the peripheral economies lack the stimulus necessary for creating independent research facilities.

Finally, the core gained (and this is quite ironical) skilled professional labor from the non-core. Just as unskilled workers migrated to the core to take up menial jobs, so did scientists, engineers, and doctors migrate in order to attain the higher standards of living available in the core, as well as to profit from the better working conditions that prevailed in the core. In other words, much of the periphery and semi-periphery lost educated personnel to the core, and this, of course, helped to perpetuate economic inequality.[10]

These advantages should not be exaggerated. It is possible that the core would have survived quite well without them. But rates of growth would have been a bit lower, the cost of life would have been a bit higher, and the technological superiority of the core would have been a bit less secure if these advantages had not existed.

Even if the gains of the core at the expense of the periphery have been small, they are worth maintaining, at least in the view of the major core investors who have interests in the periphery. Policy makers in core states who believe in a modified Leninist theory also believe the opposite of that theory, namely, that if peripheral societies were to join the chief enemies of the capitalist world system (the Soviet Union or China), then these advantages would accrue to communist states. Even those in the core who might be willing to give up the direct advantages of control over peripheral economies would be loathe to see these advantages going to the communist world system. Consequently, the only observers who can calmly watch the increasing revolt against core domination are either those who wish to see the capitalist world system destroyed, or else those who take a radically anti-Leninist position and believe that all these advantages are small indeed, and in fact basically irrelevant. So far, few politicians or entrepreneurs in the core have been willing to accept such a radically anti-Leninist view of the world.

At the same time, outside the core, the Leninist position has gained such wide acceptance that revolutionary development efforts have become increasingly anticapitalist and anti-core. The whole complex of advantages extracted by the core from the periphery has come to be labelled neocolonialism, and has been assailed as being even more pernicious than the old colonialism, because it is so much more subtle.

Since the revolutionary struggle in the periphery has become increasingly directed against the core, and recently, specifically against core economic investments, maintaining open societies (open, that is, to the capitalist system) in the periphery has become increasingly costly. The period in which subtle, indirect control could be maintained by core economies and investors is coming to an end just as surely as the period of direct, open colonial control came to an end. As costs rise, the benefits will correspondingly shrink. The overwhelming proportion of citizens in core societies will refuse to pay the military and aid costs needed to keep peripheral societies open and nonrevolutionary. Business itself will ultimately lose its enthusiasm and cease to invest in the periphery (this has already happened in much of Latin America where North American investment has been decreasing). The core will lose its willingness to fight the "small" wars that previously kept peripheral revolutionaries out of power. In short, the very identification of neocolonialism as the main device used by the core to keep control over the periphery makes the survival of neocolonialism that much less likely. In today's world, it provokes many of the same responses provoked by open colonialism three decades ago. It has become evident that for all their economic power, the core's giant multi-national corporations are politically weak and incapable of defending themselves unless they can persuade core states to act for them. This has now become very difficult. Core states, most recently the United States, have lost their enthusiasm for colonial wars.

The mark of this change has been changing American policy since Vietnam. For over a decade, Vietnam was a primary test case that would determine whether or not the United States would be able to keep peripheral societies open. The failure of that effort has served to sour the United States on such ventures by demonstrating how hopeless and costly they can actually be.

The New International Situation

The labels *core, periphery,* and *semi-periphery,* have been used throughout this book as guides to understanding the evolution of the world system in the first half of the twentieth century; they are not as applicable to the second half. Changes occurring within the last thirty years or so, particularly during the late 1960s and early 1970s, have confused the situation, and it is no longer possible to analyze the world quite so neatly. The present world system is more complicated than the one that prevailed in 1900, or even in 1950. The capitalist core, enlarged by a number of former rich peripheral societies (Canada, Australia, New Zealand) and joined as well by much of the old semi-periphery (Italy, Japan, and in the near future, Spain) persists intact, rich, and in the economic sphere, as powerful as ever; its political power, however, is greatly diminished. Aside from the rival communist societies (which now include one-third of the world's population) a large number of formerly peripheral societies have become nationalistic, development-oriented challengers of the core's supremacy. This challenge represents the major change in the world system over the last several decades. Only a few societies remain purely peripheral in the old sense of that term.

Nationalistic revolutions have occurred in much of what used to be the periphery. Many of these revolutions have been only partial successes, but the tendency toward the creation of strong nation-states and the push toward diversified, independent economic growth have become almost universal. Not only have the European colonial empires come to an end, but in many cases the classes allied to the core in the periphery have been fatally weakened. The old controllers of the land have been losing their grip throughout much of the peripheral world, and the middle-class compradors, particularly the pariah capitalists, have hardly fared much better. Even where these groups have survived, it has been in much stronger state structures which have limited their power as well as the power of core states to intervene directly in local affairs.

Which societies remain purely peripheral in the old sense of that term? Certainly a few small (in terms of population) Latin American, African, and Asian societies remain weak nation-states with weak, virtually helpless economies dependent on the export of a few primary products. But the Guatemalas and Nigers of the world are exceptions in the late twentieth century, not the rule as they were at the start of the century.

Some very wealthy, or at least potentially very wealthy primary producers (mostly those states with large amounts of petroleum) have remained well within the capitalist system but have centralized their own state machineries and then banded together to raise the price of their resources. Many of them have also initiated ambitious (perhaps overambitious) industrialization plans. (In 1976 Iran and Saudi Arabia were prime examples.) Thus these states have come to act quite like the members of the old semi-periphery, particularly Japan at the start of the century. Still within the capitalist world system, they are challenging the power of the old core. At the same time, they are undergoing a modernization process that might one day make some of them the system's real powers.

Some other states, like Brazil, and from time to time, Mexico, Turkey, Egypt, Indonesia (until Sukarno's overthrow), have also behaved in recent decades like classical semi-peripheral societies. Others, like India, have remained desperately poor, but have also challenged the political supremacy of the old core and established themselves as strong regional powers, again like the old semi-periphery. In other words, there has developed a large new semi-periphery that is still within the capitalist world, but which threatens the political and, even in a small way, the economic supremacy of the core.

A number of other former peripheral societies, like Guinea or Burma, have withdrawn from the world system and have become bitter, though helpless, enemies of that system. Small, economically and politically weak, these countries have nevertheless succeeded in excluding core power. This itself is a measure of the basic change that has occurred in the system since 1910; then only the most remote, inaccessible peripheral areas could resist core encroachment.

Finally, a few peripheral societies, like Taiwan and South Korea, have become highly integrated nation-states, have industrialized to a substantial degree, but have remained client states of the United States. Nevertheless, even these societies are no longer like the members of the old periphery: they have stronger economies and stronger political systems.

In short, the distinctions between the two categories of non-core societies have become so blurred that such labels as *peripheral* and *semi-peripheral* are dated and can be applied to the present only with great care. On the criteria sent forth early in this book, virtually all the noncommunist world is divided into core and semi-periphery, with a small, disappearing periphery. The drive toward internal consolidation and balanced economic growth has become almost universal. That massive core investments and economic control through multi-national corporations will survive in the old periphery seems unlikely. Even poorer societies that fail to industrialize (and most are not succeeding very well at all) will continue to gain increasing political independence. Nationalism, the ideological force that propelled the Western core to world supremacy, has now spread to the rest of the world and eroded if not yet totally ended that supremacy.

Even within the core, the situation is no longer similar to what it was in the earlier parts of the century. There is, properly speaking, only one core power, the United States. The rivalries that tore apart the core until 1945 are no longer a factor within the world system. Members of the core may bicker with each other from time to time, but wars waged by core powers for control of the world system are now a thing of the past. The issue has been settled by a much tighter economic, social, cultural, and political integration of the core than ever seemed possible in earlier decades. This has been, in many ways, the major triumph of the capitalist system, as well as a major rebuttal to the Leninist theory that predicted the inevitable occurrence of endless wars between core societies.

Instead of a world dominated by struggles between core powers, the world has become a battleground between the united capitalist core and its assailants, the two major Communist powers and a growing number of new semi-peripheral societies. In effect, international relations now consist of a jockeying between the core, the Soviet Union, and China for power and influence in that growing semi-periphery which, however, remains free to play off the major powers against each other. The American world system can therefore be said to be ending in the 1970s even though the United States and its core allies will remain rich and powerful for a long time to come.

VII

Internal Stratification, Politics,

and the *World* System

in the Late Twentieth Century

The world system has changed a great deal in the twentieth century, but it remains as true today as in the past that a society's position in the system is likely to correlate highly if not perfectly with its level of development and its internal political and class division. The core has become quite homogeneous in this respect. All core societies are highly industrialized, wealthy, and have similar stratification and political patterns. The differences between them seem relatively minor when compared to variations within the new semi-periphery or the communist societies.

The contemporary patterns of internal stratification and politics can be examined by means of the same categories used in Chapter III. Again, it will be necessary to concentrate on those patterns most closely related to the changing world system and neglect much of the fine detail.

Culturally Based Stratification

The years since the end of World War II have witnessed a curious phenomenon, one that has confounded most theorists. Ethnic, regional, linguistic, and religious tensions between various parts of non-core societies have remained high, and increased in those societies trying to create strong nation-states; these types of culturally based tensions have also increased quite markedly within the core itself. Presumably, according to older theories of nation-building and development,[1] culturally based tensions were bound to decrease with further industrialization, urbanization, and the increase in national integration. In effect, wherever class stratification has continued to coincide, even very partially, with cultural stratification, reactive, culturally based politics have come to play an important role in national political systems.

The persistence of culturally based divisions of labor has produced protest, and even violence, in the United States, Canada, Belgium, the United Kingdom, and even, to a slight extent, in France. In the United States Blacks, Chicanos, and certain descendants of white immigrant groups have become increasingly active as distinct cultural groups. In the United Kingdom, Celtic nationalism, even leaving aside the old and still-festering sore of Catholic Irish nationalism, has produced powerful separatist movements in Wales and Scotland. Belgium has been the scene of bitter struggles between the Flemish (Dutch) and Walloon (French) populations, and Canada has seen the birth of a powerful French nationalist reaction against English domination.[2]

There has even been, to a small but discernible degree, a tendency for core minority groups to identify their struggles with the anti-core struggles of peoples in the periphery and new semi-periphery. This has been evident, for example, in racially based cultural divisions in the United States where radical Black and Chicano groups have to some extent identified with the growth of intense nationalism in the old periphery. The enemy has been labeled "capitalism," that is, the prevailing world system, dominated not even by the whole capitalist core, but by a limited segment of the core societies.

In the long run, it is likely that this putative identification of angry cultural subgroups in the core with the nationalists in the new semi-periphery will prove to be as tenuous and inconsequential as the older, now weakened identification of core working classes with the struggles of colonial peoples against Western domination. Even the most hostile culturally defined groups in the core have profited immensely from the wealth and economic power of the core, and the likelihood of a common front against world capitalism remains both dim and highly unrealistic. But again, the degree to which this identification between certain groups in the core and groups outside the core has occurred demonstrates the existence of a world system in which political action in any part of the system is somewhat linked to actions in other parts of the system. The identification of a common, capitalist enemy by relatively disadvantaged groups is the product of greatly increased awareness of the existence of worldwide links in the capitalist system. The extent to which the claims of certain relatively disadvantaged culturally defined groups in the core have been accepted as legitimate by core polities betrays unease with the legitimacy of the capitalist system itself. The weakening of legitimacy is the product of the political reverses suffered by the core and of the new, widespread understanding of the links between core capitalism and the actions of the core outside its borders. In other words, while reactive cultural nationalism within the core has reasons of its own for existing (the inferior position of Blacks in the United States, of Celts in the United Kingdom, of French speakers in Canada, and so on), it has gained strength from the example of nationalism in the old periphery.

On a worldwide scale, lower-class protest, culturally based nationalism, and a growing anti-capitalist movement have produced a series of linked (even if weakly linked) groups united by their anti-capitalist, anti-core ideology. Even if it is unlikely that this trend will go very far, it could grow; and if it does, it could fatally weaken the core.

The reason that such a development is unlikely, despite events of the last couple of decades, is that the new semi-periphery is only superficially internationalist in its ideological orientation. There is talk of a united anticapitalist front, joined not only by deprived minorities in the core, but also by alienated intellectuals (particularly young ones) in core societies. But within the new semi-periphery, the goal is the very opposite of creating a strong international movement. Rather, the goal is the strengthening of the nation-state, the integration of regions, ethnicities, religious, and linguistic groups into a single cultural entity. Paradoxically, the strong core has witnessed the revival of forces hostile to the nation-state at the same time that the new semi-periphery has tended to move in the opposite direction, toward creating much stronger nation-states. At some point the conflict between these two opposite goals will break apart whatever international movement has developed, just as earlier the internationally oriented working-class movement, theoretically united under the banner of socialism, broke up as a result of strong nationalist forces within core societies.

In the new semi-periphery, the problem of culturally based hostilities remains much stronger than in the core. Just as the semi-peripheral states of the early twentieth century saw salvation in national integration and cultural unity, so do contemporary semi-peripheral societies pursue the same goal. And as in the past, this provokes strong reactions. It remains true that in the semi-periphery substantial portions of the population do not accept the definition of nationalism provided by their states. It is, however, increasingly difficult for core interests to take advantage of this, as they did earlier, because most contemporary states are so much stronger than old peripheral states used to be.

In 1900, for example, it was easy for the British to play on Muslim-Hindu and regional rivalries in order to "divide and rule" in India. By 1975, these cultural, regional, ethnic, and religious divisions in India had produced several nasty wars and split India, first into two parts (India and Pakistan) and then into three (as East Pakistan became Bangladesh). Such disputes have hardly helped the core powers to retain control over events, and manipulation by outside forces is both more costly and less certain of success than in the past. The goal of aspiring nationalist groups in the old periphery has been to create strong states, and even as they fight each other, these groups have shared hostility to core interference.

To a large extent this hostility has been the result of a spectacular growth in the number of Westernized, or partially Westernized
intellectuals in the old periphery. As discussed, much of the leadership for the century's early anticolonial revolts came from such individuals. Since World War II, peripheral intellectuals, educated by
long years of contact with Western thought, have increasingly espoused
radically anticapitalist, anti-Western (that is, anti-core) ideologies. As
more and more of the young in new semi-peripheral societies turn to
such ideologies, the likelihood of successful core interference in the
affairs of the new semi-periphery diminishes.

One attack made against the members of the core, particularly
the United States, has been that they have encouraged cultural splits
within the new semi-periphery in order to prevent the emergence of
strong, ultimately anti-core nation-states. To a certain extent, this
charge is correct. In Indochina, for example, the United States played
the card of cultural separatism to the maximum. Montagnards were
organized against Vietnamese, Thai tribes in Laos against the Pathet
Lao, the separatist religious groups in South Vietnam against the
Vietcong. Similarly the French encouraged and supported, even if
they did not create, Ibo secessionists in Nigeria (presumably for the
purpose of gaining control of Eastern Nigerian petroleum resources),
and Belgium certainly supported Katanga's secession in the Congo in
1960 in order to ensure Belgian control of some of the area's mineral
resources. Such actions are part of the old colonial pattern of divide
and conquer; they have tended to fail more and more, just as the old
forms of colonialism have increasingly faltered.

Even discounting interference by the core, cultural separatism
in the non-core remains a very serious problem, just as it has always
been in relatively weak states trying to strengthen their power and
create strong nation-states. Not all or even most of the culturally
based conflicts in the semi-periphery can be blamed on core interference. A number of bitter civil wars have occurred, and in many
cases, deep hostilities remain. Even without core influence, these hostilities would be strong. Yet, insofar as they have been resolved (as,
for example, in Nigeria after a civil war), the power of the core to
influence developments in the old periphery has tended to diminish.

Many of the states in the new semi-periphery have used outright
force to create stronger nation-states; their military machines have
been utilized primarily to promote national unity and cultural homogeneity. Since internal division is one of the most severe, probably
the single most immediate, problem of semi-peripheral societies,
domestic armies have become the main instruments of contemporary
nation-building. This has given the military forces in semi-peripheral
societies a great deal of power, and they now rule a very substantial

portion of what used to be the peripheral world. (In this respect the semi-periphery is a marked contrast to the core and the communist societies where the military almost never assume political control.)

These observations lead one directly into another category of this analysis of the contemporary world—namely, economic stratification and politics in different types of societies. The discussion of culturally based stratification can be summarized by saying that even while problems of national integration remain severe in the semi-periphery, virtually all non-core states are combating them. In the core, on the other hand, cultural divisions have become more important than in the recent past, a development broadly associated with the core's partial loss of world political power and self-confidence.

Class and Politics in the Core

Theorists who view the capitalist world system as strictly stratified see a core (upper class) dominating and exploiting a periphery (lower class). These theorists, the "power-elite" theorists, tend to accept a parallel image of internal stratification within the core itself: a small group that controls capital dominates and exploits a large working class. There are many variants of this view, and few scholars would claim that the parallel is perfect since the periphery in the world system consists largely of primary producers while the working class located in the core is involved mostly in manufacturing (secondary production) or services (tertiary production). But, as the power-elite theorists see it, the parallel exists because in both instances the same small elite dominates the situation to its advantage.

In this view, the rise of a new semi-periphery represents a mortal peril to the capitalist system, since it threatens to loosen the bonds of exploitation on which core power rests. At one time, the organized working class within the core also seemed to threaten the position of the capitalist elite. But as the twentieth century has advanced, this internal threat has decreased. The Leninist explanation for this (for present purposes, identical to a power-elite theory of the world system) is that, by means of extra profits generated in the periphery, the ruling capitalists have "paid off" the core working classes. Exploitation by the power elite at the international level is thus an important part of the group's continuing power at home. *Labor in the core, at the sensitive nerve center of the capitalist world system, can receive relatively high wages because the periphery remains exploited.*

Whether or not this view is correct returns one to the central question: Is the Leninist view of the world correct? Previous chapters have shown that there may be something to the argument, though perhaps not as much as the original theory maintains. The theory seems to work because the major international actors have behaved as if it were true. That, at least, has been the tentative conclusion of earlier parts of this study.

The obvious question to ask about the nature of stratification and power in the core is whether or not it is correct that a small power elite dominates the core itself. In general, theorists who say yes to this question (for example, C. Wright Mills, Gabriel Kolko, Maurice Zeitlin) see the domestic pattern as a strong confirmation of their Leninist view of the world system.[3]

Data presented in earlier chapters showed that wealth was quite concentrated in capitalist core societies in the early part of the century. Since then, the distribution of income (wages from direct labor and from return on capital) has become more equal. The elite, the top 5 percent of the population, has lost some of its dominance in the distribution of income throughout the core. This loss is among the changes indicated in Table 40, a look at the pattern of income distribution in the United States from 1929 to 1970. (Not only is the United States the most important core society, but in many ways, it is quite representative in that it sets many of the prevailing social and economic patterns throughout the core.)

Although *income* in the United States is clearly less concentrated than in the recent past, there has been little, if any change in its distribution since 1950. In addition, *wealth* (in terms of capital assets) *remains far more concentrated than income;* and some writers argue that ownership of certain kinds of decisive, economically powerful wealth may be higher than ever.

TABLE 40
Percentage of National Income
Received by Families in the United States, 1929–1970

	1929	*1950*	*1960*	*1970*	*Percentage of change* *
Lowest Fifth	3.5	4.5	4.8	5.4	+54%
Second Fifth	9.0	11.9	12.2	12.2	+36%
Third Fifth	13.8	17.4	17.8	17.6	+28%
Fourth Fifth	19.3	23.6	24.0	23.8	+23%
Top Fifth	54.4	42.7	41.3	40.9	−25%
Top Five Percent	30.0	17.3	15.9	15.6	−48%

SOURCE Edward C. Budd, "Inequality in Income and Taxes," in Maurice Zeitlin, ed., *American Society, Inc.: Studies of the Social Structure and Political Economy of the United States* (Chicago: Markham, 1970), p. 144; U.S. Bureau of the Census, *Statistical Abstract of the United States: 1974* (Washington: U.S. Government Printing Office, 1974), p. 384.

* Percentage of change = [(percentage in 1970 ÷ percentage in 1929) − 100 percent].

In 1972 there were about 70 million family units in the United States (including one-person families). Of these, less than 0.3 percent (about 200 thousand millionaire families) owned 15 percent of all assets; they owned 35 percent of all corporate stock, 73 percent of all state and local bonds, 27 percent of all corporate bonds, and 68 percent of Federal Government treasury notes.[4] The intricacies of tracing actual ownership of assets make it virtually impossible to say whether or not the degree of concentration is higher now than in the past. There is some evidence that ownership of stock and corporate bonds became more concentrated from 1922 to 1953,[5] and some estimates (which seem too high) suggest that the top 0.2 percent of all adult Americans own up to two-thirds of the country's stock.[6] The absolute numbers are not as critical as the general impression, which confirms the notion that a very few individuals own a decisive share of all wealth and economic power. Recent work also shows that of the 200 thousand families of millionaires, most inherited their money; and that if their share of all wealth has not increased since about 1945, it has not decreased either.[7]

There is more to the concentration of economic power than ownership. Within the top corporations that dominate the economies of the United States and the capitalist world, there exists a clear pattern of interlocking directorships. The top managers, lawyers, and financiers who run these corporations are either members of a small upper class or its highly rewarded servants. As G. William Domhoff, a psychologist turned sociologist, has observed:

> Our findings on all corporate boards can be summarized as follows: Interlocking directorates show beyond question that there is a national corporate economy that is run by the same group of several thousand men.[8]

Nor is there any doubt that a small number of corporations do actually dominate the American and world economies (a pattern quite similar to that in the United States exists in the other core economies). In 1929, the 100 largest manufacturing corporations owned 40 percent of all assets owned by American manufacturing corporations; in 1970, they owned 49 percent. In the entire American economy in 1970 a mere 1,349 corporations (less than 0.1 percent of the total number) owned about 60 percent of all corporate assets.[9]

Some branches of the economy are not highly concentrated in the hands of a few large corporations, notably agriculture, and to some extent, construction, but a small number of large corporations have a high degree of control in manufacturing, transportation, communications, utilities, finance, insurance, and mining. In wholesale and retail trade, and in services, several hundred large corporations hold a dominant position, but do not control a majority of assets.[10] In general, however, the strength of the largest 1000 or so American corporations, both in terms of assets and in terms of share of the market, gives them a large amount of economic power.

Economic power and political power, however, are not identical, though they are related. At the start of the twentieth century, the top controllers of corporate wealth held preponderant political power. Since then, three major changes have occurred in core societies that have severely limited the political power of the capitalist upper class, even if they have not diminished the concentration of wealth. (Again, while considering these changes in the United States, one should remember that analogous changes have occurred throughout the core.)

First, the middle class has grown to include about one quarter of the population. In advanced industrial societies the dividing line between the lower-middle class (primarily clerical and sales workers) and the working class is not particularly sharp. In many families, some members work in lower-middle-class occupations and others work in blue-collar occupations. It would be somewhat misleading to claim that about half of the working population of the United States in 1970 was in the middle class. But it is not farfetched to say that some 25 percent of the country's population was in the middle class, a far larger group than in 1910. This 25 percent of the working adults in the United States were well educated, and on the whole, prosperous. Only a tiny proportion of that class held significant economic power in terms of ownership of stock or control over capital; but the class as a whole tended to be well organized and politically active. It is impossible to speak of a "united" middle class, but certain segments of this class have provided the money and manpower for major political movements that have opposed the political power of the corporate elite. (The consumer movement that developed in the United States in the 1960s and is spreading to other core societies is only one recent example.) The point is that in political democracies, this large, relatively aware segment of the population pursues its own interests, initiates political action, and often holds veto power over unpopular government and corporate acts. Resistance to the Vietnam War within the United States came almost entirely from this middle class and its children in the universities (see Table 41).

The large middle class is surely not revolutionary in the traditional sense of that word; but because it owns little of the critical means of production, it is not firmly attached to corporate privileges either. It serves, therefore, as an important obstacle to corporate control of the United States and other core societies and as a potentially decisive bloc capable of exercising a veto in the conduct of foreign wars, particularly colonial ones.

TABLE 41
Changes in Class Distribution in the United States, 1910–1970

	1910		1950		1970		
	Number†	Relative percentage‡	Number	Relative percentage	Number	Relative percentage	Percentage of change§
Middle Class*	4,220	11	10,236	17	19,429	25	+127
Lower Middle Class	3,742	10	11,365	19	18,568	24	+140
Working Class	17,797	48	30,445	52	37,503	48	no change
Agriculturalists	11,983	31	6,953	11	3,162	4	−87
Total	37,291		58,999		78,627		

SOURCE U.S. Bureau of the Census, Statistical Abstract of the United States: 1972 (Washington: U.S. Government Printing Office, 1972), p. 230; U.S. Bureau of the Census, Historical Statistics of the United States, Colonial Times to 1957 (Washington: U.S. Government Printing Office, 1960), p. 74.

* For definition of classes, see Table 12 (page 60).
† In thousands of employed persons.
‡ Percentage does not include the military or the unemployed.
§ Percentage of change = [(Percentage in 1970 ÷ percentage in 1910) − 100 percent].

The working class has become much better organized and much more powerful than it was at the start of the century. This is the second important change that has occurred in core societies. Reforms on the order of the New Deal have now spread widely throughout the core (more occurring in Western Europe than in the United States); and although a large portion of the working class remains outside unions, the large unions hold a key position of power in government policy making. They hardly hold a monopoly of power, but they can frequently make their political wishes effective; and they can, on occasion, serve as a powerful bloc capable of obstructing policies they do not favor. This veto has reduced the power of the controllers of capital.

Strike activity has not declined noticeably in the second half of the twentieth century. In fact, after World War II, industrial societies were subject to the largest wave of strikes in their history, larger, even, than that which occurred after World War I.[11] But the increasing wealth of core societies, the significant share of power gained by unions, and acceptance of strikes as a legitimate economic and political weapon have reduced the revolutionary potential of strikes. In the core today, except for Italy and such marginal members of the core as Spain, working-class organizations pose almost no threat to the survival of the capitalist system itself. What the appeasement of the working class has done, paradoxically, is to stabilize the capitalist system at the same time that it has reduced the power of the capitalist elite. Even in France and Italy, where Communist parties are strong, there is real doubt about whether they have any revolutionary fervor left at all. When the Italian Communist Party eventually gains a share of formal political power, it will use it in order to carry out conventional social reforms, an area in which Italy has lagged somewhat behind the rest of the core.

The third major change in core societies has been the enormous growth of government bureaucracies. These have effectively come to comprise a "new class," a group with its own interests, its own organizations, its own demands, and its own political and economic power. In this area the United States actually lagged behind other core societies for much of the twentieth century, but since World War II, it has experienced an important degree of public bureaucratic growth. Tables 42 and 43 demonstrate this point.

The figures given in Table 42 show that increase in government spending is neither a temporary, short-run phenomenon, nor one that is likely to be reversed, even though as a proportion of GNP this sort of expenditure has not grown as rapidly as most Americans believed in the 1960s and early 1970s.

Again, the historical trend has been quite strong. Growth may be slowed in the future, but a sharp reversal is virtually impossible.

TABLE 42
**Government Expenditures in the United States
as Percentage of GNP, 1913–1974**

	State and local expenditures (in billions of dollars)	Federal expenditures (in billions of dollars)°	Percentage of GNP
1913	2.3	0.7	7.5
1927	8.6	3.0	12.0
1938	11.5	6.8	21.5
1950	28.0	42.0	24.6
1960	61.0	90.0	30.0
1970	148.0	185.0	34.1
1974	206.0	255.0†	33.0

SOURCE   U.S. Bureau of the Census, *Historical Statistics of the United States, Colonial Times to 1957* (Washington: U.S. Government Printing Office, 1960), pp. 139, 711, 718, 728, 730; U.S. Bureau of the Census, *Statistical Abstract of the United States: 1974* (Washington: U.S. Government Printing Office, 1974), pp. 242, 306, 373; Council of Economic Advisers, *Economic Report of the President, 1975* (Washington: U.S. Government Printing Office, 1975), pp. 249, 328–329.

° Of which the following amounts were for military spending: 1913: 335 million; 1927: 688 million; 1938: 1.24 billion; 1950: 21.9 billion; 1960: 52.3 billion; 1970: 89.0 billion; 1974: 94.0 billion. These figures include the cost of veterans' benefits, which totaled $8.8 billion in 1950, $5.4 billion in 1960, $8.7 billion in 1970, and $13.3 billion in 1974; this cost is expected to rise to over $15 billion by 1977. Federal spending for 1977 has been estimated at $400 billion, with military spending in the $110-billion range. These estimates represent a sharp relative decline in military spending, from over 50 percent of the budget in the 1960s to slightly over 25 percent.
† Actual federal expenditures in 1974 were $298.6 billion, but $43.7 billion were grants-in-aid to local and state governments.

The growth of government spending and employment did not occur randomly. The depression of the 1930s stimulated the creation of numerous New Deal reforms; the permanent assumption of worldwide security burdens led to the creation of a large defense establishment after 1945; and in the late 1950s and 1960s, the extension of education and welfare opportunities to large portions of the poorest segments of the population caused rapid growth of state and local government as well as more restrained growth at the federal level. Very specific political pressures were responsible for these costly policies; and as long as such pressures remain, the size of spending and the size of the government bureaucracies will not markedly decrease.

Similar political pressures, particularly from the organized working classes and middle classes, caused parallel rises in government

TABLE 43
Government Employees in the United States, 1909–1973

	State and local governments	*Federal civilian*	*Federal military*	*Percentage of total labor force*
		(in thousands)		
1909	?	372	142	?
1919	?	794	1173†	?
1929	2532	580	255	6.8
1939	3090	954	334	7.9
1950	3948	1961*	1460‡	11.4
1960	6387	2430*	2494	15.7
1970	10147	2928*	2874§	18.6
1973	11353	2778*	2202	17.8

SOURCE   U.S. Bureau of the Census, *Historical Statistics of the United States, Colonial Times to 1957* (Washington: U.S. Government Printing Office, 1960), pp. 70, 710, 711, 736; U.S. Bureau of the Census, *Statistical Abstract of the United States: 1974* (Washington: U.S. Government Printing Office, 1972), pp. 235, 265, 315, 336.

* Includes civilian employees of the military equal to: 1950: 988,000; 1960: 1,032,000; 1970: 1,152,000; 1973: 1,026,000.
† World War I high in 1918 = 2,897,000.
‡ World War II high in 1945 = 12,123,000. Korean War high in 1952 = 3,636,000.
§ Vietnam War high in 1968 = 3,408,000.

spending and employment throughout the core. The very growth in corporate power and wealth, both in the United States and in other core societies, created pressures for a countervailing government force that has, by and large, limited the extent of corporate power. Most of this limitation has been achieved through regulations imposed by government and through the financial power of the government and its ability to control money supply, contracts, and even to some extent the direction of economic growth and private investment.

Aside from the specific ends intended, the creation of immense government bureaucracies has created centers of power partially independent of other forces in the society. For example, in recent years, civil service unions have developed at all levels, and they can both effectively push for their interests and limit the power of other groups. *A bureaucracy, merely by existing, develops interests directly related to the survival and prosperity of its members and independent of the original purpose for which the bureaucracy might have been created.* Government bureaucracies are not necessarily the allies of any class or interest group in the society at large.

The common tendency of bureaucracies to serve themselves before their intended clients has been known for a long time. Before World War I, Robert Michels, a socialist theorist, discussed it with respect to the bureaucratization of European socialist parties.[12] The fact that large bureaucracies tend in this direction adds a new element to class structures, since twentieth-century societies have become increasingly bureaucratic. The new bureaucratic class does not fit into the old typology of upper, middle and working classes; it forms a distinct group whose presence must be taken into account in contemporary social analysis. (The full impact of government growth, as well as the reasons for that growth, are of intrinsic interest, but better saved for another occasion; this discussion must continue to focus primarily on the consequences of that growth for the world system.)

As described earlier, increasing middle-class and working-class power make foreign adventurism less likely, since those who have to bear the primary burden of foreign wars are not likely to accept the price of entanglement very happily. The growth of a large federal bureaucracy, much of which is primarily involved in the conduct of foreign and military affairs, has had a very different impact on the international situation.

During World War II, a large armed force was drafted into service in the United States. Most of that army was quickly disbanded after the end of the war, and by 1947 the American military had shrunk to about one and one-half million men, where it remained until the start of the Korean War in 1950. From that time until the end of the Vietnam War, American military personnel included between 2.5 and 3.6 million. (Since the Vietnam War, the armed forces of the United States have shrunk to their smallest size since 1950.) Civilian employees of military agencies during all these years have numbered about one million. As the military and related institutions have become a major part of the government and of the society as a whole, the higher civilian employees of the defense establishment, plus the career officers in the military, have turned into an immense bureaucratic interest group, regardless of how well or how poorly they have accomplished their primary goal. Furthermore, that bureaucracy controls vast amounts of money—through most of the 1950s and 1960s, over half of the federal budget. (Recently, military expenditures have fallen to one-quarter of federal expenditures.) This money was used not only to pay soldiers and employees of the military but also to purchase vast amounts of equipment, to fund research, and to procure some of the most expensive and complicated machines produced by the economy. The private companies and the research institutes, both privately and publicly owned, that participated in these expenditures became, in effect, adjuncts to the military bureaucracy, or at least interested parties in promoting the bureaucratic health of the military.

The claim has been made that the corporate interests that have made large profits from military contracts are strong supporters of an active American role in the world system that ensures continuing high military spending. It has also been pointed out that the personal and financial ties between many high military officers, civilian employees of the military, and the main military contractors are close enough to suggest that there exists a "military-industrial complex" inexorably pushing for continuous foreign involvement in order to boost military spending. Some go so far as to claim that this complex is the main source of international tensions and war, and that it has become the dominant elite of the entire capitalist world system. The extreme Leninist variant of the position claims, of course, that without all this military spending the United States and subsequently the entire world capitalist economy would go bankrupt and break down through revolution.

It is quite true that the large defense contractors include many of the largest American corporations and that some large companies rely almost exclusively on military work for their business. There is no doubt that this combination of entrenched bureaucratic and corporate interest is one of the main forces active in making foreign policy.

So powerful is this combination of interests that disputes within the various branches of the military-industrial complex (air force versus navy versus army, as well as the competition between various corporate contractors) have an effect on certain policies. The sociologist and China specialist Franz Schurman (*The Logic of World Power*) has persuasively argued that internal conflicts within the armed forces, and between the State Department, the Presidency, and the armed forces played a predominant role in getting the United States involved in Vietnam in the 1950s and early 1960s. His argument is complex, and to summarize it does it an injustice. But the heart of the argument proposes that the basic reason for the first massive American intervention in Vietnam, planned in 1964 and executed in 1965, was the effect of bureaucratic pressures within the American government. Fights were going on between the civilian wing of the Pentagon, the branches of the armed forces, the CIA, and the State Department, and all sides were appealing to their supporters in the population at large in an effort to extend their influence. When a crisis arose over the imminent collapse of South Vietnam, a series of bureaucratic compromises were worked out that gave each of the participants a partial victory. The escalation was not something done by an "imperial presidency" but the result of confusion and Presidential weakness by Lyndon Johnson after John Kennedy's murder in 1963.[13]

The compromises produced a massive but poorly planned, poorly coordinated effort designed to minimize the government's internal rivalries. When the war began to be costly, public opinion, which is never properly informed about foreign events until a major crisis occurs, turned against the war, and the United States was forced out of Vietnam because it could not win there quickly and cheaply.[14]

The corporate interests allied with the military, the nation's ideologically committed anticommunists (a fairly small if vocal and influential group), and widespread acceptance of a Leninist view of the world in the bureaucratic and corporate elite all played a major role in getting the United States involved in Vietnam in the first place. But the decisive input, the actual planning, and the subsequent course of events were determined by the existence of a large, permanent, internally bickering military bureaucracy, and by the President's failure to control his bureaucracy. The war was therefore pursued far beyond the point of strict rationality. Profit motives, the potential for direct economic gain, were secondary from the start of this adventure and became irrelevant by 1965. Fundamentally, the top decision-makers were obliged to rely on the information given them by their various bureaucratic services, which invariably falsified their information in ways consistent with their bureaucratic interests. The President and his top aides received biased information and became arbitrators between the various bureaucratic interests within the nation's military and foreign policy establishments rather than independent decision-makers acting on the basis of accurate information or perception of the situation.

To be sure, pure bureaucratic infighting can never explain everything. The question remains: Why were such high and powerful military bureaucracies created in the first place? What economic interests were served by their creation? What purposes were they supposed to fulfill?—that is, before bureaucratic imperatives took over and displaced the original goals of the institution. These questions cannot be answered fully, but preceding paragraphs have already suggested a major part of the reply: namely, that after 1945 American policy-makers, corporate interests, and much of the general population accepted a basically Leninist view of the world system, and therefore feared any communist victories in the periphery; such victories would remove parts of the system from capitalist influence and put them to work helping the Soviet Union and China. This fear led to the creation of a large, permanent military bureaucracy. But after the main question, why?, is answered, the fact remains that once a large bureaucracy is established, it acts in part to advance its own interests, regardless of the original goals for which it was created. Much of what happened in Vietnam and much of what has happened in all American foreign policy in recent decades can be explained by this peculiar but universal tendency of bureaucratic organizations toward self-promotion.

Many of the domestic programs of the United States have been heavily shaped by similar, bureaucratic forces competing with each other for control of resources. The same, of course, has been true in all other heavily bureaucratized, that is, in virtually all modern, societies. It is particularly true in highly industrialized societies of the late twentieth century. All these have created vast bureaucratic machines to run their affairs.

The creation of a vast bureaucracy, then, has acted paradoxically in core societies, particularly the United States, to reduce the power of the small corporate elite which controls such a large portion of the economy. For while the bureaucracy may sometimes serve corporate interests, it always serves its own interests; and the two needs are not always identical. In almost every sphere of life (the Vietnam War is only one of dozens of important examples) bureaucracy has become a new, powerful force. Of course, massive bureaucratic failure, as in the case of Vietnam, unites many of the other forces in a society against the guilty bureaucracy. Such unification occurred in the United States after 1968, and its progress explains the considerable loss of power (both in terms of size and in terms of relative budget allocations) of the nation's military since then.

Where does this leave an evaluation of the power-elite theory of American society? In particular, where does it leave an explanation of the behavior of the United States in the contemporary world system? Several brief conclusions emerge.

First, a number of competing forces are effecting the policies of the United States. Corporate interests, various middle-class groups, segments of government bureaucracies, and the organized working class all compete for power. There is no single power elite, but rather a set of partially overlapping, and sometimes mutually hostile major forces is at work.

Second, between 1945 and the early 1970s, some (but not all) corporate interests and the military and foreign affairs bureaucracies determined American foreign policy. Their view of the world was basically one predicted by the Leninist theory of imperialism. They sought to expand their power and control over the world system—some because of the profits that could be obtained, others because that was the best way to expand their influence and command of resources within the United States itself. The ideology that came to predominate viewed the world in a Leninist way. Peripheral economies had to be kept open in order to perserve the strength of the United States. The semi-periphery was potentially very dangerous and had to be resisted. The Communist world was dangerous not only because it tended to support all anti-core activity, but also because, ultimately, it threatened to take over much of the periphery and use it to strengthen the communist centers of power. In the long run, this would weaken the United States and the capitalist core and would make the Soviet Union and China the world's great powers. In such a situation, according to those shaping American foreign policy, the United States would be cut off from vital markets, investment possibilities, and sources of raw materials; and capitalism would indeed collapse.

Third, while much of the middle class and the working class tended to remain inactive in shaping American foreign policy, these two segments of the population (comprising, after all, the vast majority, in fact, the entire population outside of the small number of elite persons controlling corporations and the key government bureaucracies) became more active whenever the costs of foreign policy began seriously to outweigh the potential rewards. Such a change occurred quite early in the United Kingdom, later in France, and only in the late 1960s and early 1970s in the United States. At that point, the elites controlling American foreign policy lost part of their control over the situation.

Fourth, all this has happened not only because of patterns of change within core societies but also because of changes in the periphery, which have created a strong revolutionary trend. Well-organized peripheral revolutionists can now fight quite successfully against the core, and thus make the cost of direct and indirect colonialism unbearably high. Furthermore, the support given by the Soviet Union and China to a number of critical peripheral revolutions has helped drive up the costs of core intervention.

In a real sense, the American world system and the entire capitalist world system has been in a state of decline since at least the early 1970s. Core societies have lost the will, if not yet the ability, to intervene with the impunity they once enjoyed. The rise in oil prices in 1973–1974 has been only one, if the most visible, immediate consequence of America's defeat in Vietnam. More serious consequences will follow.

That leaves a major question unanswered: What will be the outcome? If the Leninist view of the world has been correct all along, the decline of the core in the world will inevitably produce economic decline. The whole social and political structure of the core will crack. Before that final crack up, however, one may expect to see a set of political reactions quite similar to those that occurred in Germany and Japan in the 1930s, when threatened capitalist societies turned to virulent fascism in order to salvage their positions. According to believers in the Leninist theory, such desperate change is the coming trend among contemporary core societies as well.

Throughout this book, however, considerable skepticism has been indicated about the validity of the Leninist theory, even though the book acknowledges that the world has behaved as if the theory were correct. If in fact the core derives only small advantage from its control of the periphery, then the coming loss of control over the periphery need involve only a small reduction in economic growth rates, minor disruptions, and eventual adjustment to the changing world system.

The matter cannot be allowed to rest there. The "Thomas Theorem" (if people define situations as real, they are real in their consequences), is correct, but it is not sufficient. Ultimately, if mistaken perception were the only cause of core, particularly American, imperialist behavior, the problem could be solved through a careful open debate on the nature of reality in world affairs. But real interests are at stake, not simply imaginary ones. Certain groups—the military and foreign affairs bureaucracies, that part of the industrial complex which services military needs, and some corporations that control important investments outside the core—perceive their interests correctly when they urge intervention against revolutions in the periphery and new semi-periphery. Whether or not these groups serve the entire national interest is another matter. The nature of organized groups is that they promote their interests and confound their desire with the interests of the society at large.

If the "Thomas Theorem" has any validity, it is not because the theorem says that all groups have misunderstood reality. Rather, the theorem suggests that the most interested groups, those with the strongest interests in preserving core imperialism, have falsely convinced electorates that they are serving the entire national interest. Bitter wars can change this perception of reality by driving up the costs of intervention. But the way in which the foreign policy debate in the United States, and throughout the core in general, will be resolved remains uncertain.

Over the last thirty years or so, the capitalist core has experienced a kind of peak in its power and prosperity, even as it has gradually begun losing control over much of the periphery. High standards of living have permitted rapid extension of benefits to previously disfavored portions of the society. To a certain extent, the amazing proliferation of demanding groups within core societies (women's groups, culturally defined minorities, consumer groups, and a host of less valid pressure groups) has come about because of the recent historically unique burst of prosperity. These groups have produced much of the drama of political competition within the very rich core in the 1970s. *But their survival depends on the Leninist theory of imperialism being false; for if the theory is correct, the coming crisis will make core societies both unable and unwilling to continue to hand out benefits to all those who claim them.* In a situation of great wealth, it is easier to give in to pressure groups, even small ones, than to repress them. In a situation of long-term decline, conciliation becomes too costly, and protest produces repression rather than new benefits. The direction of social change in the wealthy core now depends on the future direction of the world system and on the not yet fully answered question about the validity of the Leninist theory.

Only one thing is certain. Core democracies, including the United States, are sufficiently bureaucratized, and economic power is sufficiently concentrated, that any massive crisis could lead quickly to the assumption of power by a small elite. A frightened middle class could conceivably concur if the crisis were severe enough. This, of course, is exactly what happened in Germany in the 1930s. It is this kind of thinking, and an awareness of the political fragility of the capitalist world system which led Samuel Huntington to say in 1967:

> This is preliminary to saying that in the year 2000 the American world system that has been developed during the last twenty years will be in a state of disintegration and decay. Just as American influence has replaced European influence during the current period, so also during the last quarter of this century American power will begin to wane, and other countries will move in to fill the gap. . . . Unlike the end of European empire which was relatively peaceful, the decline of American influence will involve numerous struggles because the relationship between the rising powers and the U.S. will be much less close (in terms of values and culture) than was the relation between the U.S. and the European powers. . . . The struggles accompanying the disintegration of the American world order will have profoundly stimulating effects on political development in the participating states. These struggles are, indeed, likely to play a major role in generating national cohesion and institutional development. At the same time, the decline of American influence will tend to undermine and disrupt American politics. The American political system could be less likely than that of the Fourth Republic [of France, which collapsed in 1958 as a result of the war in Algeria] to adjust successfully to the loss of empire.[15]

This gloomy or cheerful prediction (depending on which side one happens to be) leads directly to a discussion of internal stratification and power within the rising new semi-periphery which is challenging the American world order.

Class and Power in the New Semi-periphery

Achieving balanced industrialization, strengthening the nation-state, raising the skills of the population, and generally disciplining a society while having it make these efforts are not easy tasks. Westerners tend to forget the extent of poverty, human displacement, and popular resistance to change that occurred in their own past. The major core societies experienced prolonged periods of internal struggle, violence, and external war before they reached the high levels of affluence that now characterize them.

In some ways the process should be easier today because technology is so much more advanced, and because it can be imported quickly. But the process is also more difficult than ever because the world system is different from what it was in the past. The core has an immense economic-technological advantage over the non-core, and it continues to progress so rapidly that the non-core barely has time to assimilate certain technologies before these are replaced by newer ones. In a relatively free world market, no economy can compete successfully with the core in many of the key areas of production, particularly those that require a high technological input.

A list of items produced almost entirely by core economies (and to a certain extent by the more advanced communist economies) would be lengthy. It would include not only complex machines—airplanes, computers, nuclear power plants, large earthmoving machinery, automobiles, telephone systems, and so on—but also many drugs, tools, and instruments, as well as many luxury items consumed by elites throughout the world. These, and many more goods, are produced almost entirely in the core (although some are assembled in satellite plants of multinationals outside the core). Even many key agricultural products are now produced so much more efficiently in the core (wheat, soybeans, meat) that the world is becoming dependent on the core for survival. To be sure, non-core economies have an advantage in the production of labor-intensive products, that is, products that require relatively simple technologies and cheap labor (for example, many types of textiles); but these products are not in the forefront of technological advances, and specializing in them restricts an economy's ability to absorb higher technologies. Only the Soviet Union and some of the European communist economies can compete with the core in some, but hardly all of high technology products. Finally, advanced military machinery is produced almost exclusively in the core or in the major communist economies; the non-core remains a heavy buyer of their expensive hardware of destruction.

The issue of closure

It may not be correct to say that the core needs to exploit a periphery in order to maintain its technological advantage, although as discussed, such exploitation may help keep the core ahead of the non-core. The internal cultures of the core, particularly its highly skilled levels, probably surpass peripheral exploitation in maintaining the core's overwhelming advantage. The competition from the core is so overwhelmingly strong that today's semi-peripheral economies are as likely as ever to remain technologically dependent if they remain open to core imports. The argument is an old one, and despite many attacks made against it by classical economists, it still seems to hold. Except for a few odd cases, in the early stages of industrialization, it is better for an economy to close itself off from the world system in order to nurture its infant industries. Otherwise, dependency promotes unbalanced economic growth and detrimental social effects.

Borrowing technology can be useful, but it is often better for an economy to build a relatively inefficient plant than simply to purchase one. Adapting local technologies may be more productive than importing overly sophisticated machines. Local effort begins the whole process of internally generated technological advance, which may be stifled by reliance on core imports. The ideal, in a sense, is to follow the example set by Japan in the late nineteenth and early twentieth centuries, when an industrializing Japan bought foreign technology but controlled its use for domestic purposes, kept out foreign finished products, and developed a strong industrial base on its own. Nor is the problem purely economic; social structures outside the core worsen the problem of technological inferiority.

Consider, for example, military rule, which is very common outside the core. The reason for this is readily apparent. Relatively weak nation-states with small middle classes and weakly developed internal markets are not cohesive. In a semi-peripheral society that is trying to increase cohesion, only state bureaucracies have the strength and machinery necessary for maintaining and furthering unity. Military officials in particular have the capacity to impose order, not only because they have the weapons but also because they are often among those best acquainted with Western technology. The military in the semi-periphery tend to be among the most nationalistic of groups precisely because they have been exposed to core ideas and influences. So, in case after case, as political regimes have fallen to pieces trying to pursue the twin goals of greater national cohesion and balanced economic growth, the military have taken over. But once they are in control, they must maintain control. In effect, this means using the state's resources to buy some of the complicated and expensive military hardware produced in the core (or, in some cases, in the Soviet Union). Such resources might, perhaps, be better used to develop domestic industry, but the transition from importing military hardware to producing your own is long and complicated. In the interim, the military would be weak and liable to expulsion. Thus, in many cases, imports remain important, and in effect, resources are wasted. This is even more the case today than it was when Japan first developed its military industries. If military, particularly naval, technology in the West was expensive and advanced in 1900, it is much more complicated and advanced today. In fact, four countries make almost all the world's expensive military hardware today, the United States, the Soviet Union, France, and the United Kingdom. Other core economies and, to a limited extent, China, also make some military hardware; but throughout most of the old periphery, to have such weapons means to import them and thus to reduce native resources for investment.

Consider another example, the elites in the new semi-periphery that become consumers of luxury goods produced primarily in the core. State bureaucrats in high positions, both military and civilian, and the small middle class in these societies use automobiles, telephones, televisions, watches, even some foods produced in the core, to say nothing of such seeming trivialities as drinks, tampons, and tissues. Closure would involve the loss of many of these products, or at the very least, the substitution of inferior domestic varieties. Yet, to import these products takes resources away from domestic investment. If there is anything that capitalism has succeeded in doing it is to produce thousands of goods that cater to human desires, and elites throughout the semi-periphery are loathe to give up use of such products. Still, by using them, they keep their economies dependent, technologically inferior, and deprived of investment funds.

There is another disadvantage to remaining open. The world of today, unlike the world of the past, is one in which means of communication are so good that large numbers of people throughout the world are quite aware of the wealth of the core. They are, moreover, also aware of the fact that their own elites live well and with the help of core imports. They learn this not only by seeing foreign movies or hearing radio programs but, as uprooted peasants, by moving to cities where they can observe firsthand the meaning of a high standard of living. People in poor societies are thus less likely to tolerate poverty than they have been in the past. The more open a society to outside cultural influence, the higher the likely level of internal discontent among those who do not enjoy the benefits of core imports.

Rising demand for these products can have two obstructive consequences. First, it can produce political discontent, and thus, frequently, violent protest. Second, it can put pressure on the government to expand benefits given to the population. But if such benefits are handed out too quickly, too widely, they only result in too much importation of core luxury, and therefore in a further drain on resources. A vicious circle can develop, one that leads to economic stagnation and eventual collapse. It is exactly this sort of pattern that seems to have occurred in the most prosperous (or formerly most prosperous) parts of Latin America, that is, in Argentina, Chile, and

Uruguay. Handing out too many benefits to the population, and relying too heavily on core imports to satisfy demands, bankrupted these semi-peripheral economies without creating the solid industrial infrastructures that might maintain higher domestic standards of living.

The general label given this explanation in favor of closure is "the theory of *relative deprivation.*" Basic to the theory is the notion that the expectations of individuals are regulated by what they think is obtainable. The poor who know nothing but poverty are less discontented than those who see much wealth. One of the most destructive aspects of cultural imperialism in the world today is the degree to which the capitalist core has unwittingly advertised its wealth and aroused expectations outside the core that cannot be met. Closed communist societies have more or less successfully combated rising expectations by prohibiting or at least closely controlling cultural imports from the core.

The matter is not simply culture. The larger and more cohesive a class, the more strongly it will push its demands. In semi-peripheral societies and the most developed peripheral ones, middle-class and working-class organization is more advanced than it is in the poorest parts of the periphery. Higher demands imply more imports from the core, because local industries cannot satisfy a high level of consumption. Imports can be paid for only by exporting primary goods, and this further retards balanced industrialization. Labor unions in such countries as Argentina have become so powerful that national imports have run out of control, and balanced economic growth will require severe repression of working-class organizations. In other words, the richer a peripheral or semi-peripheral society, the more political repression it requires to make continued progress.

Closure, however, has its own problems. Foreign investment dries up, imports vanish, and for some key sectors of the population, the standard of living falls. This is, of course, true for the old colonial elites, for the controllers of the land, and for the comprador capitalists. But even after these groups have been politically and economically destroyed by a more nationalistic new middle class composed largely of state bureaucrats and entrepreneurs protected by the state, the problem remains: the members of the new group also come to value the imports that maintain their life style. Closure thus involves a struggle not only against old colonial elites but often against the very classes who have replaced them. Insofar as large portions of the population use some core products, or work for foreign investors, or produce export goods, their standards of living is also threatened. This means that while discontent runs high in an open semi-peripheral economy, it also runs high in a newly closed one.

The only solution is the imposition of tight controls and political repression. The middle classes that resist closure must be fought, but the general population must also be kept in line during the period of industrialization. Wages must be kept low in order to accumulate the surplus that must be invested in economic construction (in part to replace outside investment, in part to generate larger, more diversified investment).

Gunnar Myrdal has suggested that the key difference between poor societies today is not a matter of "left" or "right" but of "hard" and "soft." He writes:

> The term "soft state" is understood to comprise all the various types of social indiscipline which manifest themselves by: deficiencies in legislation and in particular law observance and enforcement, a wide-spread disobedience by public officials on various levels to rules and directives handed down to them, and often, their collusion with powerful groups of persons whose conduct they should regulate. Within the concept of the soft state belongs also corruption. . . . The laxity and arbitrariness in a national community that can be characterized as a soft state can be, and are, *exploited for personal gain by people who have economic, social, and political power.* While the opportunities for large-scale exploitation opened up by the soft state are, of course, only at the disposal of the upper class, even persons quite low on the social ladder often find such opportunities for petty gain. But even aside from those personal interests, *there will in a soft state be a much wider spread, in all strata, of a general inclination of people to resist public controls and their implementation.* [Myrdal's emphasis][16]

But if "left" means "closed" and "right" means open, "hard" and "soft" are part of the same concept. An open society finds it much harder, if not impossible, to root out the laxity and corruption which come from being open. Foreign investors and governments bribe officials, foreign goods seduce the population and spark a race for their acquisition, and foreign cultural influences increase demand for imports and for unattainable luxury. Closure, as important for cultural reasons as it is for economic reasons, is also important politically in that it makes it difficult for foreign bribery and economic seduction to split the elite and divide a polity struggling to advance itself. The recent disclosures of bribery throughout the world by multi-national corporations have revealed only the tip of the iceberg of international corruption.

Not all closed economies manage to impose the cultural and political discipline that creates a hard state. But if closure is seldom sufficient, it is a necessary condition of hardness. This fact is sadly acknowledged by Myrdal who found that in all of Southeast Asia (including India and Pakistan) there was, in the 1960s, only one hard state, North Vietnam.

Hard closed societies are characterized not only by internal discipline and self-reliance but also by an ideology that may be called a form of nationalistic puritanism. Self-denial is extolled in order to encourage investment and to postpone luxury today for the benefit of future generations. To make poverty more bearable for the masses and to keep the state bureaucracy from being corrupted, egalitarianism is much more rigidly enforced than it is in open societies. The closed society is held together in part by fiercely nationalistic appeals, generally directed against an outside world accused of threatening internal development. The ideological form that best exemplifies the puritanical nationalism is one usually known as communism, specifically the kind of communism that was practiced in the Soviet Union in the 1930s and 1940s, and which is practiced today in China, North Korea, Vietnam, and Cambodia (though Japan also went through a period of puritanical nationalism without being communist). It may not be too clear what this ideology has to do with Marx (since he never foresaw that his main success would be in the poor parts of the world), but it is very clear why it has such appeal among intellectuals throughout the semi-periphery and why it seems to succeed so well in organizing people to resist core influence and to develop their own societies. The price paid is high; but the price of inaction, in terms of persisting poverty and dependence, is often higher in the long run.

The conditions and price of open development

Does this mean that only communist (or closed and hard, or puritanical nationalist) societies can escape poverty? Does it mean that the open and soft societies inevitably become poorer? Rigorous ideologues of the left argue affirmatively, but in reality the answers are more complicated. First, virtually all the semi-periphery is more closed and harder than the old periphery used to be. The difference may be only a matter of degree rather than dramatic, but it is real. The most successful noncommunist semi-peripheral societies have all experienced partial revolutions that have put foreign investment in their economies under much tighter domestic control, and they have all established repressive state machines designed to keep consumption lower than it would otherwise be. What is different is the extent of closure and hardness, and the degree to which it is applied to some rather than to all classes.

Mexico is a good case in point because it has had a major political revolution, a period of ideological self-reliance and nationalism, and because the country has made attempts to spread the benefits of economic growth to much of the population. Mexico is also a good example because, close to the United States, it has been an attractive place in which to invest. Today it is a relatively open and soft society. Open economies that have no exploitable resources or no cheap but relatively skilled labor force have no chance to develop at all. But societies that do offer good investment opportunities and which also manage to exercise some control over how these investments are placed do not thereby become poorer. They experience economic growth. That growth, however, is limited by the disadvantages discussed earlier. It does not decrease inequality, but increases it, and it keeps that growth slower than in the core. It is possible, within limits, to remain open and to prosper, but the combination does not remove many of the old problems of peripherality.

One can see the extent to which this is the case in Mexico. In 1910 Mexico had a population of about 15 million of which, according to Wilkie's calculations, 57 percent were poor. Wilkie's definition includes a combination of illiteracy, inability to speak Spanish, going barefoot, living in a small community, not having sewage disposal, and eating only tortillas with no wheat supplement.[17] Although any one of these indicators can be variously interpreted, together they are a fair reflection of poverty defined by Mexican standards. By 1960, some fifty years after the start of the Revolution, there were about 35 million people in Mexico, and the number below the poverty level had decreased to 33 percent (though one must remember that many of those above this level remained very poor according to core standards). The two richest regions in 1910 (those with the least poverty) not only remained the richest in 1960 but extended their superiority over the poorer regions; thus, on a regional basis, inequality grew markedly in the intervening fifty years.

Whereas the two poorest regions in Mexico had only about three times as many poor people as the richest region in 1910, by 1960 they had about five times as many poor people. Every region except the North (the region closest to the United States and, except for the capital itself, the one receiving the largest amounts of domestic aid and foreign investment) lost ground economically relative to the capital. This regional decline has been accompanied by increased migration out of the poorest regions into the richest, particularly into the capital (see Tables 44 and 45.)

What has happened, naturally, is that the two richest regions have attracted the most migrants. But the migrants who move into the wealthier areas, even if many of them escape the absolute poverty level they experienced in their native villages, remain very poor and, by the standards of the advanced industrial societies, miserable.[18] While these regional statistics do not prove that economic inequality has increased at the individual level, they correlate with other knowledge about Mexico that supports this contention.

In another major Latin American country, economic inequality

TABLE 44
Regional Poverty in Mexico, 1910 and 1960

	Percentage of population poor		Percentage of decrease in poverty°	Ratio of percentage of poor in area†	
	1910	1960		1910	1960
North	47	21	−55%	2.35	2.33
West	57	32	−44%	2.85	3.55
West Central	56	37	−34%	2.80	4.11
East Central	62	45	−27%	3.10	5.00
South	68	51	−25%	3.40	5.67
Gulf	59	35	−41%	2.95	3.89
Federal District (Mexico City Area)	20	9	−55%	1.00	1.00
Total Mexico	57	33	−42%	2.85	3.56

source James W. Wilkie, *The Mexican Revolution: Federal Expenditure and Social Change Since 1910* (Berkeley: University of California Press, 1970), pp. 236–237.

° Percentage of decrease = [(percentage in 1960 ÷ percentage in 1910) − 100 percent]
† As compared to Mexico City's poverty rate (Mexico City = 1.00)

TABLE 45
Percentage Division of the Mexico Population by Region, 1910 and 1960

	1910	1960	Absolute change in percentage (1960% − 1910%)
North	11	16	+5%
West	16	14	−2%
West Central	21	17	−4%
East Central	22	16	−6%
South	14	12	−2%
Gulf	12	12	0
Federal District	5	14	+9%

source James W. Wilkie, *The Mexican Revolution: Federal Expenditure and Social Change Since 1910* (Berkeley: University of California Press, 1970), p. 241.

also seems to be high and probably growing, even in the midst of economic growth. In Brazil in 1965 the top 1 percent of the population received 19 percent of all income (as large a percentage as came to the top 5 percent of the population in the United States), and the top 10 percent of the population received 42 percent of all income (a bit more, relatively, than the top 20 percent of the population in the United States). Since 1965 Brazil has experienced a significant economic boom, but the most eminent expert on the Brazilian economy, Celso Furtado, is convinced that inequality has grown significantly, though it was already very great in 1965.[19]

Gunnar Myrdal, writing about South Asia (other than Vietnam), notes that economic inequality there is not decreasing, but in all likelihood, increasing. Much of the problem exists among migrants who have fled the poorest regions for the cities, where they wind up inhabiting shanty towns and living miserable existences. He observes:

> The underclass in the cities may easily become the majority in most cities in underdeveloped countries. Even in the cities the overwhelming problems will be that labor becomes increasingly superfluous and goes to waste, with mass poverty as a result.[20]

The problems of economic inequality and mass poverty do not vanish as economic growth takes place. On the contrary, they become relatively more severe, at least in the open or even partially open economies in the new semi-periphery. Since the level of discontent among the poor increases in open societies exposed to core standards of living, the political consequences of these problems are potentially explosive.

What is happening within societies is analogous to what is happening in the world system as a whole. Earlier chapters noted that while former peripheral economies seem to be experiencing rapid economic growth on a per capita basis, they not only remain very poor, on the whole, but also fail to catch up to the core. *Resentment, envy, and political frustration increase as economic inequality becomes more visible; this is true both within poor societies and within the world as a whole.*

Even Mexico, a relatively successful semi-peripheral economy, is a good example. Because it had an early partial revolution, because it is also an attractive site for core, particularly North American, investment, and also because it is a large and basically well endowed country, Mexico has done rather well over the last half century. Its GNP per capita grew by 188 percent (in constant 1965 U.S. dollars) between 1910 and 1960. But during this time, the per capita GNP of the United States also grew. In percentage terms, Mexico's grew a bit faster than that of the United States (though more slowly than the per capita GNP's of most other core societies). In this respect, Mexico has been one of the fortunate few of the old periphery. Yet in 1910 the per capita GNP of the United States was only about $1200 higher than that of Mexico, while in 1960 it was more than $3000 higher. (See GNP figures and growth rates in previous chapters.) Even if one allows for the fact that Mexico has had one of the higher growth rates among the poor parts of the world in this century, and that the United States has had one of the slower growth rates among the rich parts of the world, one is still forced to conclude that it will take thousands of years for Mexico to catch up to the United States (though to extend trend lines of this century forward for such long periods is quite pointless).

Does this mean that Mexico, and by analogy, all the open semi-periphery, has failed? Yes and no. Class structure in Mexico has changed quite drastically since 1910. Using the definitions of class adopted in Chapter III, one finds that Mexico's middle class has grown significantly, thus providing at least one anchor of greater stability. The old elite, the big land companies, and the major hacienda owners, no longer play a major role, and the managerial and professional new upper middle class has grown from 1.5 percent to 6.5 percent of the population. The lower middle class and working class have also grown, but by 1960 the proportion of agriculturalists had fallen from 70 to 59 percent of the population.[21] Change has indeed occurred since 1910. There is much new industry, the population is far more literate, and the state is much stronger; the general course of the nation has hardly been one of stagnation or regression. But along with these advances there seems to be increasing economic inequality and a large new class of urban poor; neither in terms of wealth per person nor in terms of its overall class structure has Mexico even come close to reaching the level of development of the United States in 1910. In other words, by 1960, Mexico had not only failed to catch up to the United States of 1960, but it had not even caught up to the United States of 1910.

It is, naturally, inappropriate to compare the Mexico of 1960 to the United States of 1910; the difference is far more than a matter of wealth. The very social and economic structure of Mexico in 1960 or for that matter in the late 1970s does not resemble that of the United States in 1910. Far from being an independent, advanced society at the very center of world technological change and progress, Mexico remains somewhat peripheral, even if it is less peripheral than it was at the start of the century. Position in the world system is an important aspect of domestic change, and the fact that Mexico remains open has proved to be a mixed blessing.

Does this, therefore, mean that Mexico is about to have another, this time more thorough, revolution? Not in the short run, since the bureaucratic and business elite that has gradually taken over the developmental process in Mexico is not only larger but much better equipped to control the country than the elite of 1910. The new elite is nationalistic. From time to time, it exercises its nationalism by making international gestures that displease the United States. It has promoted much greater cultural cohesion than existed in 1910, is more carefully attuned to the desires of the Mexican people than the small enclave elite of 1910, and is also much better armed, both in terms of weapons and in terms of administrative state machinery. This "successful" semi-peripheral, open society has achieved a relatively high degree of political stability (punctuated by fairly frequent and bloody protests). In the long run, the inequality and urban poverty, as well as the failure to catch up to the neighboring United States, will exacerbate problems and create new political instability. For the time being, Mexico does not threaten core interests except in occasional symbolic ways. In the future, that is likely to change.

Again, while Mexico is a major case in point, similar statements might be made about almost all the relatively open members of the new semi-periphery. These societies are no longer outright colonies of the core, but they are not fully freed of dependency; their continuing ties promote inequality, "softness," and ultimately, a high potential for a new round of revolutions. Turkey could have been used as an example instead of Mexico. Egypt, Indonesia, India, Nigeria, Pakistan, or Brazil would also make good examples. All these countries are potential major economic and political powers (at least, all have sufficiently large populations, adequate resources, and a high enough percentage of educated, technologically competent people to be powerful). But all of them suffer many of the same problems as Mexico, and most of them suffer these problems to a much greater degree. Even some of the newly-rich oil states, such as Venezuela and Iran, are also faced with these problems. Both these societies are trying to industrialize rapidly, but they are also becoming more inexorably bound to the core-dominated world economy, more dependent on imports, and more dependent on the export of one, ultimately nonrenewable resources. Only the creation of a technologically advanced, highly diversified, and competitive (on the world level) economy will enable them to escape dependency, But to achieve such an economy while remaining open may simply not be possible. As economic growth occurs without the resolution of domestic economic problems, long-term pressures for revolutionary action (conversion to hard closed states) increases among the leftist intellectuals and the growing urban poor.

In a sense, an open strategy can work only if two conditions are met. A society's population must already be quite advanced (and thus provide many skilled workers), and the investment climate must be very good (good enough to encourage core investments in a wide array of enterprises). To the extent that these conditions are not met, low wages can make up some of the deficiencies; this alternative remains the hope of such avowedly open semi-peripheral societies as Brazil. It is a strategy that worked for Puerto Rico (which is, however, small and the recipient, on a per capita basis, of very substantial aid and investment from the United States), and it works quite well in societies that have almost reached core levels of development (for example, Ireland, Spain, and Italy, at least northern if not southern Italy). That an open strategy worked so very well for Canada and Australia reflects the fact that they were resource-rich and had highly skilled populations even while they were economically peripheral: strict suppression of working-class demands was not necessary. But let the levels of skills be too low, or opportunities for investment be reduced, or wages rise uncontrollably, and the strategy fails. In Mexico, partial success has been offset by partial failure. In India, Egypt, Indonesia, or Nigeria, the likelihood of any success at all, if an open strategy is followed, remains dismally small. The total number of non-core societies capable of following an open strategy and succeeding is not only small but shrinking because the overpopulation problem now threatens to engulf many poor societies.

The Problem of Overpopulation

Non-European societies in the second half of the twentieth century face a major problem never experienced by the core societies or even by the European communist societies—overpopulation. This problem is the direct result of their absorption into the capitalist world system as peripheral societies and is linked to the process of economic growth and partial modernization in the absence of balanced development. Relative overpopulation has been a problem in many societies, but at no time before the contemporary period has it reached such severe levels.

The nature of the problem can be unambiguously represented by basic demographic statistics, and the explanations are fairly clear, though the possible solutions are much debated.

One reason the death rate is as low as it is in poor countries is that very large portions of the population are young. In Africa and tropical Latin America 44 percent of the population is under 15 years old; among Asians that age group represents 38 percent. In Europe, the United States, and Japan, only about 25 percent of the population is under 15.[22] Since young people have lower death rates than old people, the death rates of poor countries seem low. This youthful age

TABLE 46
Rates of Population Growth in the Mid–1970s

	Crude birth rates (per 1000 inhabitants per year)	Crude death rates	Annual rate of natural increase	Years needed to double population at rate of growth
World	33	13	2.0%	35
Africa	46	19	2.7%	26
Asia (except Japan)	38	14	2.4%	29
Latin America (tropical)	38	8	3.0%	23
United States	15	9	0.6%	117
Japan	19	7	1.2%	58
Europe	16	11	0.5%	140
Soviet Union	18	8	1.0%	70
Canada, Australia, New Zealand, Argentina, Chile, and Uruguay	22	8	1.4%	50

SOURCE Ronald Freedman and Bernard Berelson, "The Human Population," in
Scientific American, *The Human Population* (San Francisco: W. H. Freeman
and Co., 1974), p. 11.

structure will persist if birth rates remain high, but even if they begin to decline it ensures that a large supply of potential childbearers
will already be on hand to perpetuate rapid population growth for a
period of a generation. Not even a sharp decline in fertility could
halt the population explosion in poor societies in the near future (although in the longer run it would slow growth), and these societies
can be expected to double their populations before the end of the
century. In contrast, fertility in all industrialized societies has fallen
quite sharply in the last ten years; and it is likely that, for these populations, the estimated time of doubling calculated from crude rates is
too low. In other words the population totals of industrialized societies
are rising more slowly than seems apparent from crude birth and
death rates, and those of poor societies are rising at least as fast as
seems apparent from these measures.

Population growth has already had severe negative repercussions
in the most overpopulated poor societies, among them India and Bang-

ladesh. In all poor societies, it is a severe barrier to economic growth since much of any increased economic power must be used to feed the growing population. Given the absolute economic growth rates experienced by the new semi-periphery since 1950, there would have been much more substantial per capita gains had population growth been limited to the levels that predominate in industrial societies. In some of the poorest societies, not only the ones mentioned above but many of the very poorest cases in Africa (particularly the belt of countries just south of the Sahara Desert), the potential for catastrophic famine is very high. Local famines have already occurred, and only gifts of food from the industrial world (primarily the United States) have prevented worse ones. The continuing growth of population makes it unlikely, however, that the United States and the rest of the industrial world can long maintain the ability to provide helpful amounts of food.

The basic causes of rapid population increase in the West in the nineteenth century and in the peripheral parts of the world in the twentieth have already been discussed here (see primarily Chapter V). Since 1950 the population problem has become more serious. Transportation has improved in this period (allowing food to be more easily transported to areas that have temporary shortages), and medicine and hygiene have vastly improved in poor parts of the world, but human fertility has not declined, and population growth accelerates at a geometric rate. Where population doubles every quarter century, it increases 16 times each century ($2 \times 2 \times 2 \times 2$).

From the standpoint of technology, the outlook is not as bleak as it may seem. The productivity of agriculture outside the core remains much lower than agricultural productivity within the core, and could be improved substantially. Not only fertilizer (which may come to be in short supply) but increased irrigation and more rational use of land could improve fod production and diminish the probability of famine. In fact, agricultural technology has improved in many former peripheral societies.[23] On the population side, effective methods of birth control exist, and if applied thoroughly, could cause rapid decreases in fertility. Even if population continued to grow over the next quarter to half century (because of the abundance of young females reaching puberty), reduced fertility would eventually result, as it nearly has in many core societies, in slow, or even zero population growth.

The problem is not that the world has insufficient space or insufficient technological knowledge. Overpopulation continues to plague certain parts of the world because of the uneven distribution of space and technology in the world, and because of the social structure of many poor societies. *As long as better distribution of income does not occur, poor peasants have neither the incentive nor the capacity to invest in improved technology. As long as radical transfor-*

TABLE 47
Population Growth and Urbanization, 1950–1975

	Population in millions			Urban percentage		
	1950	1975†	Percentage of growth	1950	1975†	Percentage of growth*
World	2486	4147	67	28.6	39.3	37.4
Africa	217	420	94	13.2	24.5	85.6
Egypt	20.5	37.2	81	21.4	49.9	133.2
Asia	1355	2407	78	?	?	?
India	435 {	636.2 } 787.4	81	17.0	21.5	26.5
Pakistan		71.6		15.4	26.9	74.7
Bangladesh		79.6		4.2	6.8	61.9
Indonesia	76.5	137.9	80	11.8	19.3	63.6
Latin America	162	328	102	40.9	60.4	47.7
Mexico	26.3	59.3	125	42.1	63.2	50.1
Brazil	52	113.8	119	35.4	59.5	68.1
United States	151.3	219.7	45	63.5	76.3	19.4
Soviet Union	180	254.3	41	54.8	67.2	22.6
Europe	392	474	21	39.4	60.5	53.6

SOURCE For 1950 populations: United Nations, *Demographic Yearbook: 1970* (New York: Statistical Office of the U.N., 1971), pp. 105, 126–132. For 1975 populations and for urbanization 1950–1975: The Environmental Fund, "World Population 1975." Their estimates are from projections in U.N., *Demographic Yearbook: 1973*, Table 4. These estimates and those for 1950 vary slightly from some others given in this book; this is because of variation in estimation procedures from source to source, and also because various estimates are from different parts of the same years.

* Percentage growth = [(percentage in 1975 ÷ percentage in 1950) − 100 percent]
† All figures are mid-year estimates for 1975.

mation of the economy does not occur, the social transformations that lead to declines in fertility cannot occur.[24]

This last point is very important. In the advanced industrial societies, increased education, increased wealth, growing participation by males and females in the nonagricultural sector of the economy all combined to lower fertility, even before the advent of advanced methods of mechanical birth control. Individuals in a modern society *want* to have fewer children because children increase the expenses of their parents without bringing them significant economic help. Once children become adults, they leave the family home. Having many children lowers the living standard of parents in advanced societies. In poor rural economies, as discussed in former chapters, children have always been regarded as potential or contributing laborers; and the expenses of schooling and taking care of them until they become adults are offset by their economic contributions to the family. Moreover, in poor societies, there are no social security schemes, no pensions, no welfare programs, and children are the only insurance that exists for old age. It is thus necessary and quite rational for parents in such societies to desire large families.[25]

One of the factors that has decreased fertility quite rapidly in both core and European communist societies has been increased participation by women in the wage-earning labor force. Employment opportunities outside the home are an incentive to women to limit births. The larger the percentage of women who work at home, the greater the birth rate (other things being equal): it is easier for such women to take care of a child, and pregnancy does not cost them lost earning capacity.

Actually, declines in fertility have begun in many poor societies; but largely among the urban (and still small) middle classes. For many of the urban poor, family size is still based on expectations brought from the rural villages. Too often, having extra children is viewed as a source of eventual income; and large families remain important as old-age insurance. Also, even among the urban sector of the population, relatively few women are in the wage-earning labor force of most poor societies.

One key problem of most new semi-peripheral societies, as well as of the remaining peripheral ones, is that urban employment is not growing rapidly. Population is exploding, but job opportunities are growing much more slowly. This lag not only prevents the spread of greater prosperity among the population; it also keeps women out of the wage-earning labor force; and it slows the spread of education, economic security, and the accompanying attitudes that cause individuals to want fewer children. The more difficult it is to find jobs for the growing population, the more slowly will the population problem be solved. The more severe the population problem, the longer it will take to find the necessary number of new jobs. This vicious circle is very closely tied to the failure of poor economies to diversify and promote balanced industrial growth.

In a real sense, the improvements in industrial technology in the core have contributed to this problem. When semi-peripheral societies import machinery for factories, they tend to import machines designed to save as much labor as possible. In core societies, labor is expensive; in poor countries it is cheap and abundant. The more advanced the world system, the less useful are imports of machinery into poor economies from rich ones. Whereas early industrial Europe had labor-intensive factories, contemporary core economies have capital- and technology-intensive factories. Yet, establishing labor-intensive factories is not a perfect solution for semi-peripheral societies either, since this would put them at a long-range disadvantage relative to core economies. The very act of remaining open multiplies all the development problems of semi-peripheral economies, and makes the problems of economic inequality, population growth, unemployment, and technological inferiority more severe.

Balanced economic growth in the new semi-periphery would create more new jobs, stimulate agricultural production (by better rewarding producers of food), involve more women in the labor force and thereby reduce fertility, and provide the surplus necessary in establishing social insurance schemes that allow individuals to worry less about their security in old age or periods of illness. *The population problems of poor societies are intimately tied to all their other problems, and it is reasonable to conclude that the solutions will come as a package rather than as a series of partial solutions, none of which can succeed alone.*

Rapid industrialization has caused birth rates to drop fairly quickly wherever it has occurred. The semi-peripheral societies of the early twentieth century had birth rates much higher than those of the core; but as these areas have industrialized, their birth rates have fallen to core levels, or even below in some cases. For example, at the start of the century, Russia's birth rate was on the order of 45 per thousand inhabitants per year, and it remained high through the 1920s. In the 1930s the Russian yearly birth rate began to fall below 40 per thousand, and after World War II it fell quickly to its present level of about 18 per thousand. Japan's birth rate, also very high in the early part of the century, had fallen to about 29 per thousand per year in 1940, and is now about 19 per thousand per year. Even those societies that began to industrialize later than the old core have experienced rapid demographic change from high to low birth rates.[26]

Most of the decreases in birth rates that have occurred in the past have not been helped by planned, government-sponsored birth-control programs. On the contrary, they occurred spontaneously as people's wishes with respect to family size changed. In recent years, however, a number of states have pushed population control programs. *Where these programs have been accompanied by fairly rapid social and economic change, they seem to have had some success.*

Taiwan and South Korea, both recipients of large amounts of American aid and investment, as well as of Japanese investment, have consequently experienced significant industrialization and economic growth. These two economies, with Hong Kong and Singapore, are the outstanding examples of economies industrialized as adjuncts to core needs. Some observers therefore consider progress in these economies fragile, since they are neither sufficiently diversified nor sufficiently independent to withstand the shocks that might occur if demand for their products drops. While rapid transformation has occurred in these economies, the fact that they received such large amounts of aid and investment per capita from abroad makes it unlikely that larger societies can hope to follow this route. *But in any case, rapid change has occurred; and birth rates have fallen.*[27]

Another, in a sense, more surprising case, has been China. There, tight social and political discipline, and mobilization of the entire population in order to carry out economically beneficial "investment" activities and in order to enforce government plans have also brought birth rates down. After years of hesitation the Chinese Communist Party finally decided that rapid population growth would hinder rather than help development, and a campaign was begun to lower birth rates. One of the most effective techniques has been to discourage young men and women from marrying early, while also enforcing rather puritanical sexual behavior among the young. This, combined with the spread of contraception, gradual industrialization, mobilization of the female as well as the male labor force, and spread of social insurance benefits (thus lessening the need for children as insurance) have all combined to bring a recent but dramatic drop in the birth rate.[28]

When China is compared to other societies in Asia that are at the same low level of economic wealth, the contrast is startling. India, which has had a substantial government-sponsored birth-control program for some time, seems to have had almost no success in lowering birth rates. Of course, India has not been able, either, to discipline its population, to initiate the beginnings of rapid per capita economic growth, to equalize its distribution of wealth, or to stop major epidemics and periodic outbreaks of famine. China, in the late 1940s at an even more catastrophically low point in terms of mass poverty, has made more rapid progress than India in all aspects of development. In other words, if development is to be swift, a whole package of social, economic, and in most cases, political transformations must accompany a solution to the population problem.

While industrializing the West could tolerate a slow, spontaneous drop in fertility, since it was never faced with serious overpopulation. Most of Europe in the nineteenth century could export whatever surplus population it produced to America, and of course, huge Russia and the United States never had much problem with overcrowding. The situation is quite different in societies developing today. Those societies with rapid population growth have no outlet to which they can ship their surplus people, and many of them are already dangerously overcrowded. Waiting for the eventual, slow decline in fertility that will occur as they become more prosperous (if they become more prosperous quickly enough) will not do. Too many resources are used simply to feed the growing population; too few are left for economic advance. This makes balanced economic growth in today's poor societies difficult, and ultimately it increases the pressure for drastic domestic action. Since the South Korean or Taiwanese path to change seems neither possible nor attractive to most new semi-peripheral societies (it involves being small and remaining a permanent client of a core state), China's success in solving its population problem will have a strong ideological impact throughout the semi-periphery.

Strangely, for some states, the day of awareness has not yet come. Because Western countries, particularly the United States, have been pushing for birth-control programs throughout the poor parts of the world for the last two decades, many of the committed nationalists in the semi-periphery and even in the remaining periphery have decided that the only reason for American concern is fear, and that the predominantly white core is afraid that the black, brown, and yellow non-core will grow too quickly. Whatever conscious or unconscious fears motivate the American effort to promote birth-control programs, the fact that such programs have been tainted, ideologically, by imperialism has hurt them. Some of the semi-peripheral states, for example, Brazil, have actively promoted high birth rates in the mistaken belief that this will produce greater economic growth and greater national strength. Similar ideas about population prevail within much of Africa.

Ultimately, all poor societies that have not experienced substantial transformation will wind up with very severe overpopulation. A government's attitude toward the population problem is less important than the efficacy of its general development program. Since, in most cases, successful development involves the creation of a closed, hard state, it is this achievement, rather than the number of contraceptives handed out, that is most critical in determining a society's future.

Most demographers believe that rapid population growth will produce an inevitable catastrophe by the end of this century. Not only does absolute overcrowding threaten many societies, but beyond a certain point, the resources necessary for the improvement of standards of living do not exist. If most of Asia, Latin America, and Africa had a standard of living as high as those of Europe, North America, the Soviet Union, and Japan, world demand for energy and resources would far exceed supply. If, as seems correct, birth rates will drop only when the standard of living increases, and if the standard of living cannot increase because of a shortage of resources and energy, the only possible outcome is, indeed, catastrophe. Fed by years of resentment against core imperialism, the social and political tensions produced by this catastrophe will produce virulently anti-core activity and demands for help. Wars will erupt outside the core, and the new semi-periphery, armed with advanced weapons, perhaps even nuclear bombs, will try to force the old core to sacrifice its high standard of living for the benefit of the overcrowded poor societies. This stress will increase the pressure within the core for militarization, and will raise international conflict to very high levels.

A Further Note on Democracy

In the early part of the twentieth century, most core societies were either political democracies, or well on the way toward becoming so. Relatively free elections decided who would occupy many of the most powerful positions in government. In the late twentieth century, democracy is more extensive within core societies than ever before. A larger portion of adults are allowed to vote (most importantly, women now vote but could not before 1914), elected officials hold more power than ever, and since the number of core states has grown somewhat, the number of political democracies has also grown. But outside the core, democracy is a rarity. Within the core, democratic regimes are effective and generally stable (with a few exceptions), but where some form of political democracy exists outside the core, it is neither effective nor solidly rooted. After World War II, the American victory democratized the major fascist states, Germany, Italy, and Japan. Outside the core, American power and influence has not had the same effect.

In a number of former peripheral societies types of democratic political systems have been tried. On the whole, they have not worked for the same reasons that made democratic regimes a failure in the old, pre–World War I semi-periphery. The pressures on government, both domestic and international, are too intense, and the class structure and low degree of national solidarity within semi-peripheral societies make democracy an unlikely form of government. Where some form of democracy has survived, at least in formal terms, it has not been a healthy sign at all, but rather, the consequence of softness and inability to mobilize society in order to carry out improvements.

A hard state cannot be a democratic state, and while many soft states are not particularly democratic either, Westerners have often mistaken political laxity, corruption, administrative incompetence, and deep internal political divisions within a society for democracy. In such cases as Lebanon (at least until 1976), or India (at least until 1975), formally democratic but also deeply corrupt regimes reflected a balance of forces that paralyzed the state and prevented action toward reform rather than reflecting the strength of democratic institutions.

There are many reasons for the absence or failure of democratic government in today's new semi-periphery. First, whereas historically modernization in the core was promoted and led by an independent capitalist middle class which fought against the old aristocracy as well as against the restrictive power of the state, modernization in the twentieth century in the semi-periphery is promoted and led by bureaucratic elites within governments. Rather than being a decentralized, economically independent set of actors joining together for political ends (the situation of nineteenth-century core capitalist classes), today's leaders in the semi-periphery operate out of centralized, hierarchical organizations. This is true of civilian as well as of military elites, although it is particularly evident in the case of the military.[29]

Second, the cultural diversity in many new semi-peripheral societies means that substantial portions of the population still do not accept the legitimacy of the state. This not only opens states to meddling in their affairs from the outside, it makes their very survival problematic. If free elections were held today in many African or Asian states, there would be instant secession as some regions would vote to leave the state. Such a vote is exactly what provoked the Pakistani civil war that led to Bangladeshi independence. Although it would have happened sooner or later in any case, the precipitating event was the election of 1970 in which East Pakistan (Bengal) overwhelmingly voted for a secessionist party. This was the first free election in many years in Pakistan, and is likely to be the last for a long time to come.

Relatively democratic India managed to hold itself together until 1975, though it, too, frequently resorted to military force to prevent secession. But insofar as enforced integration did not occur, and certain regional minorities retained a large degree of self-rule, this maintenance of the status quo also blocked development of a strong nation-state and made it that much more difficult for India to solve some of its major economic problems. Since 1975, India has abandoned formal democracy and now conforms to the general pattern of the semi-periphery.

Third, the power of the core, both of core governments and of the large multi-national core businesses, is so great, and its ability to seduce, corrupt, or otherwise influence policy in weak states is so high, that only relatively autocratic governments can resist.

Fourth, the discontent prevalent in semi-peripheral societies makes democratic compromise unlikely. Peasants, urban poor, revolutionary students, comprador middle classes, remnants of the old controllers of the land, new bureaucratic middle classes, and the various culturally defined groups clamor for scarce resources and for control of the weak state. But there are few benefits to pass around, and the critical hardships that must be enforced in order to carry out closure, direct investment, and prevent excessive spread of resources into wasteful consumption cannot be made in the political flux of a democracy.

Again, India is an example of the phenomenon of "democratic paralysis." Because its anti-British revolution was less than thorough, much of the land remained in the hands of a relatively small number of prosperous peasants and small landowners who have consistently thwarted reform. The alliance between this rural elite and the business class in the cities has produced a conservative, immobile, incapable government. The survival of parliamentary democracy for so many years, until 1975, was neither beneficial to India nor, in the long run, destined to last, since it could not solve the problems left by the colonial legacy.[30]

A semi-peripheral state run on democratic principles is likely to meet failure since it will not be able to control foreign investors, keep the cost of consumption low enough to generate significant investment, or unite diverse cultural groups into a strong nation-state. Such relatively advanced and prosperous societies as Argentina, Chile, and Uruguay (all of which have had fairly long, ultimately disastrous experiences with democracy) are unfortunate proof of this contention.

Fifth, it follows from all this that the most likely form of effective government in the semi-periphery will be bureaucratic control, by civilians or by the military. Where lengthy revolutions against the core have taken place (as in China, Vietnam, Algeria, or more recently, Mozambique), the revolutionaries develop a tight organization capable of running a hard, closed state. Elsewhere, the process is more difficult though rarely more democratic. Where tight, ideologically united ruling bureaucracies have not come to power, government tends to be more lax, more corrupt, and less efficient, rather than genuinely more democratic.

Thus it appears that in order to escape their problems, semi-peripheral societies need to be closed, hard, and *frozen*. That is, internal politics must be controlled by a small, tight elite that freezes debate and imposes its will on the majority. The choice is not, in any case, between Western-style democracy and something else, but between Indian-style stagnation and effective change.

In many ways, this is unfortunate. Once a bureaucratic or military elite has seized power and consolidated it, it is loathe to give up the privilege of such power. In the Soviet Union the grip of the Communist party is as tight as ever, and the prospects for democratization are slim, even though after sixty years of Communist rule the country could well afford considerable internal relaxation. In Japan, only the defeat in World War II brought about democracy. It is quite likely that successful ruling groups throughout today's semi-periphery will resist democratization, even at some future time when politics can be safely unfrozen. Bureaucratic machines created to promote progress will not dissolve themselves once the original goal has been reached.

It would therefore be prudent for Westerners to get used to the idea that "democracy" as they know it will not spread. It may be a pleasant luxury created by a set of unique historical circumstances that will not be repeated.

Democracy in the core, however, will not necessarily persist either. As noted above, democracy persists because of the balance of forces in core societies. There is no doubt that this balance and its resultant democracy make life easier and more pleasant for most people in core societies. But if, as seems likely, the core continues to lose control over its old periphery, and if many people in core societies, particularly in the large middle classes, begin to perceive this as a mortal threat to their prosperity, change in the core could occur quite quickly. This, of course, is what the Leninist prediction is about. But rather than having working-class revolutions, core societies put in desperate circumstances would, more likely, hand power over to the large government bureaucracies and to the dominant corporate elites that already control such a large part of the economy. It was exactly this kind of alliance of the middle class, the corporate elite, and the bureaucracy that produced fascism in Germany in the 1930s. One may hope that the Leninist prediction will turn out to be wrong and that the loss of control over peripheral areas will not produce panic. The last quarter of the century will tell.

A Communist World System?

*M*any of the international problems of the capitalist world system in the latter part of the twentieth century are exacerbated, and even partly caused, by the presence of strong societies explicitly hostile to world capitalism. The preconditions for peripheral revolutions were created by capitalist exploitation and by the patterns of colonial development, but peripheral revolutions have a much better chance of success when they can count on support from certain great powers in struggling against others. This support the Soviet Union, and, to a lesser extent, China, have been willing to provide. Despite the great advances in revolutionary organization in the periphery, Soviet aid has been a key ingredient of several successful revolutions. This has been particularly evident in the recent histories of Vietnam (during the war against the United States) and of Cuba (in maintaining a revolutionary regime in power during the 1960s in opposition to the United States). In many other cases, for example, the anti-Portuguese wars in Africa, Soviet support has also been important. If nothing else, the threat of possible Soviet intervention restricts the amount of force the United States has felt itself able to use in such areas as the Middle East and southern Africa.

The destabilizing effect of communist (particularly Soviet) power, however, should not be exaggerated. The conditions for revolution within the periphery would have been strong in any case; and had there been no strong communist power, it is conceivable that the capitalist core would have been far less united than has been the case. Conflict between core powers, or between core and semi-peripheral powers, can also create opportunities for peripheral revolutionary movements. This was amply demonstrated during World War I and World War II when the various sides encouraged and aided peripheral revolutionaries to advance their own cause. Arab nationalism was given a boost during World War I by the British in their fight against the Ottoman Empire, then an ally of the Germans. Indian nationalism was indirectly helped by Britain's weakness during World War II, and Indonesian nationalist movements gained power with Japanese help during the same war. Even the Vietnamese Communist movement received some support from the United States during World War II because it promised to fight against the Japanese. In other words, any conflict or merely intense rivalry among great powers leaves maneuvering space for peripheral revolutionary movements.

But the presence of several communist societies has had more of an effect than this. It has also provided an ideological model for revolution which has become even more widespread than direct Soviet or Chinese power.

In view of the importance of communist societies as a source of international and domestic change in much of the world, two series of questions arise. First, has there emerged in the late twentieth century a communist world system? Are there connections and exchanges between communist societies such that an alternative world system exists, or are communist societies merely a series of successful semi-peripheral, development-oriented societies, societies that may one day rejoin the capitalist world system, as did Japan after its prolonged transforming experience? Are communist societies, if they form a system at all, themselves divided into core, semi-periphery, and periphery? Does the Soviet Union (the core) seek to exploit a communist periphery (Eastern Europe and Cuba), while a communist semi-periphery (China) seeks to replace the Soviet Union as the core communist power? (This is not an idle question since it reflects exactly what the government of China has been claiming for the last fifteen to twenty years.) Or do such relationships not arise in communist economic relations? Or, perhaps, has the Soviet Union already made an attempt to create a communist world system and failed? In short, do big communist states tend toward imperialist behavior, as do capitalist states?

A second series of questions, related to the preceding one, is: what has been the pattern of domestic social and economic change in communist societies? In what respects has communist development succeeded or failed? What explains the great ideological influence of communist societies in the former peripheral world, and even among certain groups within the capitalist core? Or these questions might be phrased more succinctly as: How is it that a semi-peripheral society, Russia, and a divided, chaotic, peripheral one, China, transformed themselves between 1910 and 1970 into the second and third most powerful states in the world (in the late 1970s, some would say, the first and third most powerful states in the world)?

The Absence of an International Communist System

An answer to this question might well begin with a list of all the communist societies in the world, the dates on which they became communist, and their recent populations.[1]

TABLE 48
Communist Societies

Country	Date of communist regime	Process by which communist regime took power	Population in 1975 (in millions)
Soviet Union	1917	Revolution	254.3
Mongolia	1924	Revolution with Soviet aid	1.4
Yugoslavia	1945	Revolution (broke away from Soviet alliance in 1948)	21.3
Albania	1945	Revolution with Yugoslav aid (broke away from Yugoslavia in 1948 and from the Soviet Union in 1960)	2.5
Poland			34
German Democratic Republic (East Germany)			16.8
Czechoslovakia	1945–1948	Occupation by Soviet Army	14.8
Hungary			10.4
Romania			21.2
Bulgaria			8.7
North Korea	1945	Occupation by Soviet Army	15.9
China	1949	Revolution	942
North Vietnam	1954	Revolution	24.5
Cuba	1959	Revolution	9.2
South Vietnam	1975	Revolution and North Vietnamese military action (joined with North in 1976)	19.9
Laos	1975	Revolution and North Vietnamese military action	3.3
Cambodia (Khmer Republic)	1975	Revolution with Vietnamese aid	8
Total Population in 1975		(34% of world population)	1,408.2

Many former peripheral societies have adopted a formally socialist mode of government patterned, in part, on a communist model and have become close allies of the Soviet Union or China. But it is premature to call them communist since, as the experiences of Egypt and Indonesia demonstrate, a tendency in this direction can be abruptly reversed by counterrevolutions (peaceful in Egypt and very violent in Indonesia) which can bring societies back into the capitalist orbit. In the late 1970s, a list of "partially communist" societies strongly sympathetic to the model of communist development would include Syria, Iraq, South Yemen, Somalia, Congo-Brazzaville, Guinea, Equatorial Guinea, Guinea-Bissau, Mozambique, and Angola. In some respects, Algeria and Libya are tending in that direction as well; Chile was also until the Allende government was brutally overthrown by the military. Various other countries might be mentioned, but all of them, including the short list above, are dubious cases so far. Proclamation of socialist ideals and voting with the Soviet Union in the United Nations are not sufficient grounds for labeling a state "communist," or even part of the world communist movement. Rather, communism implies certain immense social transformations, which have not been accomplished, or even attempted on a massive scale, in any except the seventeen societies listed in Table 48. Counterrevolutions that might turn any of these societies into noncommunist societies are extremely unlikely in the foreseeable future.

Does the existence of a substantial number of powerful communist societies mean that there is a united international communist political system? In the late 1970s the only certain allies of the Soviet Union (and that in large part because of the presence of Soviet troops within their borders) are the East European communist states, minus Albania, Yugoslavia, and Romania. Mongolia and Cuba are also firm Soviet allies, the latter entirely by choice rather than because of Soviet military pressure. Yugoslavia is neutral in the capitalist-communist conflict, and Romania tends toward neutrality. Albania is hostile to the Soviet Union but allied to China. China, of course, has been openly hostile to the Soviet Union since the early 1960s. The various Asian communist states are either neutral in the Sino-Soviet hostility (like North Korea), relatively pro-Soviet (Vietnam), or pro-Chinese (Cambodia). But all these patterns of political alliance could shift quickly, and even the pro-Soviet European communist states are only precariously loyal. In other words, in international politics there does not exist a communist world system, at least not a unified one. Even if China and the Soviet Union cease to be as hostile to each other as they have been in the recent past, a firm alliance between them, at least in the immediate future, seems unlikely. By comparison, the core capitalist states are far more united.

In terms of economic exchanges, the communist world system is also a myth. COMECON, the communist version of the European Common Market, has been a failure. Its East European members have directed an increasing, and critical portion of their trade away from the Soviet Union, and were it not for direct Soviet pressure (based, ultimately, on military rather than economic power) all the East European economies would be more highly integrated with Western European economies than with the Soviet economy. West Germany has played a particularly important, growing role in commercial and financial exchanges with Eastern Europe, and the Yugoslav economy is almost a part of the Common Market's economy. China, which is more self-sufficient than the small East European economies; nevertheless has a large and growing trade connection with capitalist Japan, its main trading partner. Even the Soviet Union has recently become a major trading partner of the capitalist world, particularly with respect to the purchase of grain and advanced technology.[2]

No pattern of classical core-peripheral exchanges has developed between various portions of the communist world. The Soviet Union does not rely on other communist economies for raw materials (rather, the other members of COMECON tend to purchase raw materials from the Soviet Union), and little specialization by society has occurred among communist economies. Evidently, in the late 1950s the Soviet Union attempted to impose such a pattern of specialization on its allies and to turn the weaker communist economies (that is, those that were still primarily agrarian) into raw material and agricultural exporters. The attempt failed when it provoked strong Chinese and Romanian hostility.[3]

The absence of an international communist political or economic system does not, however, mean that communist societies are integrated parts of the capitalist world system either (except for Yugoslavia). The two largest communist powers, the Soviet Union and China, are so highly self-sufficient and so large by themselves that they constitute virtually autonomous systems of their own. The Asian communist societies are following almost classical programs of "closure" to the outside world in order to develop diversified domestic economies, as did the Soviet Union until very recently; and even in Eastern Europe, as long as the Soviet Union remains the dominant military and ideological force, full reintegration into the capitalist world system will not occur. Although they deal with the capitalist world, the Soviet Union and China continue to be ideologically hostile to that world and to expect its ultimate demise. If no unified communist international system exists, this does not lessen the long-range revolutionary threat to the capitalist system posed by communist powers. Nor does it decrease the probability that an increasing number of former peripheral societies will take the communist path to development and closure from the capitalist world system.

Despite the great progress of most advanced communist economies, their standards of living remain lower than those in core capitalist economies; and the communist societies seem incapable of building mass-consumption economies that can cater to as many economic desires as the capitalist economies. For this reason Westerners find it difficult to understand why the communist model of development should seem so appealing to intellectuals and revolutionaries in former peripheral societies. The answer, actually, is not hard to find. *Communist development means elimination of core influence, eradication of the "enclave classes" that benefited from colonial relationships,*

*an end to humiliating dependency on the core, an end to gross in-
equality, and a chance to create balanced economic development.* For
those who do not think it possible to attain these goals within the
context of a capitalist world system, the example of the Soviet Union
and China have obvious appeal. Moreover the Soviet Union, and to a
lesser extent, China, have been willing to extend aid and protection to
those trying to develop in this way, and this help has reduced the disadvantages of breaking away from the capitalist network. In the perspective of a peripheral society, the Soviet Union and China look like
magnificent successes. There has not emerged a "world communist
system," ready to absorb new revolutionary societies into an integrated
fold. But as long as the main goal of revolutionaries in former peripheral societies is closure to capitalist influence, the presence of a complete new alternative system is not necessary.

This does not answer the question of whether or not communist
societies have imperialist tendencies. Evidently, in pure economic
terms, the Soviet Union does not have such tendencies in the same
sense as capitalist societies because it is so large, so resource rich, and
relatively poor in investment capital. China has even fewer such tendencies. But politically, the question cannot be answered so easily.
The following brief look at social change within communist societies,
particularly the Soviet Union and China, should not only help to
illuminate this particular question but also answer the second large
question raised at the start of this chapter; In what respect has communist development succeeded or failed, and in what direction will
Soviet and Chinese societies move in the near future?

Soviet Society and International Policy

As discussed in Chapter IV, during the 1930s the Soviet Union succeeded in closing itself from the world system, industrializing rapidly,
and creating a large modern army with which to fight World War II.
It emerged from the war as the second strongest power in the world,
though considerably weaker, and much poorer than the United States.
Stalinist terror was ended in the 1950s, but the basic system of Soviet
government has changed little since then. The Communist Party continues to repress dissent; and economic growth, concentrating on
heavy industrialization and armaments, has continued. The Soviet
standard of living is high compared to what it used to be, but remains
low compared to the capitalist core. Still, total Soviet economic
strength is enormous. This can be seen by comparing the Soviet
economy to the economy of the United States.

The Soviet Union has achieved enormous advances in the trans-

TABLE 49
American and Soviet Economic Statistics, 1975–1976

	United States	*Soviet Union*
Total GNP	$1,499 billion	$873 billion
Per capita GNP	$6800	$3400°
Steel production	117 million tons	155 million tons
Oil production	457 million tons	590 million tons
Coal production	693 million tons	771 million tons
Auto production	6.7 million	1.2 million
Average monthly wage	$820	$191°
Electrical-power production	1,903 billion kwh	1,038 billion kwh

SOURCE   Fay Willey, Alfred Friendly Jr., Lloyd H. Norman, Steven Shabad, "The Soviet Surge," *Newsweek* (March 1, 1976), p. 40.

° The Soviet per capita GNP in this estimate seems artificially high. Yet, comparing it to the GNP of the United States and comparing Soviet and American average wages reveals an interesting fact: a much lower percent of GNP goes to personal wages in the Soviet Union than in the United States. Correspondingly more of Soviet GNP goes as investment in heavy industry and military spending. This is confirmed by comparative military statistics. In almost every respect, the Soviet Union has a larger military machine than the United States.

formation of its class structure as well as in sheer economic production. In 1900 it was an overwhelmingly agrarian society (78 percent of the population was in agriculture); only 11 percent of the population was in the working class, and 8 percent of all inhabitants comprised the various middle and upper classes. By 1959 Soviet class structure had changed to the extent reflected in Table 50, and as Table 51 indicates, by 1968 it had evolved still further.

Applying the same categories used in discussing American class structure in the twentieth century to Soviet class structure is misleading in some respects. There is very little privately owned business in the Soviet Union, and what there is consists of very small operations; Soviet agriculture is also organized very differently from agriculture in capitalist societies. Yet analogies remain, although they would be denied by official Soviet social science. The functional requirements of modern industrial economies promote similarities across different political systems, and it is quite clear that Soviet class structure is moving in the direction of American class structure. Developments in the Soviet Union during the first half of the twentieth century show a change from a largely nonindustrial society with a typically "backward" pattern of stratification to an industrialized society with stratification patterns roughly equivalent to those in the United States in the early 1900s. Surprisingly, when all differences in political systems

TABLE 50
Class Structure of the Soviet Union, 1959

	People in the labor force	Percentage of total
Middle Class (professional, managerial, higher white collar)	12.2 million	12.8%
Lower Middle Class (sales and clerical)	6.2 million	6.5%
Working Class (blue collar)	38.7 million	40.5%
Collective Farmers	31.1 million	32.6%
State Farmers°	6.4 million	6.7%
Other Agriculture (mostly private)	900,000	0.9%
Total Labor Force	95.5 million†	100.0%

SOURCE   G. L. Smirnov, "The Rate of Growth of the Soviet Working Class and Changes in Its Composition with Respect to Occupation and Skill," and V. S. Semyonov, "Soviet Intellectuals and White-collar Workers," both in G. V. Osipov, ed., *Industry and Labour in the U.S.S.R.: Sociological Problems in the U.S.S.R.* (London: Tavistock Publications, 1971), pp. 26–27 and 132. Warren W. Eason, "Demography," in Ellen Mickiewicz, ed., *Handbook of Soviet Social Science Data* (New York: The Free Press, 1973), p. 55.

° Includes 500,000 "agrotechnicians," though some should be listed as "collective farmers." State farms are large, modern, and generally highly mechanized farms. Collective farms include the peasant class, and tend to be less efficient and less mechanized. On collectives, peasants also own small private plots which produce much of the Soviet Union's food. Whereas state farms are really "industrial" enterprises in agriculture, collectives are much like traditional peasant villages subjected to state control. Soviet statistics normally list state farmers as members of the working class, except for managers and technicians, who are listed in the "intelligentsia," or middle class.
† Does not include 3.6 million in the military.

and methods of organization are taken into account, the population percentages in each broad class for the Soviet Union in 1959 are remarkably similar to those in the United States in 1910. By 1968, this similarity was even more evident; and as more collective farmers and children of collective farmers leave the land to enter industry, Soviet class structure will increasingly come to resemble contemporary American class structure.

Aside from the political differences between the two societies, other obvious differences exist in stratification. The lower (clerical and sales) middle class is not being developed as quickly in the Soviet Union as it was in the United States, probably because the

TABLE 51

Class Structure of the Soviet Union, 1968

Middle Class	15%–16%*
Lower Middle Class	8%– 9%
Working Class	47.3%
Collective Farmers	22.3%
State Farmers†	6.7%

SOURCE   David Lane, *The End of Inequality? Stratification under State Socialism* (Harmondsworth: Penguin Books, 1971), pp. 56 and 121; V. S. Semyonov, "Soviet Intellectuals and White-collar Workers," in G. V. Osipov, ed., *Industry and Labour in the U.S.S.R.: Sociological Problems in the U.S.S.R.* (London: Tavistock Publications, 1971), p. 132; L. A. Gordon and E. V. Klopov, "Some Problems of the Social Structure of the Soviet Working Class," in Murray Yanowitch and Wesley A. Fisher, eds., *Social Stratification and Mobility in the U.S.S.R.* (White Plains: International Arts and Sciences Press, 1973), p. 28. (Some of Gordon and Klopov's figures have been adjusted to fit with the figures of Semyonov.)

* All the totals in this list include the military.
† Includes forestry workers and might better be labeled "rural working class and middle class."

Soviet system does not place a premium on services to individual consumers. It is also likely that because of the emphasis on heavy industrialization, the blue-collar working force of the Soviet Union will eventually become proportionately larger than its counterpart in the United States. Also the inefficiency of Soviet agriculture prevents a more rapid exodus from the countryside, and it will be a long time before the Soviet Union has as low a percentage of its labor force in agriculture as does the United States. Greater similarity is likely with respect to the managerial, professional, and supervisory white-collar class (called the "intelligentsia" by communist societies); the Soviet Union will probably duplicate the American population proportion in this category fairly soon. This class, both in the United States and in the Soviet Union (and in any industrial society), is the key source of economic leadership, and from its ranks come the members of the new elite of advanced societies.

   Distribution of wealth is much more equal in the Soviet Union than it is in the United States or other capitalist societies; private individuals in communist societies are not allowed to own the means of production. A few individuals, celebrated artists, writers, athletes, and the like, have accumulated small private fortunes, but there is no class of extremely wealthy capitalists. Probably income is also distributed much more equally than in the United States, but no reliable statistics on this point are available.

   Insofar as power and privilege are concerned, however, the

Soviet Union has a small elite class that is as favored as the elites in capitalist societies. Members of the Soviet bureaucratic elite live very well. Nice homes, special stores in which they can purchase goods not available to the general public, summer cottages, automobiles, special hospitals, restaurants, and special schools for their children are placed at their disposal. These gratuities are not formally "income"—they are not included in salary calculations; nor are they "wealth" in the capitalist sense of that term, since they end with an individual's official position in the society and cannot be inherited or sold. If one seeks an analogy with capitalist societies, it is probably correct to say that members of the Soviet elite have huge "expense accounts." Because they can send their children to favored schools, members of the elite can even pass on their "wealth" to some extent. But inheritance of these extras is not direct; the children of the elite have more opportunity to succeed, but they are not guaranteed success. In many ways, their position is similar to that of many upper-middle-class children in a capitalist society. Parents in the Soviet elite can afford the best schools for their children; but unlike the top capitalist elite, they cannot automatically pass on their material success to their young, only a better opportunity to succeed.[4]

Despite the comparative evenness of the Soviet distribution of wealth the material well-being of the upper-middle class is still much higher than that of the working or lower-middle class, and the collective farmers are worse off than any of those in these broad categories. Such gaps place immense pressure on children in the Soviet school system, for success in school is the key to entry into the middle class. Yet in the Soviet Union as in the capitalist world, the position of one's parents in the society has much influence on the probability of one's success in school. There is a strong tendency for the children of the "intelligentsia" to do better than others in school. Sociologist Martin Lipset has found this tendency to be even stronger in the Soviet Union than it is in the United States.[5]

The principle of communist social organization that makes for major differences between the class structures of the Soviet Union and the United States is that almost all high- or middle-level positions in this social organization are gained by success in the bureaucracy. Even the most important Soviet individual can lose everything material if he or she is demoted. The state and Communist Party bureaucracies are all-powerful. In the United States and other capitalist societies, bureaucracies are also important; and one might even argue that all large private enterprises work like big bureaucracies. *But in capitalist societies, there remain several different centers of power.* Big business, labor unions, government bureaucracies, and the general electorate each wield their own power, and new alliances are always forming within and between these power centers. *In the Soviet Union, there are virtually no "independent" sources of power outside the single state and Party hierarchies.* This means that it is much more difficult to organize a veto of state actions. Neither labor unions, private "wealth," nor the electorate have any independent power. Within the bureaucracy, various departments have disputes, and various political tendencies manifest themselves in struggles at the top. But outside the bureaucracy, there is no recourse; and few Soviet members of any class dare organize themeselves in the same way that American middle-class or lower-class political activists routinely organize themselves for political action.

By understanding that the Soviet Union is a much more heavily bureaucratized society than the United States, one is more able to understand some of the motives for Soviet behavior in international affairs as well as the continuing push of the Soviet Union toward heavy industrialization and world military supremacy.

It goes almost without saying that the Soviet elite believes in the Leninist view of the world, that it agrees that in the long run capitalism will fail as it loses control over the peripheral world. World war is not considered necessary to defeat capitalism. A strong military that can deter the United States from intervening with impunity against anti-core revolutions in the third world is sufficient to ensure the ultimate demise of capitalism. This has been Soviet policy at least since the middle fifties, when the Soviet Union realized it no longer needed to fear direct attack by the United States. Recently the policy has begun to yield impressive results, first in Southeast Asia and now in southern Africa.

Success toward the ultimate goal, a communist world system to replace the capitalist world system, is one of the two fundamental legitimatizing principles of the Soviet state. The other is to have the Soviet Union "catch up" to the richer capitalist core. But whereas the goal of catching up, in terms of material welfare, remains elusive, the goal of destroying the perceived base of the capitalist world system is beginning to seem much more realistic; and much of the energy of the Soviet Union is now devoted to this goal. Internal bureaucratic imperatives demand some visible form of success, and in the bargaining for resources that goes on within the Soviet bureaucracy, those branches that favor an increased military and heavy industrial strength (which are closely related) have a strong card to play. They can claim, and seem to have claimed successfully, that in the long run, if they get the resources they want, they will bring about the ultimate goal of the communist system. Some Western observers keep on hoping that in their drive to improve their standard of living, the Soviets will abandon foreign adventures; but this is a false hope. The Soviet Union will continue to make certain that its standard of living increases quickly enough to prevent massive social discontent (which, however, can be controlled rather easily by the police), but catching up will always be a secondary goal.

In other words, the Soviet Union has a "military-industrial complex" that is even more strongly entrenched than its equivalent in the United States. As mentioned earlier, at least some portion of American adventurism in foreign affairs has been promoted by the bureaucratic interests of such a "complex" rather than by a national profit motive. The Soviet military-industrial complex has far fewer domestic constraints on it than its American equivalent. For this reason, it holds much more power than its counterpart in determining foreign and domestic policies.

A great many conclusions follow from this supposition. As long as the Soviet Union remains so heavily bureaucratized, and a relatively small bureaucratic elite, imbued with a Leninist world view and measuring success in international terms, retains control, the prospects for democratization of the nation are slim. Furthermore, the large and growing middle class in the Soviet Union has no independent sources of power, unlike similar classes in capitalist societies. Despite its privileges and size, the Soviet middle class remains part of the bureaucracy and is unable, even unwilling, to act independently. If the middle class were frustrated in its desires for improved material rewards, a potential for protest might exist. But in fact the Soviet middle class is materially pampered, and while it has few political liberties, still benefits from the system. It is unlikely, therefore, to become a major source of opposition to that system.

All this makes it easier to understand why the Soviet model seems so appealing to former peripheral societies. These societies also have a desire to "catch up" to the core, and they, too, hold an anticore ideology based on the last century of Western domination. As in the Soviet Union, the classes in the former periphery that are pushing hardest for progress, in order to catch up, are state bureaucrats and intellectuals. Societies in much of the old peripheral world have weak capitalist middle classes and see bureaucratic control as the only method of success. The Soviet Union consequently holds more of an appeal than Western societies. Even in former peripheral societies where there is a significant capitalist middle class (such as Brazil or South Korea), state protection of business is critical; and the government is much stronger than any aggregation of independent capitalists. Intellectuals in these societies, who associate capitalist development with colonialism, core domination, and inequality, tend to idealize socialist (that is, bureaucratic, state controlled) regimes and to see in them hope both for personal advancement and for ultimate national success against the core. So, for them, too, the Soviet example of development looks more promising than the capitalist Western example. The long and short of it is that Marxist ideology has become the dominant ideology of intellectuals, and increasingly, of bureaucrats in the former peripheral world, even if it has not yet triumphed everywhere.

Once a communist system has been established in a society, the effective bureaucratization of that society, combined with accelerated economic and social change, make a return to another system unlikely. Well-organized bureaucracies are hard to overthrow, and the onset of communist-inspired industrialization creates many new openings for intellectuals and newly-schooled children of former peasants and workers. Communist social change involves the creation of a large class that supports the regime, and the creation of organizations capable of maintaining control of society against opposition. Communism is not the "dictatorship of the proletariat"; it is the "dictatorship of the intelligentsia," or rather, a segment of the "intelligentsia" (the bureaucratic middle class).

The Eastern European communist societies, though smaller, are organized in much the same way as the Soviet Union. They have the same goals (to "catch up to the West") and are run by the same sorts of bureaucracies. To be sure, they constitute much less of a danger to the capitalist world system than does the Soviet Union, but only because they are smaller. Yet, because they have their own programs for development, they can even be anti-Soviet at times, especially when the Soviet Union demands too high a price in the anticapitalist struggle. But basically, excepting Yugoslavia, the communist societies of Eastern Europe have no international political significance apart from their relationship with the Soviet Union.

The Yugoslav "Model"

Because Yugoslavia is so different from other communist societies, it merits some further consideration here, if only a brief one. Since its break with the Soviet Union in 1948, Yugoslavia has evolved a much more open economy and a more democratic political system than the other communist societies. It had no choice, since after 1948 it was threatened by the Soviet Union and had to build domestic popular support in order to avoid Soviet subversion and possible invasion. But by becoming much more of an open economy, highly integrated with the Western European capitalist economies, Yugoslavia has reaped both benefits and severe problems. The Yugoslav regime is certainly more popular at home than other East European regimes, but any economy that is part of the capitalist world system cannot concentrate on heavy industrial development and forced national integration as thoroughly as can a closed economy. The requirements of the capitalist system have to be taken into account. This means emphasizing market rationality over political and social objectives. It also means opening the population to all the seductive influences of capitalist wealth. Consequently, while Yugoslavia has more consumer goods than other communist economies, it also has more problems with unemployment and greater internal inequality, both between classes and between regions; it remains the last society in Eastern Europe threatened by deep regional and ethnic divisions. Many Yugoslav workers have left the country to work in Western Europe, and in that respect, Yugoslavia remains, in part, a peripheral adjunct to Western economies, as do other capitalist societies in Southern Europe, such as Greece, Spain, and Portugal.

The fact that Yugoslavia continues to suffer from many of the problems typical of peripheral economies serves as a warning to bureaucratic elites in the rest of Eastern Europe. Romania, for example, which is relatively independent of the Soviet Union in international affairs, follows a strictly Soviet model of development, and fears the probable effects of becoming more open. Even if Soviet military power were weaker, the communist bureaucrats of Eastern Europe would no doubt remain loathe to copy the Yugoslav model. It is, however, an important example to them, for it emphasizes the dilemma of communist development: any communist society that becomes reintegrated into the capitalist system is threatened by renewed problems of peripherality; yet, closer ties with the West also promise access to more consumer goods, and in the short run, greater popular support. The leaders of the Soviet Union know this appeal well, and to prevent the emergence of more wayward regimes, they are willing to invade communist societies that stray too far from the accepted path. This explains their military intervention in Hungary in 1956 and in Czechoslovakia in 1968. Romania, despite its independent foreign policy, has not been invaded because, internally, it follows the Soviet model of development.[6]

Even within the Soviet Union the problem of seduction by capitalist economies remains serious. Greater integration with the capitalist world would raise the Soviet standard of living, but it would also weaken the hold of the political bureaucracy on the population and introduce the divisive influences to which relatively weak economies in the capitalist system are subject. In a multi-ethnic society like the Soviet Union, in which the government does not yet have a high degree of legitimacy among large segments of the population (particularly among European minorities in the Ukraine, the Caucasus, and the Baltic), opening the economy to Western influences could well produce the kind of internal tension now present in Yugoslavia. Since greater integration with capitalist economies requires that economic decisions be made on the basis of world market considerations, rather than on the basis of domestic political and social considerations, it is very unlikely that the Soviet elite will make the decision to rejoin the capitalist world system, if only out of a sense of self-preservation.

The real problem of reintegration into the caiptalist world system, combined with the prevalence of the Leninist world view within the Communist Party of the Soviet Union, and the stake that party has in seeing the demise of world capitalism, make any kind of permanent peace between the Soviet Union and the capitalist world system unlikely. Whereas some in the capitalist world hope that greater trade with the Soviet Union will ultimately return that country to the world system, much as Yugoslavia has returned to the fold, this is a most improbable prospect. Through trade and better economic relations the capitalist world can only expect to retain slight leverage over the Soviet Union; and only for a time. Such measures will not alter the basic policy of the Soviet bureaucracy.

China and Maoism

What then is one to make of China, which is an enemy of the Soviet Union in international relations and which is somewhat differently organized domestically? Unfortunately, much less is known about the workings of modern Chinese society and politics than is known about the domestic functioning of the Soviet Union. There are far fewer published data, and the Chinese revolutionary experience is more recent than that of its large communist neighbor. In recent years, China has been idealized to an extraordinary extent by Western leftist intellectuals seeking an alternative to the heavy-handed bureaucratization of the Soviet Union; and, this popular conception makes it all the more difficult to evaluate events objectively. China, unlike the Soviet Union, remains a poor, primarily agrarian society, and this too makes comparison difficult. Still, a try at analyzing the basis of Chinese society seems indicated here, as does an attempt to understand both why China has become so anti-Soviet and what its future in the world system is likely to be.

The Chinese communist revolution differed from the Russian communist revolution in one major respect. The Chinese revolutionary party gained control from the countryside rather than from the cities, and it contained an important peasant component. Even after their victory in 1949, the Chinese communists did not have the degree of centralized control that a communist revolution had established in Russia, primarily because they controlled China through local, rural organizations rather than through a few key urban nerve centers. The difference in the means to power of the two major communist regimes reflects historical differences between China and Russia. Whereas Russia had a centralized communications and industrial network in 1917, China in 1949 did not. Whereas in prerevolutionary Russia the state was already highly centralized, and there were no centers of local power, the exact opposite was true in prerevolutionary China.[7]

The presence of a strong peasant component among the Chinese communists spared postrevolutionary China such excesses as the purges of peasants that disrupted Soviet agriculture in the 1930s. The Russian Communist Party always viewed the peasants as a hostile group to be conquered and controlled for the benefit of the cities, but this was not the view of the new Chinese party. When in the 1950s it began a rapid program of heavy industrialization, based in part on Soviet aid, China seemed headed for the same kind of development the Soviet Union had experienced. It subsequently changed its course, however, and opted, instead, for more-balanced rural development and the simultaneous development of light industry and heavy industry. This policy fit the "peasant" interests of the Chinese Communist Party, but it also engendered severe internal disputes. In the late 1950s and early 1960s, when it became evident that the Soviet Union was interested in using China for its own purposes—that is, as a help to Soviet economic development and political aims—and not in sacrificing large amounts of aid for the sake of China, the "peasant," as opposed to the centralizing "heavy-industrialization" line gained supremacy in China. The Chinese disillusionment with the Soviet Union (because of insufficient aid), the fact that the Soviet Union relegated China to the status of a junior partner, and the Soviet distrust of developmental policies that did not stress heavy industrialization led to the Sino-Soviet split.

But an emphasis on decentralized development and a deemphasis of heavy industrialization also meant that China would be unable to tolerate prolonged war with the capitalist world. The preoccupation of Mao Tse-tung, the Chinese Communist leader, with preventing rigid bureaucratic control over China also implied a recognition that the Chinese would not launch the kind of full-scale mobilization necessary for war. Thus, the triumph of Mao over Liu Shao-ch'i (and his ally Teng Hsiao-p'ing) in 1966, at the start of the great Cultural Revolution, meant that China would not take an activist role in foreign affairs. It also meant, more importantly, that China would develop without creating a "dictatorship of the bureaucratic intelligentsia."[8]

Nineteen sixty-six was also the year in which the Chinese realized that going to the direct help of North Vietnam in its war with the United States would push them toward bureaucratization, alliance with the Soviet Union, and development along Soviet lines. Not only Mao but the Chinese Communist Party as a whole decided against direct intervention, and Vietnam was left to fight its own war with increasing Soviet help but only minimal Chinese help.[9] The Chinese decision, it should be emphasized, was based on the desire to create a more genuinely egalitarian, and in the long run, more humane society in China than existed in the Soviet Union. It also followed naturally from the rather different balance of forces within the Communist parties of the two countries.

Since 1966 it seems that the Maoist line has again been challenged, and is again being reaffirmed in the struggle against the same Teng Hsaio-p'ing who was discredited in 1966, but who briefly came back to power in 1975.

Chinese development has been extraordinary in many respects, not least of which has been the mobilization of the society toward raising the standard of living and preventing the recurrence of famine. China is slowly industrializing; but as long as the Maoist line holds, China will try to avoid giving full power to its state and political bureaucracy and will allow considerably more decentralization of power than other communist societies.

The dispute between the Soviet Union and China, therefore, is not simply one between the putative "core" and "semi-periphery" in the communist world system. Rather, the dispute is fundamentally about what kind of society communist revolutions should build. China does not present much of a military threat to the Soviet Union, but it does present a major ideological threat in that it questions the entire basis of Soviet social organization. The Chinese recognize that a heavily bureaucratized military-industrial society tends to become involved in the big power game, and that such a society thus tends toward imperialist political behavior. *If the basis of imperialist behavior is not merely the capitalist profit motive, but also the expansive tendencies of competing bureaucracies, then, if capitalism collapses, a new, possibly more dangerous form of communist imperialism (that is, Russian imperialism) may prevail.* However, if Chinese social organization were to be accepted by the revolutionary movements of the future, the Soviet Union would not be able to control world communism and become a nasty bureaucratic dictatorship surrounded by a world as hostile to it as the present capitalist world. If Soviet social organization comes to prevail, China's attempt to develop a better kind of society will fail; for bureaucratic forces within China will receive increasing help from the outside, and ultimately triumph. Westerners who analyze the Sino-Soviet dispute purely in terms of power within the communist system have failed to recognize that at stake in the dispute may be nothing less than the future of the world.

Will the Maoist line prevail in China in the long run? Not only Mao's death in 1976, but general social theory make it seem unlikely that Chinese society will escape the worldwide trend toward bureaucratization. It is probable that in the future China will turn into a copy of the Soviet Union. China will then, no doubt, establish better relations with the Soviet Union and begin to take a more active role in international politics. Such a unified challenge would present a severe danger to the capitalist world system, which is already struggling with other troubles. But the bureaucratization of China is not inevitable, and one can hope that it will not happen. Strangely, both from the perspective of "new left" radicals throughout the world (basically, those opposed to the bureaucratization of any society) and from the perspective of capitalist conservatives, the permanent victory in China of the Maoist "radical" line seems desirable. Perhaps this helps to explain to observers of world affairs the otherwise strange alliance that has prevailed for much of the 1970s between the conservative Republican Party of the United States and the radical Maoist Communist Party of China.

IX

The Future
and the Study of Social Change

T his review of social change in the context of a changing world system is now near an end. Many questions remain unanswered; some because no brief account can cover all important issues, and others because there are no known answers. But several important problems have been explored in sufficient detail to suggest some tentative conclusions.

The End of the Liberal Theory of Social Change

The liberal hope of the early 1960s that engendered the "Peace Corps" era has turned out to be a false hope. In retrospect, it was based on a poor reading of twentieth-century history and on a mistaken projection for the future. In 1966, historian Charles Wetzel wrote:

> The American experience has indeed created an American practical idealism which holds that all men can achieve dignity and freedom in a world laden with opportunity. If only, some have reasoned, others would duplicate our history. Perhaps they cannot, or do not wish to. But insofar as success in the style of the West or of the United States is possible elsewhere on the globe, Americans may especially qualify as its conveyers. Our Peace Corpsmen are not divided or conditioned to respond in terms of class distinctions. They are not impeded by the attitude that work is undignified. They are not discouraged by beliefs in closed societies where a recognition of limitations meliorates against an open universe or pragmatic choice, trial, and creation. . . . If, indeed, the will can triump over circumstances, and a classless world of hard-working, self-confident, harmonious brothers is possible, Americans may be able to point the way.[1]

Speaking of that period, the early Kennedy years, Franz Schurman has written:

> President John F. Kennedy came to power with a grand design to do what Roosevelt had dreamed of: spread a Pax Americana

over the entire world which would guarantee security from war, stability for all, and development for the poor. Kennedy's progressivism and his imperialism were inseparable. The progressivism which gave rise to the Peace Corps reawakened an American idealism. . . . The imperialism, however, was manifest in a kind of hard, unsentimental rationality common to those who regard power as a technical instrument for achieving goals superior to all other instruments in society.[2]

In the end, neither approach worked: neither American "idealism" nor American "imperialism," neither the Peace Corps nor the doctrine of limited war in defense of developing societies "threatened" by communism.

The reasons for this double failure are now evident. In a capitalist world system, the core and the periphery have contradictory interests. Peripheral development is not merely escape from "old-fashioned," traditional attitudes, but involves destroying the economic, political, and cultural monopoly of the core. The Peace Corps may have been created out of the best intentions, and some foreign aid programs may have been idealistically motivated, but in the end, revolutions in the periphery were perceived in the core as threats to the prevailing capitalist, that is, American, world system. Fighting communism came to mean fighting revolution in the periphery, and at that point, it came to mean rejection of the aspirations of nationalist reformers. Since American, French, and British public opinion could not tolerate drawn out, ultimately hopeless colonial wars, and since Soviet military power prevented unlimited military intervention in order to crush revolutionary movements, the Kennedy policy failed.

The liberal world analysis accepted by most Americans in the 1950s and 1960s has turned out to be a poor interpretation of historical events. The great nationalist uprisings that have occurred in the twentieth century have been aimed at accomplishing the very things the Peace Corps and at least some designers of American foreign aid claimed they were trying to do. But the means used by revolutionary nationalist movements have been very different from those envisioned by the proponents of liberal developmental policies. What was once thought to be a "temporary" disease of development, communism, has turned out to be one of the main strategies available to peripheral societies attempting to catch up to the core. There are other strategies, but closure from the capitalist world system, domestic repression in order to keep down consumption and waste, and forced investments in economic modernization have produced the desired result, economic development, in a number of important societies. The struggle by the core against what seemed to be a superficial disease has turned out to be a fight against the fundamental process of change. This fact is particularly evident in the American involvement and dramatic failure in Cuban and Vietnamese affairs in the 1960s and early 1970s. To a great extent, the same attitudes that then prompted the United States to involve itself against revolutionary movements persist in the way Americans view such movements today in Asia, Africa, and Latin America.

But would the "communization" of the third world be such a disaster? Since communist revolutions and the variety of third-world socialist revolutions turn out to be primarily nationalistic, it certainly seems unlikely that the revolutionary process will create an effective political and economic system united against the core, except in a purely formal, ideological sense. So far, not even the Soviet Union has succeeded in creating a communist world system.

Furthermore, "conservative" new semi-peripheral societies, such as Brazil, Iran, or Saudi Arabia, turn out to be dubious allies of the core, since their own plans for development are based on a challenge to core hegemony. In the 1970s, Iran, more than any other semi-peripheral society, has helped to organize an anti-core cartel of oil-producing states and has thereby threatened the core even more than the so-called radical states in the third world. Yet, Iran remains firmly anticommunist and ideologically more attuned to capitalism than to socialist modes of development. The experience of Japan also serves as an example. As long as it was a striving semi-peripheral society, Japan was a dangerous enemy of the old core, even though it was formally "capitalist." In other words, even promoting development of the Japanese type is no guarantee that the old core, particularly the United States, will remain unchallenged.

Development in the former periphery will challenge core hegemony to an ever greater degree. But does this fact necessarily threaten core prosperity? Is it correct that the core needs to exploit a periphery? This is the key question, and one this book has not yet answered. The evidence of previous centuries strongly suggests that in the early days of the capitalist world system, colonial exploitation was a vital ingredient of Western success.[3] The evidence from the present century is much more ambiguous, and that presented in this analysis suggests that the hysterias which caused World War I and World War II were probably ill-founded. The need for colonies, whether direct or indirect, has not been established. It can be demonstrated, however, that the capitalist world system has consistently behaved as if it needed to maintain a dependent periphery, and various capitalist states have fought hard to maintain and extend their spheres of economic influence. Some of the major interest groups in the capitalist core have promoted imperialism, but it is not certain that their particular interests coincide with those of capitalist societies as a whole. Soon, since the old core will invariably lose control of ever greater portions of its former periphery, the question will be answered. If the Leninist contention is correct, then the world is headed for disaster. Endless small wars, spreading panic, and the gradual transformation of capitalist democracies into militaristic fascist states lie ahead.

But suppose that the Leninist theory has been wrong all along, and that sufficient numbers of influential people in the core capitalist democracies come to realize this? In other words, suppose that core states, particularly the United States, come to practice an enlightened form of isolationism with respect to revolutions in the old periphery. That is, suppose the United States learns to tolerate such revolutions, to trade with revolutionary regimes on a limited basis (as it does with the communist world today), and to wait for them to go through the convulsions of nationalist development? Then, as long as the original Leninist theory turns out to be wrong, a much more peaceful, balanced world can emerge in the next century.

Any discussion of the core's need, real or imagined, to control a periphery hinges in part on an issue this book has not discussed in detail—the industrial world's need for raw materials and particularly for oil. The capitalist world could conceivably do without Ghanaian cocoa, or Brazilian coffee, or Malaysian rubber; but can it do without Arabian oil, Zaire copper, South African uranium and gold, or the host of other minerals exported from the periphery to the core? Are raw-material cartels, on the model of the oil cartel, the wave of the future, and will they cause massive transfers of wealth from the core to the old periphery, transfers such that the core economies will be ruined? This line of questioning is at the crux of evaluations of the Leninist theory and is also closely related to the increasing environmental concerns over pollution and the waste of raw materials.

One thing is clear. The capitalist core has used cheap raw materials from the periphery to fuel the Western world's extravagant economic growth in the twentieth century, and the social and economic institutions that have developed in the core during this century have been partly based on the increasing, wasteful use of these resources. At the same time, scientists are agreed that core societies could maintain high standards of living with far less wasteful habits.[4] The question then becomes, will the giant corporations that control manufacturing in the core make the technological adaptations necessary for a less wasteful use of resources? That the technological capacity for this adaptation exists is not in doubt. *That the economic and political will exists is in question.* It may be easier, and in the short run, more profitable for core economies to continue their waste and then panic when the former periphery begins to jack up the price of raw materials. Such a reaction, a repetition of old habits that led to world war earlier in the century, would bring the kind of massive political catastrophe that the Leninist theory predicts. Political catastrophe would strike the core even before environmental catastrophe. Many of the leading corporations and the bureaucratic elites that make social policy must either be persuaded that the world system has so changed that continued exploitation of cheap peripheral resources is neither desirable nor profitable in the long run, or their power must be curtailed by the broader interests of society.

In the past, core societies could assuage civil unrest due to domestic inequalities by simply providing more benefits to all citizens, through continuous economic growth. Since limits on growth are now apparent, core societies must reorder the process of domestic change and learn to accommodate the demands of various pressure groups within a slowly growing, or stagnant GNP.

Others have written about the technological limits of wasteful growth, a matter that is in the fore of much contemporary social and economic debate.[5] Suffice it to say that the analysis in this book brings in another, possibly more critical dimension. Even if capitalism solves the technological problems of pollution and energy waste, the political problems of the world system will go unsolved unless the core learns to do with fewer and more expensive imports of raw materials from the old periphery. Changes in the world system will impinge on core economies and force considerable social and economic change. Not only political, but relatively greater economic isolationism is indicated. The core can at the very least, continue to exchange goods and services within itself; but it must learn to do without the profits it formerly extracted from the periphery, and it must learn to trade with new revolutionary regimes on a more limited and more equitable basis than in the past. Such regimes are proliferating and will soon test the extent to which the core has adapted.

For example, after a decade of revolution, Angola and Mozambique achieved independence from Portugal, in 1975 and 1976 respectively, and established Marxist, revolutionary regimes. In Angola, the Marxist faction won with considerable Cuban and Soviet military aid. Both Angola and Mozambique are deeply committed to extending their revolutions to Rhodesia, Namibia, and South Africa, where old forms of colonialism still prevail and where white minorities rule large black majorities. South Africa in particular contains many vital raw materials and high American and British investments. With Soviet and Cuban help and with the ideological support of most of Africa and the third world, a war will eventually be launched against South Africa. For all its military might, the South African regime is hopelessly outnumbered within its own borders by the resentful black majority. Will the capitalist world, particularly the United States, be drawn into this war? Will the reflexive tendency to defend foreign investments and sources of raw materials prevail? Will the war in Southern Africa mark the start of a new, more desperate, and economically much more vital struggle than that which occurred earlier in Algeria, or the more recent one in Vietnam? Or will the United States and the rest of the capitalist core cut their losses and give in to the nationalist current in Africa, even though that current is so obviously influenced by communist ideology and supported by capitalism's main international enemy?

All of the arguments in this book suggest that on practical grounds, the capitalist core should abandon its remaining hold over the periphery rather than risk becoming hopelessly involved in colonial wars. But whether or not such reasoning will prevail is not certain.

These conclusions are neither widely accepted nor obvious. The old liberal dream of constant improvement through increasing integration of the world's societies into the capitalist system dies hard, particularly because increasing integration within the core has brought some societies greater prosperity. The recognition that the former periphery must be left alone to conduct its development is acceptable neither to governments in core societies nor to major corporate interests. Since this book offers these ideas only as tentative conclusions and since its main purpose is to provide an analytical framework within which to study social change in the context of an evolving world system, it will refrain from pressing these conclusions beyond this point and will leave the question of future policy to others.

The Paradox of the Leninist Theory

The way in which this analysis differs from the "liberal" view of the world elaborated in the 1950s and 1960s has been made evident. In what way, then, does it differ from the "Marxist," or better, "Leninist" mode of analysis?

The Radical Left predicts that the capitalist social and economic system in the United States will come to its demise because of revolutions in the periphery. Falling profits caused by the loss of overseas investments, resources, and markets are expected to initiate a depression far worse than the Great Depression of the 1930s. Large segments of the working and professional middle classes, united with oppressed minorities, would then rise against the system and create a revolutionary socialist society. Since the end of the political protest that occurred in the middle and late 1960s, it has been obvious that in the United States the only realistic source of revolution is external. Left alone, American society is too rich, and too many of its people are too satisfied and have too much at stake in the present system, to engage in revolution. Since the situation in the former periphery is precisely

the opposite, and a long chain of revolutions can be expected, the intelligent radicals know that they must wait for the collapse of the
entire capitalist world system before they can expect to see its main
bastion, the United States, undergo radicalization.[6]

It has been the contention of this final chapter that loss of control over the periphery need not cause economic collapse and revolution in the core, particularly in the United States. The book as a
whole has demonstrated that a version of the Leninist theory accounts
for many of the key international events in this century and that the
theory deals with the interaction between a changing world system
and domestic social change more adequately than the "liberal" theory.
But the discussion has not been able to answer the fundamental question: Is the theory correct? Rather it has only been able to suggest
that in the long run the theory will turn out to be wrong, that is, if
core societies are willing to make certain difficult adaptations to their
changing circumstances.

Suppose, however, that the Leninist theory is correct, and that
the economy of the United States begins to suffer significantly because
the periphery is liberating itself from core control. What will be the
consequences for social change? It seems certain that the type of revolution expected by the Radical Left will not occur. The entrenched
interests of the capitalist upper class, the government bureaucracies,
and large portions of the general population motivated by fear of
change and intense nationalism will produce a sharp shift to the right,
not to the left.

A shift to the right, toward a form of fascism, could occur for
one of three reasons or a combination thereof. Conceivably, the American electorate could be panicked into believing that economic disaster
and social ruin face the nation because of the deteriorating international situation. This conviction seems improbable unless a realistic
threat does occur. Second, a series of economic boycotts (such as the
Arab oil-boycott of 1973–1974) directed by a hostile alliance of semi-
peripheral societies could provoke a military reaction by the United
States. In order to contain the popular discontent that would result,
American business and bureaucratic elites could move to restrict protest and control the political process. This would, of course, be accompanied by appeals to nationalism. Third, lengthy depression could
occur. This would confirm the Leninist theory. Barrington Moore has
observed:

> [I]t is necessary to specify more clearly just what a thoroughly
> reactionary neo-fasist regime might mean: it would force down
> wages, repress any shadow of racial equality, put actual and
> suspected dissidents in jail with no "nonsense" about letting
> them go around the country making speeches while their cases

were under appeal, and unleash the military with an end to "half-measures" in coping with America's foreign involvements. We are a long way still from such a situation. That there is considerable popular support for some such program is reasonably clear.[7]

This is the paradox of the Leninist theory. It is an excellent tool of analysis, but it need not be an accurate prediction of the future. If it does predict correctly, however, the outcome in the capitalist core will not be socialist revolution but its opposite.

Social Change: How to Study It

There are many types of social change that this book has not discussed, just as there are many aspects of social life that it has not examined. Books have been written about social change in America, for example, that discuss changing sexual mores, changing residential patterns, changing artistic tastes, changes in general life style, and so on. All of these concerns are interesting. This book has emphasized something else, not because it is the only type of social change, but because it establishes limits to other, secondary changes.

According to the theory presented, the primary aspect of social organization is internal stratification: who in the society has what forms of power—economic, cultural, and political—and to what ends are these types of power used? A society controlled by a very small capitalist elite behaves differently than one in which power is shared by a number of other groups. A society in which a plurality of interests compete with each other for resources behaves differently than a society in which a united bureaucratic elite makes all critical decisions. As economies change, as they grow or develop in particular directions, stratification patterns change as well. So it is that peripheral societies, semi-peripheral societies, and core societies have different forms of stratification. Revolutions, economic development, and political crises of various sorts change the balance of power in a society. This is social change. Other types of change follow.

Internal stratification, however, is not independent of changes in the world system. Earlier chapters have shown how colonialism created certain types of stratification systems, and how these have led to an increasing number of revolutions. They have also compared the various types of development that have occurred in former peripheral societies in the twentieth century. These societies have in common: the creation of strong nation-states, of unified cultures, of balanced economic development, and primarily, attempts to catch up to the core. At the same time, the discussion has examined how prosperity has changed social stratification in the core and created the democratic, affluent societies in which Western Europeans, North Americans, and Japanese people live. The changing fortunes of the capitalist world system, and the rise of enemies of that system have been traced as well. Recognizing that all these developments are closely tied to the positions of societies in the world system should alert one to the international dimensions of social change: social change is also change in the world system. Internal stratification and international stratification interact with each other, and studying one without the other leads only to inconclusive results. No twentieth-century society is independent of the world system, or rather, of the various world systems which coexist, compete, and occasionally make war on each other. Studying social change without studying its international context is theoretically unsound, and also dangerous, because it leads to the illusion that a contemporary society can be the complete master of its fate.

The illusion is particularly dangerous when it involves advanced capitalist societies; because from the start of the capitalist world system, the core has always interacted a great deal with the periphery. But core-peripheral relations have changed drastically in the twentieth century, and any analysis of the future must take this fact into account. Any new policy for guided social change must accommodate itself to the changing international context and recognize that in the future the capitalist world system, if it is to survive at all, must shrink and count on its own resources.

Notes

Chapter I
1. Walt W. Rostow, *The Stages of Economic Growth: A Non-Communist Manifesto* (New York: Cambridge University Press, 1960).
2. Max Millikan and Walt W. Rostow, *A Proposal Key to an Effective Foreign Policy* (New York: Harper & Brothers, 1957).
3. The most comprehensive summary of these opinions is the set of brief essays in Myron Weiner, ed., *Modernization: The Dynamics of Growth* (New York: Basic Books, 1966).
4. Immanuel Wallerstein, *The Modern World-System: Capitalist Agriculture and the Origins of the European World Economy in the Sixteenth Century* (New York: Academic Press, 1974).

Chapter II
1. Carlo M. Cipolla, *Guns, Sails, and Empires: Technological Innovation and the Early Phases of European Expansion* (New York: Minerva Press, 1965).
2. Mark Elvin, *The Pattern of the Chinese Past* (Stanford: Stanford University Press, 1973), Pt. 3.
3. Colin McEvedy, *The Penguin Atlas of Modern History* (Harmondsworth: Penguin Books, 1972), pp. 9 and 22.
4. Immanuel Wallerstein, *The Modern World-System: Capitalist Agriculture and the Origins of the European World Economy in the Sixteenth Century* (New York: Academic Press, 1974), Ch. 2.
5. J. H. Elliot, *Imperial Spain 1469–1716* (New York: St. Martin's Press, 1964).
6. Max Weber, *Economy and Society* (New York: Bedminster Press, 1968), pp. 1094–99.
7. Lynn White, Jr., *Medieval Technology and Social Change* (New York: Oxford University Press, 1964); and Cipolla, *Guns, Sails, and Empires.*
8. Wallerstein, *The Modern World-System,* Ch. 4.
9. Ibid., pp. 91–97.
10. Eugene D. Genovese, *The World the Slaveholders Made* (New York: Vintage Books, 1971), pp. 3–102.
11. Herbert Passin, "Japan," in James S. Coleman, ed., *Education and Political Development* (Princeton: Princeton University Press, 1965), pp. 272–77.
12. An excellent review of theories of state-building is found in Charles Tilly, "Western State-Making and Theories of Political Transformation," in Charles Tilly, ed., *The Formation of National States in Western Europe* (Princeton: Princeton University Press, 1975), pp. 601–38.
13. Samuel P. Huntington, *Political Order in Changing Societies* (New Haven: Yale University Press, 1968).
14. On the important role of French investment in the peripheral and semi-peripheral parts of Europe and in the Near East, see Rondo E. Cameron, *France and the Economic Development of Europe 1800–1914: Conquests of Peace and Seeds of War* (Princeton: Princeton University Press, 1961). Other figures are from William Woodruff, *Impact of Western Man: A Study of Europe's Role in the World Economy 1750–1960* (New York: St. Martin's Press, 1966), pp. 154–55.
15. Simon Kuznets, *Economic Growth of Nations* (Cambridge: The Belknap Press of Harvard University, 1971), p. 30, and Woodruff, *Impact of Western Man,* pp. 110–11 and 154.
16. Calculation of GNPs from Kuznets, *Economic Growth,* pp. 11–50 and Woodruff, *Impact of Western Man,* pp. 110–11. All investment figures are from Woodruff, *Im-*

pact of Western Man, p. 154. For the United States, see also U.S. Bureau of the Census, *Historical Statistics of the United States, Colonial Times to 1957* (Washington: U.S. Government Printing Office, 1960), p. 139. This source also evaluates depreciation of the U.S. dollar (through inflation) to 1957. For more recent evaluations, see U.S. Bureau of the Census, *Statistical Abstract of the United States* (Washington: U.S. Government Printing Office, 1974), p. 404. For estimates of the most recent (1970s) GNP of the United States, see various editions of the *Abstract.*

17. For a discussion of investment in various peripheral economies, see W. Arthur Lewis, ed., *Tropical Development 1880–1913* (Evanston: Northwestern University Press, 1970); and Woodruff, *Impact of Western Man,* Ch. 4.
18. For Argentina, Tomás Roberto Fillol, *Social Factors in Economic Development: The Argentine Case* (Cambridge: The M.I.T. Press, 1961), p. 43. For Russia and the Balkans, Cameron, *France,* pp. 275–83, and 320–25. For India, Helen B. Lamb, "The 'State' and Economic Development in India," in Simon Kuznets, Wilbert E. Moore, and Joseph J. Spengler, eds., *Economic Growth: Brazil, India, Japan* (Durham: Duke University Press, 1955), p. 475.
19. Andre Gunder Frank, "The Development of Underdevelopment," in Robert I. Rhodes, *Imperialism and Underdevelopment* (New York: Monthly Review Press, 1970), pp. 4–17.
20. See import-export tables in Woodruff, *Impact of Western Man,* Ch. 7.
21. Donald Coes, "Brazil," in Lewis, *Tropical Development,* pp. 106–7.
22. Ralph W. Harbison, "Colombia," in Lewis, *Tropical Development,* p. 85.
23. Celso Furtado, *The Economic Growth of Brazil* (Berkeley: University of California Press, 1965), pp. 193–203. For Senegal, see Ernest Milcent, "Senegal," in Gwendolen M. Carter, ed., *African One-Party States* (Ithaca: Cornell University Press, 1962), pp. 111–16.
24. Rupert Emerson, *From Empire to Nation: The Rise to Self-Assertion of Asian and African Peoples* (Boston: Beacon Press, 1962), pp. 197–98; and Bernard Fall, *Last Reflections on a War* (New York: Doubleday & Co., 1967), pp. 59–90.
25. Furtado, *The Economic Growth of Brazil,* pp. 176–77.
26. W. Thomas Easterbrook, "The Entrepreneurial Function in Relation to Technological and Economic Change," in Bert F. Hoselitz and Wilbert E. Moore, eds., *Industrialization and Society* (The Hague: Mouton-UNESCO, 1963), p. 59.
27. Edwin O. Reischauer, *Japan: Past and Present* (New York: Alfred A. Knopf, 1965), pp. 108–41.
28. The sense of the times and the preoccupation with expansion is captured in many diplomatic history books of the first quarter of the century. A good example, which includes the most important cases, is G. P. Gooch, *History of Modern Europe* (New York: Henry Holt and Company, 1922).
29. See the essays in Kenneth E. Boulding and Tapan Mukerjee, eds., *Economic Imperialism* (Ann Arbor: The University of Michigan Press, 1972), particularly Richard Koebner, "The Concept of Economic Imperialism," D. K. Fieldhouse, "Imperialism: An Historiographic Revision," and Harold and Margaret Sprout, "Rising Demands and Insufficient Resources."
30. See the essays in George H. Nadel and Perry Curtis, eds., *Imperialism and Colonialism* (New York: Macmillan, 1964), particularly J. Gallagher and R. Robinson, "The Imperialism of Free Trade"; Henry Brunschwig, "The Origins of the New French Empire"; Thomas Power, Jr., "Jules Ferry: Imperial Activist"; and Mary E. Townsend, "Commerical and Colonial Policies of Imperial Germany." On international tensions, see Gooch, *History of Modern Europe.*
31. V. I. Lenin, *Imperialism, the Highest Stage of Capitalism* (New York: International Publishers, 1939).
32. Woodruff, *Impact of Western Man,* p. 150.
33. William A. Williams, *The Tragedy of American Diplomacy* (New York: Dell/Delta, 1962), pp. 53–61.
34. Cited in Fieldhouse, "Imperialism," in Boulding and Mukerjee, *Economic Imperialism,* p. 120.
35. Robert K. Merton, *On Theoretical Sociology* (New York: Free Press, 1967), p. 19. Fieldhouse's interpretation is exactly this—that "psychological necessity" was paramount. See his essay in Boulding and Mukerjee, *Economic Imperialism,* pp. 121–23.

Chapter III

1. Michael Hechter, *Internal Colonialism: The Celtic Fringe in British National Develop-ment, 1536–1966* (London: Routledge and Kegan Paul, 1975), particularly chs. 8–9.
2. Walter Minchiton, "Patterns of Demand," in Carlo M. Cipolla, ed., *The Fontana Economic History of Europe,* Vol. 3 (London: Collins/Fontana Books, 1973), pp. 114–15; Simon Kuznets, "Quantitative Aspects of the Economic Growth of Nations," Pt. 1 in *Economic Development and Cultural Change,* 5, No. 1 (October 1956), p. 61; Robert J. Lampman, "The Share of Top Wealth-Holders in National Wealth, 1922–1956," in Maurice Zeitlin, ed., *American Society, Inc.: Studies of the Social Structure and Political Economy of the United States* (Chicago: Markham, 1970), p. 100. Figures for Britain are for 1913, and for the United States, for the period 1913–1922.
3. William A. Williams, *The Tragedy of American Diplomacy* (New York: Dell/Delta, 1962), pp. 37–40 and 61–62.
4. Eric R. Wolf, *Peasant Wars of the Twentieth Century* (New York: Harper & Row, 1969), pp. 3–22.
5. Hsiao-tung Fei, "Peasantry and Gentry," *American Journal of Sociology,* 52, No. 1 (July 1946), p. 14.
6. Barrington Moore, Jr., *Social Origins of Dictatorship and Democracy: Lord and Peasant in the Making of the Modern World* (Boston: Beacon, 1967), p. 176.
7. On the Chinese in Southeast Asia see Gunnar Myrdal, *Asian Drama: An Inquiry Into the Poverty of Nations* (New York: Pantheon, 1968), pp. 133, 164, 169–70, 388, 402, 447, 464, 578, 813, and 841; on the Jews in Eastern Europe see Daniel Chirot, *Social Change in a Peripheral Society: The Creation of a Balkan Colony* (New York: Academic Press, 1976), pp. 107–9, 144, 146, and 150; on Indians in East Africa see Floyd and Lillian Dotson, "Indians and Coloureds in Rhodesia and Nyasaland," in Pierre L. van den Berghe, ed., *Africa: Social Problems of Change and Conflict* (San Francisco: Chandler, 1965), pp. 267–73; on the Caribbean see Leo A. Despres, "The Implications of Nationalist Politics in British Guiana for the Development of Cultural Theory," in Reinhard Bendix, ed., *State and Society* (Boston: Little, Brown, 1968), pp. 502–28.
8. Wolf, *Peasant Wars,* p. 15.
9. Moore, *Social Origins,* pp. 251 and 341–53.
10. This is a pervasive theme in Wolf, *Peasant Wars.*
11. J. H. Broomfield, "The Regional Elites: A Theory of Modern Indian History," in Bendix, *State and Society,* pp. 552–61.
12. Wilkie, *The Mexican Revolution,* pp. 45–47.
13. Woodruff, *Impact of Western Man: A Study of Europe's Role in the World Economy 1750–1960* (New York: St. Martin's Press, 1966), p. 112.
14. James S. Coleman, *Nigeria: Background to Nationalism* (Berkeley: University of California Press, 1960), pp. 11–35.
15. On Africa see Immanuel Wallerstein, *Africa: The Poiltics of Independence* (New York: Vintage Books, 1961), pp. 31–34. For other examples see Doreen Warriner, *Land Re-form in Principle and Practice* (Oxford: Clarendon Press, 1969), particularly pp. 3–10.
16. The theoretical argument is best explained by Eric J. Hobsbawm, *Primitive Rebels: Studies in Archaic Forms of Social Movement in the 19th and 20th Centuries* (New York: W. W. Norton, 1959), chs. 4 and 5. See also Wolf, *Peasant Wars,* pp. 226–302.
17. Pierre L. van den Berghe, *South Africa: A Study in Conflict* (Berkeley: University of California Press, 1970).
18. Erik H. Erikson, "On the nature of Psycho-Historical Evidence: In Search of Gandhi," in Dankwart A. Rustow, ed., *Philosophers and Kings: Studies in Leadership* (New York: George Braziller, 1970), p. 37.
19. Theodore H. Von Laue, "Imperial Russia at the Turn of the Century: The Cultural Slope and the Revolution from Without," in Bendix, *State and Society,* pp. 427–45.
20. Alexander Gerschenkron, *Economic Backwardness in Historical Perspective* (New York: Frederick A. Praeger, 1965), p. 131.
21. Ibid., p. 130.
22. Ibid., pp. 119–42.
23. Moore, *Social Origins,* pp. 228–313.
24. On the Austro-Hungarian economy see N. T. Gross, "The Habsburg Monarchy 1750–1914," in Carlo M. Cipolla, ed., *The Fontana Economic History of Europe,* Vol. 4

(London: Collins/Fontana Books, 1973), pp. 228–78. On its international role and collapse, see Barbara Jelavich, *The Habsburg Empire in European Affairs, 1814–1918* (Chicago: Rand McNally, 1969), particularly pp. 150–72.

25. Douglass C. North, "The Economic Structure of the South," in Eugene D. Genovese, ed., *The Slave Economies: Slavery in the International Economy*, Vol. 2 (New York: John Wiley & Sons, 1973), pp. 143–56; Moore, *Social Origins*, pp. 111–55; V. O. Key, *Southern Politics in State and Nation* (New York: Alfred A. Knopf, 1949), pp. 160–61 and 533–618.

26. Moore, *Social Origins*, Pt. 3.

Chapter IV
1. Paul-Marie La Gorce, *The French Army: A Military-Political History* (New York: George Braziller, 1963), p. 103; Henri Bunle, *Le mouvement naturel de la population dans le monde de 1906 à 1936* (Paris: Institut national d'études démographiques, 1954), p. 112.

2. Martin Gilbert, *First World War Atlas* (New York: Macmillan, 1970), pp. 130 and 158.

3. For an easily read, superb description of the stupidity which produced such carnage see A. J. P. Taylor, *A History of the First World War* (New York: Berkeley Medallion Books, 1966).

4. Gilbert, *First World War*, pp. 144–55 (maps).

5. Peter Gay, *Weimar Culture: The Outsider as Insider* (New York: Harper Torchbooks, 1970), pp. 19–22; Salvatore Saladino, "Italy," in Hans Rogger and Eugen Weber, eds., *The European Right* (Berkeley: University of California Press, 1966), pp. 251–53; T. L. Jarman, *A Short History of Twentieth Century England* (New York: Mentor, 1963), pp. 153–55.

6. John H. M. Laslett and Seymour M. Lipset, "Repression as a Cause of Failure," in Laslett and Lipset, eds., *Failure of a Dream? Essays in the History of American Socialism* (New York: Anchor Books, 1974), pp. 48–55.

7. Jarman, *A Short History of England*, pp. 163–64.

8. H. Stuart Hughes, *Contemporary Europe: A History* (Englewood Cliffs, N.J.: Prentice-Hall, 1961), pp. 149–58.

9. Charles P. Kindleberger, *The World in Depression 1929–1939* (London: Allen Lane, The Penguin Press, 1973), p. 292.

10. William Woodruff, *Impact of Western Man: A Study of Europe's Role in the World Economy 1750–1960* (New York: St. Martin's Press, 1966), p. 274.

11. Ibid., pp. 277–79.

12. Kindleberger, *The World in Depression*, pp. 83–107.

13. For the United States: Buerau of the Census, *Historical Statistics*, pp. 73 and 139; for the United Kingdom: Parker, *Europe 1919–1945*, p. 116. For Germany: Kindleberger, *The World in Depression*, p. 240 and Dudley Kirk, *Europe's Population in the Inter-war Years* (1968; reprint ed., New York: Gordon and Breach, 1946), p. 197.

14. Woodruff, *Impact of Western Man*, p. 272.

15. Maurice Dobb, *Studies in the Development of Capitalism* (New York: International Publishers, 1963), pp. 371–83.

16. On European fascism see Rogger and Weber, eds., *The European Right*, particularly the essays on Italy by Salvatore Saladino and on Germany by Ernst Nolte. See also S. J. Woolf, ed., *The Nature of Fascism* (New York: Vintage Books, 1969).

17. See István Deák, "Hungary" and Eugen Weber, "Romania," in Rogger and Weber, *The European Right*.

18. For investment position in the world in 1938, see Woodruff, *Impact of Western Man*, pp. 156–57.

19. Edwin O. Reischauer, *Japan: Past and Present* (New York: Alfred A. Knopf, 1965), p. 164.

20. Woodruff, *Impact of Western Man*, p. 274.

21. Reischauer, *Japan*, pp. 186–200.

22. For Japan, see Reischauer, *Japan*, pp. 142–85. For Germany see Gay, *Weimar Culture* on the short-lived liberalism of the 1920s; and Eugen Weber, *Varieties of Fascism* (New York: Anvil/Van Nostrand Reinhold, 1964), pp. 79–87.

23. The size and consequence of massive unemployment was undoubtedly the main, immediate cause of reform. See Arthur M. Schlesinger, Jr., *The Age of Roosevelt: The*

Crisis of the Old Order (Boston: Houghton Mifflin, 1957), particularly pp. 166–83.
24. Gardiner C. Means, "Economic Concentration," in Zeitlin, *American Society, Inc.*, p. 12.
25. Robert W. Campbell, *Soviet Economic Power: Its Organization, Growth, and Challenge* (Cambridge: Houghton Mifflin, 1960), pp. 7–27.
26. Warren Eason, "Demography," in Ellen Mickiewicz, *Handbook of Soviet Social Science Data* (New York: Free Press, 1973), p. 58.
27. Parker, *Europe 1914–1945*, p. 102.
28. Campbell, *Soviet Economic Power*, p. 48.
29. Eason, "Demography," in Mickiewicz, *Handbook of Soviet Data*, p. 55.
30. Mark Field, "Health"; Pool, Azrael, Pinnar, Bakulo, and Bereday, "Education," in Mickiewicz, *Handbook of Soviet Data*.
31. Campbell, *Soviet Economic Power*, p. 24.
32. Merle Fainsod, *How Russia is Ruled* (Cambridge: Harvard University Press, 1965), pp. 531–32.
33. Roy Laird, "Agriculture," in Mickiewicz, *Handbook of Soviet Data*, pp. 70–71.
34. Henry W. Morton, "Housing," in Mickiewicz, *Handbook of Soviet Data*, p. 122.
35. Roy A. Medvedev, *Let History Judge: The Origins and Consequences of Stalinism* (New York: Vintage Books, 1973), pp. 192–239. The quote is on p. 239.
36. Hughes, *Contemporary Europe*, pp. 285–94.
37. George F. Kennan, *Soviet Foreign Policy 1917–1941* (Princeton: Anvil/Van Nostrand, 1960), pp. 176–78.
38. George F. Kennan, *American Diplomacy 1900–1950* (Chicago: University of Chicago Press, 1951), pp. 74–75.
39. H. C. Darby and Harold Fullard, eds., *The New Cambridge Modern History Atlas* (Cambridge: Cambridge University Press, 1970), pp. 58–61.

Chapter V
1. Charles Issawi, "Egypt since 1800: A Study in Lopsided Development," in Charles Issawi, ed., *The Economic History of the Middle East 1800–1914* (Chicago: University of Chicago Press, 1966), p. 373.
2. Gabriel Baer, "The Evolution of Private Landownership in Egypt and the Fertile Crescent," pp. 79–90; Issawi, "Egypt since 1800," p. 373; and Issawi, "Land Policy, 1906," p. 497; all in Issawi, *The Economic History*. Also, Gabriel S. Saab, *The Egyptian Agrarian Reform 1952–1962* (London: Oxford University Press, 1967), p. 9.
3. Simon Kuznets, *Economic Growth of Nations: Total Output and Production Structure* (Cambridge: The Belknap Press of Harvard University, 1971), p. 31.
4. Simon Kuznets, "Quantitative Aspects of the Economic Growth of Nations," Pt. 2 in *Economic Development and Cultural Change*, 5, No. 4 (Supplement), (July 1957) p. 78.
5. Barrington Moore, Jr., *Social Origins of Dictatorship and Democracy: Lord and Peasant in the Making of the Modern World* (Boston: Beacon, 1967), pp. 354–55.
6. Daniel Thorner, "Long-term Trends in Output in India," in Simon Kuznets, Wilbert E. Moore, and Joseph J. Spengler, eds., *Economic Growth: Brazil, India, Japan* (Durham: Duke University Press, 1955), pp. 121–23.
7. Kuznets, *Economic Growth of Nations*, p. 31.
8. The best general short summary of the effects of colonialism is George Balandier, "The Colonial Situation," in Pierre L. van den Berghe, ed., *Africa: Social Problems of Change and Conflict* (San Francisco: Chandler, 1965), pp. 36–57.
9. Bernard Lewis, *The Emergence of Modern Turkey* (London: Oxford University Press, 1961), p. 444.
10. Ibid.
11. Ibid., p. 447.
12. Ibid., p. 350.
13. B. R. Mitchell and Phyllis Deane, *Abstract of British Historical Statistics* (Cambridge: Cambridge University Press, 1971), p. 6; U.S. Bureau of the Census, *Historical Statistics of the United States, Colonial Times to 1957* (Washington: U.S. Government Printing Office, 1960), p. 7.
14. Russell Lindman and Robert I. Domrese, "India," in W. Arthur Lewis, ed., *Tropical Development 1880–1913* (Evanston: Northwestern University Press, 1970), p. 314.
15. Kuznets, "Quantitative Aspects," in *Economic Development and Cultural Change*, p. 77.
16. Doreen Warriner, *Land Reform in Principle and Practice* (Oxford: Clarendon Press,

1969), pp. 373–92. Reform, particularly in Egypt, has increased productivity, and everywhere, it does liberate peasants. But it does not solve the overpopulation problem unless there is also industrialization. The "large estate" versus "small farm" controversy is the key theoretical dispute in the literature on land reform; it cannot be resolved because the immense variation in types of class structure, economy, and geography make it impossible to verify theories in a broadly comparative way.

17. Edward A. Shils, "The Intellectuals in the Political Development of the New States," in John H. Kautsky, ed., *Political Change in Underdeveloped Countries: Nationalism and Communism* (New York: John Wiley and Sons, 1962), p. 198.

18. Harry J. Benda, "Non-Western Intelligentsias as Political Elites," in Kautsky, *Political Change*, pp. 239 and 243.

19. Dankwart A. Rustow, "Ataturk as Founder of a State," in Rustow, ed., *Philosophers and Kings: Studies in Leadership* (New York: George Braziller, 1970), pp. 208–47.

20. Moore, *Social Origins of Dictatorship and Democracy*, pp. 188–89; Chalmers A. Johnson, *Peasant Nationalism and Communist Power: The Emergence of Revolutionary China 1937–1945* (Stanford: Stanford University Press, 1972) pp. 31–32.

21. Francis G. Hutchins, *India's Revolution: Gandhi and the Quit India Movement* (Cambridge: Harvard University Press, 1973).

22. Bernard B. Fall, *Last Reflections on a War* (New York: Doubleday & Co., 1967), pp. 59–90.

23. Ibid.

24. Samuel P. Huntington, *Political Order in Changing Societies* (New Haven: Yale University Press, 1968), p. 316.

25. Eric R. Wolf, *Peasant Wars of the Twentieth Century* (New York: Harper & Row, 1969), pp. 31–37.

26. James W. Wilkie, *The Mexican Revolution: Federal Expenditure and Social Change Since 1910* (Berkeley: University of California Press, 1970), pp. 64–65.

27. Ibid., pp. 72–79.

28. Wolf, *Peasant Wars*, pp. 32–37.

29. Population Reference Bureau, "1972 World Population Reference Data Sheet" (Washington: World Population Reference Bureau, 1972). The data source for these yearly reports is the International Bank for Reconstruction and Development, and generally run several years behind publication date.

30. See William Woodruff, *Impact of Western Man: A Study of Europe's Role in the Western World Economy 1750–1960* (New York: St. Martin's Press, 1966), p. 112, for estimates of Amerindian population in Latin America.

31. Johnson, *Peasant Nationalism*, p. 23.

32. Ibid., p. 24.

33. A good book on the rise of Mao Tse-tung is Benjamin I. Schwartz, *Chinese Communism and the Rise of Mao* (Cambridge: Harvard University Press, 1951).

34. Johnson, *Peasant Nationalism*, p. 31.

35. Moore, *Social Origins of Dictatorship and Democracy*, pp. 198–99.

36. Myrdal, *Asian Drama*, pp. 257–303, particularly pp. 300–303.

Chapter VI

1. See, for example, David Horowitz, "The Alliance for Progress," and Hamza Alavi and Amir Khurso, "Pakistan: The Burden of U.S. Aid," both in Robert I. Rhodes, ed., *Imperialism and Underdevelopment* (New York: Monthly Review Press, 1970), pp. 45–78.

2. William Woodruff, *Impact of Western Man: A Study of Europe's Role in the World Economy 1750–1960* (New York: St. Martin's Press, 1966), p. 158.

3. U.S. Bureau of the Census, *Statistical Abstract of the United States* (Washington: U.S. Government Printing Office, 1974), p. 784.

4. For a partial list, see George Modelski, "Multinational Business: A Global Perspective," in George Modelski, ed., *Multinational Corporations and World Order* (Beverly Hills: Sage Publications, Sage Issues No. 2, 1972), p. 15.

5. *Abstract of the U.S.* (1974), pp. 484, 781.

6. Ibid., pp. 373, 790, 792, 829–30.

7. See, for example, the entire special issue on "Materials," *Science*, 191, No. 4227 (20 February 1976), pp. 631–776.

8. Hugh Thomas, *Suez* (New York: Harper & Row, 1967).
9. David R. Francis, "The Multinational Corporations," *The Christian Science Monitor,* 4 November 1975, pp. 16–17.
10. On some of the effects of multinationals, see Fouad Ajami, "Corporate Giants: Some Global Social Costs," in Modelski, *Multinational Corporations*, pp. 109–27. See also, Theotonio Dos Santos, "The Structure of Dependence;" Celso Furtado, "The Concept of External Dependence in the Study of Underdevelopment;" Ronald Müller, "The Multinational Corporation and the Underdevelopment of the Third World;" all in Charles K. Wilber, ed., *The Political Economy of Development and Underdevelopment* (New York: Random House, 1973), pp. 109–51.

Chapter VII
1. Seymour M. Lipset and Stein Rokkan, "Cleavage Structures, Party Systems, and Voter Alignments," in Lipset and Rokkan, eds., *Party Systems and Voter Alignments: Cross-National Perspectives* (New York: Free Press, 1967), pp. 1–64.
2. On the United Kingdom: Michael Hechter, *Internal Colonialism: The Celtic Fringe in British National Development, 1536–1966* (London: Routledge and Kegan Paul, 1975), pp. 298–310. On Belgium and Canada: Lipset and Rokkan, "Cleavage Structures," pp. 14 and 42.
3. C. Wright Mills, *The Power Elite* (New York: Oxford University Press, 1956); Gabriel Kolko, *Wealth and Power in America: An Analysis of Social Class and Income Distribution* (New York: Praeger, 1962) and *The Roots of American Foreign Policy: An Analysis of Power and Purpose* (Boston: Beacon, 1969); Maurice Zeitlin, ed., *American Society, Inc.: Studies of the Social Structure and Political Economy of the United States* (Chicago: Markham, 1970). See also Harry Magdoff, *The Age of Imperialism: The Economics of United States Foreign Policy* (New York: Monthly Review Press, 1969).
4. David R. Francis, "Most Millionaires Start with Inherited Wealth," *The Christian Science Monitor*, 19 April 1975, p. 21.
5. Robert J. Lampman, "The Share of Top Wealth-Holders in National Wealth, 1922–1956," in Zeitlin, *American Society, Inc.*, p. 104.
6. G. William Domhoff, *Who Rules America?* (Englewood Cliffs, N.J.: Prentice-Hall, 1967), p. 45.
7. Francis, "Most Millionaires," p. 21.
8. Domhoff, *Who Rules America?*, p. 57.
9. On current concentration see U.S. Bureau of the Census, *Statistical Abstract of the United States* (Washington: U.S. Government Printing Office, 1974), pp. 483–84, and 487.
10. Ibid., p. 484.
11. Edward Shorter and Charles Tilly, *Strikes in France 1830–1968* (Cambridge: Cambridge University Press, 1974), pp. 306–34.
12. Robert Michels, *Political Parties* (New York: Collier Books, 1962), particularly pp. 342–56.
13. Franz Schurman, *The Logic of World Power: An Inquiry into the Origins, Currents, and Contradictions of World Politics* (New York: Pantheon Books, 1974), pp. 401–500.
14. Ibid.
15. Samuel P. Huntington, "Political Development and the Decline of the American System of World Order," *Daedalus*, 96, No. 3 (Summer 1967), p. 928.
16. Gunnar Myrdal, *The Challenge of World Poverty: A World Anti-Poverty Program in Outline* (New York: Vintage Books, 1970), pp. 208–9.
17. James W. Wilkie, *The Mexican Revolution: Federal Expenditure and Social Change since 1910* (Berkeley: University of California Press, 1970), p. 205.
18. Oscar Lewis, *The Children of Sanchez: Autobiography of a Mexican Family* (New York: Vintage Books, 1961).
19. Celso Furtado cited in Raymond Aron, *The Imperial Republic: The United States and the World, 1945–1973* (Cambridge: Winthrop Publishers, 1974), pp. 244–45.
20. Myrdal, *The Challenge of World Poverty*, p. 402.
21. Wilkie, *The Mexican Revolution*, pp. 193 and 203.
22. The statistics on age distribution are from The Environmental Fund, "World Population Estimates 1975 Chart," (Washington: Environmental Fund, 1975). Their estimates are

from U.S. Bureau of the Census, *World Population, 1973* (Washington: International Statistical Programs Center, 1974).

23. Thomas T. Poleman, "World Food: A Perspective;" Pierre R. Crosson, "Institutional Obstacles to Expansion of World Food Production;" Harry Walters, "Difficult Issues Underlying Food Problems;" James D. Gavan and John A. Dixon, "India: A Perspective on the Food Situation;" G. F. Sprague, "Agriculture in China;" all in special issue on "Food," *Science*, 188, No. 4188 (9 May 1975), pp. 510–30, and 541–55.

24. Kingsley Davis, "Population," *Scientific American*, 209, No. 3 (September 1963), pp. 62–71. Davis has long stressed the association between social change, economic development, and fertility rates.

25. Mahmood Mamdani, *The Myth of Population Control: Family, Caste, and Class in an Indian Village* (New York: Monthly Review Press, 1972).

26. P. K. Welpton and Clyde V. Kiser, "Trends, Determinants, and Control in Human Fertility," *The Annals of the American Academy of Political and Social Science* (January 1945), pp. 114–15. For current birth rates, The Environmental Fund, "World Population 1975."

27. For South Korea's and Taiwan's unusually low birth rates, see Paul Demeny, "The Populations of the Underdeveloped Countries," in Scientific American, ed., *The Human Population: A Scientific American Book*, (San Francisco: W. H. Freeman and Co., 1974), p. 111.

28. On Chinese development, see Sprague, "Agriculture in China," particularly pp. 550–52. On China's success in lowering birth rates, see Ronald Freedman and Bernard Berelson, "The Human Population," in Scientific American, *The Human Population*, pp. 9–10.

29. Rupert Emerson, *From Empire to Nation: The Rise to Self-Assertion of Asian and African Peoples* (Boston: Beacon, 1962), pp. 272–92; Barrington Moore Jr., *Social Origins of Dictatorship and Democracy: Lord and Peasant in the Making of the Modern World* (Boston: Beacon, 1967), pp. 430-31.

30. Moore, *Social Origins of Dictatorship and Democracy*, pp. 406–10.

Chapter VIII

1. Population estimates from The Environmental Fund, "World Population Estimates 1975 Chart," (Washington: Environmental Fund, 1975.) Their estimates are from U.S. Bureau of the Census, *World Population, 1973* (Washington: International Statistical Programs Center, 1974).

2. Roy E. H. Mellor, *Eastern Europe: A Geography of the Comecon Countries* (New York: Columbia University Press, 1975), pp. 221–48.

3. Kenneth Jowitt, *Revolutionary Breakthroughs and National Development: The Case of Romania, 1944–1965* (Berkeley: University of California Press, 1971), pp. 198–213; Jacques Lévesque, *Le Conflit sino-soviétique et l'Europe de l'Est* (Montreal: Les Presses de l'Université de Montréal, 1970), pp. 119–90.

4. David Lane, *The End of Inequality? Stratification Under State Socialism* (Magnolia, Mass.: Peter Smith, 1976), pp. 62–79.

5. Seymour M. Lipset, "Commentary: Social Stratification Research and Soviet Scholarship," in Murray Yanowitch and Wesley A. Fisher, eds., *Social Stratification and Mobility in the U.S.S.R.* (White Plains, N.Y.: International Arts & Sciences Press, 1973), pp. 359–62.

6. Mellor, *Eastern Europe*, pp. 230–31; Philip Windsor and Adam Roberts, *Czechoslovakia 1968: Reform, Repression and Resistance* (New York: Columbia University Press, 1969), pp. 80–94.

7. Theda Skocpol, "Old Regime Legacies and Communist Revolutions in Russia and China," *Social Forces*, 52, N. 2 (December 1976), p. 128.

8. Franz Schurman, *The Logic of World Power: An Inquiry into the Origins, Currents, and Contradictions of World Politics* (New York: Pantheon Books, 1974), pp. 328–400, particularly pp. 368–72.

9. Ibid., pp. 513–15. On more recent politics in China, and Teng Hsiao-p'ing, see Victor Zorza, "Chinese 'jigsaw' puzzle falling into place," *The Christian Science Monitor*, 7 May 1976, p. 3. Evidently, the "anti-Russian" versus "pro-Russian" struggle continues, with the "bureaucrats" more or less pro-Russian, and the Maoist "idealists" anti-Russian.

Chapter IX
1. Charles J. Wetzel, "The Peace Corps in Our Past," *The Annals of the American Academy of Political and Social Science* (May 1966), p. 11.
2. Franz Schurman, *The Logic of World Power: An Inquiry into the Origins, Currents, and Contradictions of World Politics* (New York: Pantheon Books, 1974), p. 419.
3. This is the central theme of Immanuel Wallerstein, *The Modern World-System: Capitalist Agriculture and the Origins of the European World Economy in the Sixteenth Century* (New York: Academic Press, 1974).
4. See, for example, William D. Metz, "Energy Conservation: Better Living Through Thermodynamics", *Science* 188, No. 4190 (23 May 1975), pp. 820–21; W. J. Chancellor and J. R. Gross, "Balancing Energy and Food Production, 1975–2000", *Science,* 192, No. 4236 (16 April 1976), pp. 213–18; Eric Hirst, "Transportation Energy Conservation Policies," *Science,* 192, No. 4234 (2 April 1976), pp. 15–20; Thomas H. Maugh II, "Natural Gas: United States Has It if the Price Is Right," *Science* 191, No. 4227 (13 February 1976), pp. 549–50; and the more fanciful article by Gerard K. O'Neill, "Space Colonies and Energy Supply to the Earth", *Science,* 190, No. 4218 (5 December 1975), pp. 943–47. There are also more pessimistic predictions, but most of these concentrate on political, economic, and social barriers to efficiency, not on technological problems. See Philip H. Abelson, "Energy Diplomacy," *Science,* 192, No. 4238 (30 April 1976), pp. 429, for a gloomy comment. If fusion power (as opposed to more dangerous fission power) is developed within this century, there is little doubt that the energy problem will be solved. But even without this, a high potential for solution exists *if* the political, economic, and social reforms can be carried out. On the availability of other raw materials, see the special issue "Materials," *Science,* 191, No. 4227 (20 February 1976), pp. 631–776.
5. See, for example, Lawrence G. Hines, *Environmental Issues: Population, and Economics* (New York: W. W. Norton, 1973); Peter R. Cox and John Peel, eds., *Population and Pollution* (New York: Academic Press, 1972).
6. Immanuel Wallerstein, "From Feudalism to Capitalism: Transition or Transitions?" *Social Forces,* 55, No. 2 (December 1976). Despite the title, this article is about the future.
7. Barrington Moore, Jr., *Reflections on the Causes of Human Misery and Upon Certain Proposals to Eliminate Them.* (Boston: Beacon, 1973), p. 152.

Index

THE WORL

■ Capitalist core

▨ Communist soci

C A N A D A

UNITED STATES

MEXICO

CUBA

VENEZUELA

BRAZIL

CHILE

ARGENTINA

WES

EUROP

ALGER

GHANA

Jean Paul Tremblay

N 1977

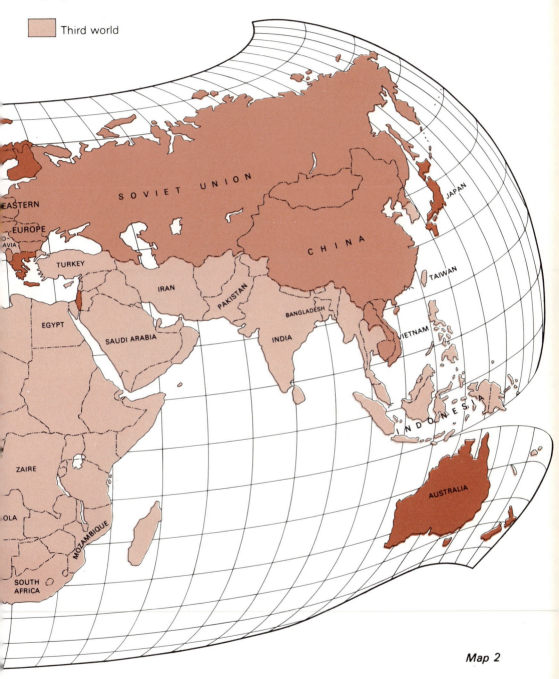

EASTERN
EUROPE
AVIA

SOVIET UNION

JAPAN

TURKEY

CHINA

IRAN

PAKISTAN

TAIWAN

EGYPT

BANGLADESH

SAUDI ARABIA

INDIA

VIETNAM

ZAIRE

INDONESIA

AUSTRALIA

OLA

MOZAMBIQUE

SOUTH
AFRICA

Map 2